THE
UNITED STATES
AND
India and Pakistan

By

W. Norman Brown

HARVARD UNIVERSITY PRESS

Cambridge, Massachusetts

1958

CONTENTS

Maps

INTRODUCTION

One of the really tragic—and much neglected—aspects of the emergence of the United States into a position of leadership in the Western world has been our pitifully restricted knowledge of those very areas which suddenly appeared in the forefront of our interest at the end of the last war. For generations the education of Americans, both private citizens and officials concerned with the foreign world, has been focused on central and western Europe, and it is in this region, too, that the vast majority of American tourists have traveled. Suddenly, in 1945, problems touching Russia and China took top priority, and at that point the number of men—official, academic, business, and other—who could qualify as "expert" on these areas could have been accommodated in a modest seaside summer theater, and with plenty of room to spare.

The Indian subcontinent, which was less immediately in the news, was in an even weaker posture so far as American knowledge was concerned. A very small and highly competent group of Americans had for decades interpreted the culture of India in a very few universities, but the author of this volume notes that, prior to World War I, "There was scarcely an American economist, sociologist, modern historian, political scientist, geographer, anthropologist who was trained in the Indian aspect of his science or knew his way around in it." Even when the second war came, the dearth of specialists was still very serious. This situation came dramatically to Professor Brown's attention when he was a leading member of the intelligence staff of the wartime Office of Strategic Services, and since then he has launched and developed, at the University of Pennsylvania, the only full-scale "area program" on the Indian subcontinent in this country. There he has gathered representation from a wide range of the social sciences and humanities, and the present volume has benefited not only from Mr. Brown's lifelong study of this area but also from the continuing discussion of his colleague specialists, each of whom brings a separate approach to the complex problems in hand.

The general significance of the subcontinent for international politics is not far to seek. It has roughly a quarter of the world's population, and a population still growing in massive annual increments. Its geographical position lends it special importance: in the north and northeast it is contiguous with China, although access overland is inhibited by the Himalayas and other ranges, and in the northwest it is not far from Soviet Russia. At the same time it is embedded in a complex of peoples ranging across South Asia from Iran to Indonesia where, in different degrees, nationalism and communism are prominent elements in a situation of endemic instability.

India and Pakistan had already made notable progress when Britain yielded independence to them, both in the fields of technological absorption and of political development. But for all this progress, India and Pakistan remain seriously underdeveloped areas. Mr. Brown has given us a deep-ranging analysis of the leading political, economic, and social problems in these two countries, some of them having roots very deep in the past, almost all of them inviting serious internal tensions.

As if these internal problems, some of them so baffling as to seem almost insoluble, were not enough, the partition of the subcontinent into the two nations of India and Pakistan at the time of independence has created additional and most menacing tensions. The division precipitated the largest exchange of population in recorded history, and much of it took place amidst violence and bloodshed. The still unresolved contest over strategic Kashmir has repeatedly threatened overt war between the two, a struggle which might have dynamic consequences in the international scene. One of Mr. Brown's ablest chapters is devoted to this very complex question.

The direct interest of the United States in the subcontinent is— as it is in so many parts of the world—largely a product of recent events. Indeed, before World War II, we had only a few consular offices in India, and carried on our relations through the British Foreign Office. During the nineteenth century, American traders had called at Indian ports, and India became a major field for American missionary effort. The nineteenth- and early-twentieth-century missionary was too often unequipped to understand the complexities of the age-old culture he met and on returning gave Americans a one-sided view. His stereotypes became lurid in presentation by American writers like Katherine Mayo. Both the United States and India meanwhile continued to have a minimum of reliable information about the other, which might have acted as a corrective. And then, precipitately, the last war brought India directly into our "world." Since then the barometer of relations between the two sides has shown wide variation.

India reacted favorably to the friendliness of the G.I., of whom it saw a good many. And Roosevelt's strong democratic pronouncements on world politics found a deep resonance in the subcontinent. On the other hand, the articulate people of India resented American "lack of understanding" of their attitude toward the whole conflict. Since the war, Indians and Pakistanis have attacked our support of French and Dutch colonial rule, and, in that connection, American domestic attitudes toward race discrimination. They have been disappointed in our unwillingness to supply capital for their industrial expansion, and have felt persistently that we fail to understand that their overriding problems are social and economic and that hungry men cannot be expected to be fully sensitive to ideological appeals. This is the heart of our difference: the Indian and Pakistani fear Russia and communism less than we, and are convinced that in the Cold War we seek our own advantage and are inclined to subordinate the greater needs of other countries to our policy; at the same time, the American press has been loud in its denunciation of the "neutrality" of India and Pakistan in the Cold War as selfish and indefensible. Mr. Brown makes a plea for more knowledge and understanding on both sides. India and Pakistan, he believes, are moving gradually toward a fuller understanding of our position in the international crisis. He urges that, in turn, we convince these peoples of the genuineness of our concern for their baffling problems by acts and sympathy rather than by exhortation.

Mr. Brown has long been a deep student of Sanskrit and the culture of India. He has had repeated, direct contact with the peoples of the subcontinent, and his wartime government service gave his experience a new and important dimension. He has placed the complex of recent problems in the deep background of a history which few men are competent to write. In discussing current problems and tensions between Pakistan and India, he has, in the view of the present writer and of various knowledgeable specialists, done so with notable detachment and urbanity. In the issues he analyzes, he does not advocate the position of any single one of the disputants —Britain, India, Pakistan. We believe that Mr. Brown has written a book which, in giving Americans the basis for an informed opinion on our relations with these two new countries, will have performed a signal service.

Donald C. McKay

FOREWORD

This book endeavors to point out the major forces affecting human development in India and Pakistan now, the circumstances that have called them into existence, the sources of their power among the people, the specific issues on which they are operating, the problems which the two nations have to solve. Such data may help us as Americans to define the associations we may profitably cultivate with India and Pakistan. Those nations mean much to us now; they will mean more as Asia's importance in world affairs increases.

In writing this book I have been indebted to the works of many scholars, of whom a number are mentioned in the bibliographical appendix. I have also drawn heavily upon the learning of my colleagues in the South Asia Regional Studies seminar at the University of Pennsylvania—Holden Furber, Daniel Thorner, William F. Christians, Richard D. Lambert, Stella Kramrisch, Marian W. Smith, Ernest Bender, Leigh Lisker, Mark J. Dresden, Suniti K. Chatterji. I have drawn too upon the work of students in the seminar. Many other persons in this country and in India and Pakistan have given me ideas and information.

The topics discussed in this book are many and each receives only summary treatment. As author I trust that readers will take the fullest advantage of the suggestions for further reading in Appendix III.

W. Norman Brown

1. Two Young Nations

On August 15, 1947, the world received two new large, self-ruling nations, India and Pakistan. They were created by partition of the old British "Indian Empire" and began their separate and independent existence as Dominions within the British Commonwealth of Nations. Both remain members in the Commonwealth. Pakistan retains the same relationship to the Commonwealth as do Canada and those other member countries which acknowledge a common allegiance to the British Crown. India, on inaugurating its new constitution on January 26, 1950, became a "sovereign, democratic republic," but remained a member in the Commonwealth in accordance with an agreement with other Commonwealth countries to recognize the King as the symbol of the Commonwealth association and as such the "head of the Commonwealth." Since the former unpartitioned India was a member of the United Nations, that membership passed to the new India as the "successor state." Pakistan on becoming eligible was promptly elected to membership in the United Nations under the terms of the charter.

The old India, before partition, had little voice in international affairs. Its foreign relations were conducted through the British Foreign Office; its internal administration was subject on the highest level to the British Parliament. What India or citizens of India thought was of slight significance outside India, and, until only a few years before 1947, of not much more within India itself. But when the new nations were created, this situation changed. Each acquired international importance as a great Asian power, whose friendship and coöperation are valuable to other nations.

What is the basis for the two nations' importance? Briefly, it lies less in their present development than in potentialities, and derives from their area, population, resources, intellectual capacity, and strategic situation. First, is the simple matter of size. The old pre-partition India, a self-contained subcontinent, well isolated from the rest of the world by difficult land barriers and seacoast, had about 1,581,410 square miles of territory, more than half the area of the United States. This is now divided unequally between India and Pakistan in a ratio of not quite 3.4 to 1, with some regions in dispute. The territorial claims of the two nations slightly exceed those of the old undivided India. India claims (Census of 1951) 1,221,072 square miles, including Kashmir, Junagadh, and Manavadar (whose status is in dispute with Pakistan), and is between one-third and one-half the size of the United States with its territorial possessions. Pakistan, with acceding princely states, claims (1951 Census estimate) 360,780 square miles (excluding Junagadh and Manavadar) and is about the size of France, Italy, Switzerland, and the Netherlands combined. Pakistan is in two sections, at opposite sides of the subcontinent, a thousand miles apart. Of these, Western Pakistan is much the larger, having approximately 307,000 square miles. Eastern Pakistan has only about 54,000 square miles but is the more populous.

The population figures of the subcontinent are more suggestive than those of area. In 1951 India counted its population at 356,891,624, excluding Kashmir (4.02 million in 1941, estimated in 1950 to be 4.37 million) and some tribal areas in Assam (estimated at 560,631). This is more than double that of the United States. Pakistan, according to its 1951 Census estimate (released March 20, 1951), has 75,687,000, of whom 33,568,000 live in Western Pakistan and 42,119,000 in Eastern Pakistan. The total population of the two nations was, therefore, estimated in 1951 at around 437.5 million, which is more than the combined populations of the United States, the Soviet Union, and the United Kingdom. It is possibly exceeded by the population of China, though there are no census figures for that country as a whole on which to base a comparison. In the two nations of India and Pakistan live not quite one-fifth of the world's total estimated population, occupying, however, only a little over 3 per cent of the world's land area, excluding the polar regions.

Economically India and Pakistan are far from having developed their industrial potentialities, though it is true that after World War II, with the eclipse of Japan, India was, for the time being, the chief industrial producer in Asia. It is doubtful that these two countries separately or together could ever assume an industrial position in Asia comparable to that which Japan held before the war and may regain. Nevertheless, they have the resources for a development of notable size. India has extensive, high-grade deposits of iron, estimated at 20 billion tons. She has deposits of coal, estimated at 60 billion tons; little of this is useful in metallurgical activities. She has excellent resources in manganese, mica, and bauxite. Her largest industry is cotton textiles. She produces cement, paper, and some other industrial products. Pakistan has far fewer economic resources than India, but does have almost a world monopoly in raising jute, though the mills for processing it are located in India, Scotland, and the United States. It is estimated that India and Pakistan have combined water-power resources of about 27,000,000 horsepower. Though the subcontinent lacks a good supply of oil and has few deposits of non-ferrous metals, these and other necessities for industry can be imported from nearby—oil from the Persian Gulf and Burma, the needed metals largely from Burma.

The population figures show that the subcontinent has a large labor supply. Not only is the source practically inexhaustible; Indian labor also has a tradition of skill celebrated in Europe since the times of classical Greece and Rome. Five centuries ago 'India was producing wares which induced technically less advanced Europe to seek a water route to that land. Hence the discovery of America! Early in the war in 1942 a United States Technical Mission to then unpartitioned India reported that, given a living wage, the Indian workman stood up well in comparison with industrial workers of western countries.

Besides economic potentiality, India and Pakistan have the prospect of significant intellectual accomplishment. In the Indian subcontinent flourish today two of the world's greatest historic civilizations—the native Indian and the imported Islamic. Of these the first has existed for more than four and a half thousand years. Islam, though younger in India, is the heir to a thousand years more of civilization in the Near East. Both of these have been supplemented in the subcontinent by Europeanism since it established itself militarily and politically in the latter half of the eighteenth century. Thought in India has never been static, nor has social custom. As Jawaharlal Nehru repeatedly points out in his *Discovery of India* (1946), it is just the adaptability of Indian civilization to new ideas and its conjunction of intellectualism with imagination which have enabled it to modify or abandon outworn institutions and maintain its vitality and strength by developing new ones. It is this same adaptability which makes India and Pakistan potentially strong for intellectual development in the modern world. It is reasonable to expect that in the future, as in the past, the Indian subcontinent will be intellectually creative and will rank with Europe and America in scientific, social, and humanistic accomplishment. It may rival, though not duplicate, the great western nations.

Together with these possibilities of achieving world economic importance and intellectual distinction, the subcontinent happens also to hold a strategic position on the globe. It lies at the top of the Indian Ocean, commanding the lanes of sea traffic between Europe and Africa on one side and on the other, Southeast Asia, the Far East, and the Pacific lands. This situation gives it marked advantages for trade in a great section of the earth. If India and Pakistan expand their industry, they will have convenient foreign markets on each side for surplus exportable manufactures. In a military crisis they could, with their large resources of population and an expanded industry, strike out in either direction.

Politically, India is the most influential nation in Southern Asia, and she assumed a measure of leadership in calling the Asian Relations Conference in 1947 and the Asian Conference on Indonesia in 1949. Since then, and especially after the outbreak of the Korean war, she has been the chief spokesman for non-communist Asia. Pakistan as the world's most populous Muslim nation might become the leader in an association of Islamic states.

But along with these potential sources of strength, India and Pakistan have serious elements of weakness. One is the conflict between the Islamic and Hindu communities which has now separated the subcontinent into two political entities and may lead to further strife. There are perilous divisions within each country between majority and minority social groups, between linguistic groups, between geographical regions. Today the economy of each is weak. Poverty is general, and sudden disaster can produce a famine, local or widespread according to the circumstances. The population problem is critical. Before these two countries can realize their potentialities, they must get these various problems under control.

India and Pakistan live today, as they have done in the past, primarily by means of agriculture, with relatively little supplement from industry. The imbalance is shown by the small number of industrial workers. Modern factories in the two nations employ only

around two million persons, or by the most liberal interpretation of
"factory" perhaps 2.5 million. This is about one-half of 1 per cent of
the total population. Whether you travel in the subcontinent by rail,
automobile, or air, you emerge suddenly from one of the few
large cities to proceed for hundreds of miles across open country,
dotted with drab little villages, lightened by only an occasional whitewashed Hindu shrine or Muslim mosque. Here and there you come
to a small town. There is nothing to compare with the Atlantic
coastal stretch of almost continuous urbanization from Boston to
Wilmington or with some other American industrial areas, as around
Pittsburgh and Chicago. Only about 6.5 per cent of India's population in 1951 and 5.0 per cent of Pakistan's lived in cities of a hundred thousand or over. In the United States the urban percentage in
1951 was 32.0. Just as there are few cities and towns in India and
Pakistan, so too there are few isolated rural dwellings like the farm-
houses of the United States. Most of the people (over 87 per cent)
live in the more than 650,000 villages, which are settlements of less
than 5000 population, averaging about 520 each. Of the villagers
much the greater part (about 70 per cent of the total population)
are cultivators of the adjacent land; the others supply services or
pursue handicrafts (weaving, pottery, metal work, oil pressing, or
other). The country, as one sees it, consists of clusters or even long
stretches of tiny fields, streaked with inarable land and jungle. Except at a few centers like Calcutta, Bombay, Madras, Jamshedpur,
Asansol, Ahmedabad, Kanpur (Cawnpore), Sholapur, Karachi, factory chimneys are solitary or absent. This is how things are in the
cultivated sections of "the plains." In the hills and mountains, where
agriculture is more difficult, villages are fewer and smaller. In the
deserts, as in Rajasthan, they are still scarcer.

Agriculture in almost every part of India and Pakistan has to
depend upon a scanty or fickle water supply, and the possession of
water is a perennial and never fully solved problem. Nowhere else
do so many people put so much labor into getting water; and nowhere else is the problem of getting it more dramatic. In a region
where great rivers can be used for irrigation, such as the Punjab or
Sind, the water is impounded by huge dams or barrages and led off
through canals. The major outlets are large; from these run off
smaller canals, and from these still smaller ones, and so by gradu-
ated decrease until the water finally reaches the fields through minute capillary-like distribution. For part of the year many of these

channels must be cut off, to save the water until it is needed later. At the latter time the peasants are busy throughout the day opening the sluices leading to their land so as to get the maximum flow during the hours for which they have contracted and to direct the water first to one part of their farms and then to another. This is the easiest of India's ways of using human labor to water fields, and the most certain. The rivers of north India are largely fed by the melting snows of the Himalayas and the rain that falls upon their southern ranges during the annual summer monsoon. At that time the clouds, after crossing the plains, have to rise, are cooled, and so are made to condense and precipitate their moisture. The flow of water in the rivers fluctuates from year to year, but in no year does it cease entirely. Hence, peasants who live in regions where there are river-fed irrigation systems are usually better off and less subject to crop failure and famine than those who must rely upon other sources.

In many parts of India and Pakistan the farmer gets water for his fields from a well. In North India he may use a great Persian wheel, filling the air with an interminable creaking, which dips an endless chain of earthenware pots into the water, raises them above ground level, and empties them into a trough from which the water flows through runlets to the land. A blindfolded camel or a pair of bullocks operates the mechanism, treading a tiny circle all day long while a man or boy stands by to keep them moving. Elsewhere a peasant may use a buffalo or a bullock or a pair of bullocks, which alternately raise and lower a leather sack into the water. There is a ramp built up to the well, rising above its mouth some six feet or more. Along it the bullocks tread forward and backward, relaxing the rope to which the sack is tied, and so letting it fall, then, when they reverse, raising it to the wooden crossbeam at the high end of the incline, where it is emptied into a channel to flow away. It takes one man to empty the sack, another to drive the bullocks. Very poor peasants who own no bullocks and cannot arrange to use those of a neighbor may operate such a well with only human labor, India's cheapest commodity, drawn from the ranks of the family.

In still other areas peasants raise the water with a sweep, like an Egyptian *shaduf*. This is a seesaw-like apparatus with a leather sack or an earthenware pot at one end of the beam and a counterpoise balanced at the other. All day long a man may walk back and forth along the beam, first lowering the container into the well and then raising it to the top, where another man empties it into a runway. Or at the extremity of the sweep there may be a bamboo pole with the vessel fastened to its end. A man stands beside the well forcing the pole down until the vessel is submerged, then letting it go so that the counterpoise can raise it to the surface. In South India one may see a channel or ditch full of water, into which two peasants, often women, jointly dip a shallow scoop, rhythmically swinging it back and forth between them, lifting the water and emptying it in a higher channel through which it flows to the fields.

Throughout the land there are hundreds of thousands of "tanks," or artificial ponds, which are filled by the annual rains and serve in the dry season for irrigation, washing, even drinking. It is important to keep these tanks in good working order. Silt must not be left to accumulate; plants, such as the rapidly spreading water chestnut, must be prevented from choking them and absorbing the water supply. A tank has to be cleaned out regularly. But when it is cleaned, it is necessary to do the work carefully, so as not to dig out the bottom and let the water seep away.

In South India there are myriads of such artificial storage ponds, varying in size from an acre or less to a square mile or more. At the lower end of a gentle slope an earthen dike is constructed, which has to be kept in constant repair; the upper end is a marsh. Seen from the air, the country sparkles with them like the embroidered garments inset with bits of glass that women wear in Cutch. This method of maintaining agriculture appears to have been used since megalithic times.

In every part of the subcontinent where rice is cultivated, from the extreme south to the steep mountains of Kashmir, the peasants have made the cultivable land into series of terraces. These are large where the slope of the ground is gradual, but on the steep sides of the lower Himalayas they seem from the air to be no bigger than one's fingernail. Around each terrace is a mud wall to retain the water that accumulates during the annual rains or is introduced by some device of irrigation.

Water brought by river or rainfall has always exercised a decisive influence on the life of the subcontinent. It has been responsible for the population concentrations, for the direction of ethnic invasions, for the development of the arts of civilization, for the songs of poets. Its importance is certified from the time of India's earliest literature. In the Rig Veda's myth of creation the cosmic Waters were at first confined by malevolent inertia and had to be released by a hero-god in fierce battle before a universe could exist and operate. In that same work and in allied literature are charms which priests recited to wake the aestivating frogs so that with the magic spells of their croaking they might summon the needed rain. Fifteen

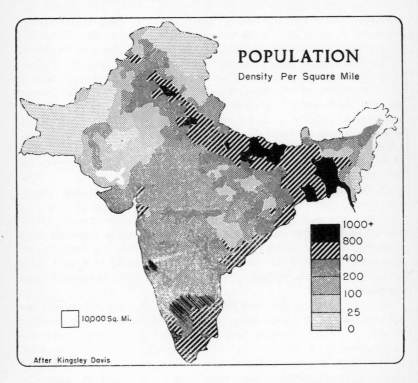

POPULATION

Density Per Square Mile

10,000 Sq. Mi.

1000+
800
400
200
100
25
0

After Kingsley Davis

hundred years later the Sanskrit poets were extolling as divine music the peacock's cry, so shrill to our ears, that heralds the approach of the rainy season. In the Rajput and Mughal miniature paintings of the eighteenth and nineteenth centuries the musical mode appropriate to the rolling thunder and serpent-like streaks of lightning that accompany the vitalizing downpour of the monsoon evokes the artist's most delicate powers of imagination.

What are the facts about the subcontinent's topography, its fertile plains, its river systems, its mountainous areas, its deserts, its basic water supply?

The subcontinent is shaped roughly like a quadrangle—or, more precisely, like a pentagon, though the fifth side is disproportionately short. One long point of the figure is the Deccan peninsula projecting sharply southward into the Indian Ocean, with the Arabian Sea on its west and the Bay of Bengal on its east. The rest is mountainbound. Along the northwestern side, now held by Pakistan, is a protective barrier of hills and desert, generally difficult for armies or peoples on the trek, yet penetrable at various points, and providing the chief means of ingress to India by land throughout recorded history. The northern side is a concave arc of lofty mountains, containing the world's highest peaks. It bars both the peoples and the cold winds of the land beyond and at the same time blocks the rainclouds of India from reaching Central Asia, where in consequence large areas remain desert. These ranges are geologically young and they and the nearby plains are disturbed by frequent tremors and occasional disastrous earthquakes, such as those in Bihar in 1934 and Assam in 1950. On the east the short fifth side is the Burma frontier, whose jungle-covered mountains and dangerous marshes are all but impassable.

Inside the northwestern and northern walls is the great plain of the subcontinent. It starts at the Arabian Sea with the peninsula of Kathiawar in the present Republic of India, and extends, first, slightly west of north to Sind in Pakistan. There it bends to a little east of north and continues for about 700 miles to the Himalayas, including all of Western Pakistan except some mountain areas. It then turns eastward into India, to follow a curved course below the Himalayan chain, crossing the breadth of the country and coming to an end against the hills of Assam and Eastern Pakistan and the coast of the Bay of Bengal.

This plain varies from 80 to 200 miles in width. In its sweeping course it contains the greatest of India's river systems. In the west is the Indus, which rises on the northern side of the Himalayas, flows westward behind them to round their end, separating them from the Karakoram and Hindu Kush ranges, and then drives inside the northwestern frontier down to the sea. The Indus is fed by the five rivers of the Punjab ("Land of Five Streams"), one of which (the Sutlej) also rises north of the Himalayas not far from the source of the Indus, but, unlike it, finds a route directly through them. The four others (Jhelum, Chenab, Ravi, Beas) rise in the range and flow directly to the lowlands. In the upper Punjab the moderate rainfall and the irrigation based upon its rivers support an extensive agriculture. Farther south, in the lower Punjab and Sind, rainfall is scanty, varying from ten to twenty inches annually and in many places being even less. Here agriculture is impossible except with the aid of irrigation. This has been practiced for millennia, but never on a scale to support a large population. Today there are great systems of irrigation in this region, and others are under construction or planned. East of the long course of the Indus is the Great Indian Desert, which has neither rivers nor rainfall. In form it is an irregular triangle with one side paralleling the river and the others forming an apex which points eastward into Rajasthan in India. Southeast of Sind in India is Kathiawar, a region with very moderate rainfall but enough to support a population of medium density.

The northern part of the Great Indian plain, often called Hindustan, contains the Ganges-Jumna (Jamna) river system, which only a low rise of ground separates from the Indus system. The soil of this region is a deep alluvial deposit. Its two main rivers, the Ganges and the Jumna, rise on the lower side of the Himalayas and curve southeast in gradually converging arcs until they unite at Allahabad. From there the Ganges continues eastward to Bengal, absorbing many tributaries, to join the Brahmaputra. This last, like the Indus and the Sutlej, rises on the northern side of the Himalayas, but, as though to polarize the Indus, flows eastward to turn and circle the eastern end of the mountain chain, where it finds an opening, reverses itself, and flows southwest. It and the Ganges unite and form an immense delta. Their waters reach the Bay of Bengal through many mouths, steadily depositing silt, and today as for millennia in the past continually projecting the land area into the bay.

The part of the northern plain east of the Punjab, already favored by its rivers, is in normal years also well watered by seasonal rains. It is the most desirable part of India and has always been the goal of invaders. Its population density is close to 600 per square mile and, though it comprises only about one-sixth of the subcontinent's total area, it contains about two-fifths of its total population.

Below the northern plain is a complex highland, the upper end of which is embraced by the two descending extremes of the plain.

Along its northern part are various ranges of low hills, of which
the highest peak, Mount Abu, is 5651 feet in elevation. These make
the Central Indian terrain difficult to penetrate and permit it to
support only a moderately dense population. Indian literature has
for 2500 years spoken fearfully of the wild jungles and the primitive
peoples in this area. The largest range of its hills is the Vindhyas,
south of which is the Narmada (Narbada, Nerbudda) River. Below this are other ranges (Satpura, Mahadeo, and Maikala), and
below them the Tapti river. These two streams flow from the center
of the Indian peninsula westward to the Arabian Sea and are the
only ones of the subcontinent's large rivers moving in that direction.

Still farther south is the part of the plateau known specifically
as the Deccan ("South"), which comprises most of the triangle of
peninsular India. This tableland (varying from about 1000 to 2500
feet in elevation) tilts gently from west to east. Its great rivers rise
on the western side, flow eastward across it, and empty in the Bay
of Bengal. It is not well watered, either by streams or by rainfall,
and much of its area is rocky or has soil of only inferior quality.
Nevertheless it supports around 200 persons to the square mile.

The Deccan is bordered on east and west by low ranges of mountains known as Ghats ("Steps"). The Western Ghats, a kind of
sea-board scarp, which have a few peaks of approximately 5000 feet
but average around 3000 feet, descend in thickly forested, bold de-
clivities to the seaboard. The southern part of this shoreline, known
as the Malabar coast, is one of the best-watered, most fertile, and
most thickly populated parts of India, having over 800 persons to
the square mile. On the other side of the peninsula the Eastern
Ghats, averaging about 1500 feet in altitude, are less picturesque.
They lead down to another well-watered, productive, and thickly
inhabited plain, wider than that on the west and known as the
Coromandel coast. The central plateau terminates in clusters of
hills called the Nilgiris ("Blue Mountains") and Palni, which
respectively have peaks as high as 8640 and 8841 feet. Finally, below these, at the extreme south, are the Cardamom Hills. Beyond
these last is Cape Comorin, the southernmost point of India, east
and south of which lies the fragrant island of Ceylon.

The Deccan highland is geologically old in comparison with the
Himalaya; hence its worn appearance and low elevation, though
Hindu myth assigns a different reason. The Vindhya mountain, says
the great Sanskrit epic Mahabharata, became jealous of Himalaya

and elevated himself, intending to surpass the latter and to interrupt the circuit of the sun and moon around Mount Meru, the mythical crest peak of the Himalayas and the assembly point of all the divine beings. The gods were alarmed but handled the problem by appealing for help to the renowned sage Agastya. He asked Vindhya to give him passage to the South so that he might carry civilization there, as he is traditionally credited with doing, and Vindhya graciously assented, bowing himself low and promising to remain so until the reverend sage should return. But Agastya never came back, and Vindhya true to his promise has never raised himself or even stirred. Being old and settled Vindhya, unlike the youthful Himalaya, is free of earthquakes; it is not only lowly but resigned as well.

The most important climatic feature of the subcontinent is the annual southwest monsoon, which brings "the rains," and gives India 90 per cent of its heaven-dispensed water. So impressive has this phenomenon been upon India's consciousness that in her languages the commonest words for "year" primarily mean "rain" or "rainy season." The southwest monsoon blows, with some variation each year, during the four months of June through September, when the high sun heats the land rapidly and the hot air rises so that a low-pressure area is created and cool air flows inland from the sea. As it comes in from across the Indian Ocean, it is laden with moisture which it has sucked up. One arm of the monsoon strikes the hills of the lower western (Malabar) coast of India, rises, cools off, and precipitates its water heavily. But by the time it has crossed the Western Ghats, it has lost most of its moisture and has little left to precipitate upon the Deccan behind them. Northerly along this coast the indrawn winds dispense their water in smaller and smaller amounts as the Ghats become lower, until they deposit scarcely any when they reach Cutch, just below the Tropic of Cancer, and Sind, which the clouds hasten across, hoarding their treasure for Kashmir seven hundred miles to the north. Hence Gujarat, which is the region north of Bombay, is productive, rich, and thickly settled, but beyond it Cutch, Sind, Rajasthan, and parts of the Punjab, being almost rainless, are dry and thinly peopled except where irrigated from the Indus.

The other arm of this monsoon rounds the southern end of India and Ceylon and proceeds north up the Bay of Bengal. It strikes the eastern coast unevenly, but gives fair coverage to the coastal plain lying between the Eastern Ghats and the Bay. When it gets to the head of the Bay of Bengal, it fans out to west, north, and east. The winds which blow westward water the inland areas of eastern India and the long northern plain of Bengal, Bihar, Uttar Pradesh, and the Punjab. They reach also into the center of the country. As they proceed westward, they steadily lose moisture until very little is left for the upper Punjab, especially the part which lies in Pakistan. They beat against the length of the first ranges of the Himalayas, rising and cooling and exhausting their last moisture on their southern side. This rainfall, in the years when it is sufficiently abundant, soaks the deep alluvial soil, fills the streams, which in the dry season are but thin trickles in wide sandy beds, transforms them into roaring floods, and happily makes the northern plain for the time a mass of fertile mud.

The currents of the monsoon which go to the north, northeast, and east drench Bengal and Assam, especially the hills in the latter area, which have the world's heaviest rainfall. Over eight hundred inches have been recorded in a single year at Cherrapunji in the Khasi and Jaintia Hills. This heavy precipitation fits the slopes of the mountains for tea gardens.

Additional rain comes to certain parts of India during the months of November and December, when there is another monsoon, this one blowing from the northeast. Over most of the country these winds are dry, with only occasional light rainfall known as "mango showers." They make the winter season in northern India a time of cool weather with almost unbroken sunshine and a comfortable temperature, ideal for tourists but of no help to the peasant if the southwest monsoon has been deficient and his crops need water. In South India the case is different. The part of the northeast monsoon which comes inland from across the Bay of Bengal carries moisture which it has absorbed from that body of water and then precipitates. It waters the coastal plain and succeeds in carrying much of its charge across the low Eastern Ghats into the rest of Madras, and into Coorg, Mysore, and Travancore. With this supplement to the rainfall of the southwestern monsoon the area is able to support a good deal of intensive agriculture. Nevertheless, neither monsoon brings the region just east of the Western Ghats very heavy rainfall, and each monsoon is fickle. There is no certainty of adequate annual rain to guarantee full crops, and often, as in the five-year stretch 1947–1951, there is short supply, and the area is in difficulty.

If "the rains," that "annual gamble" from the southwest, are "normal" and widespread, the subcontinent is prosperous. That is, people do not actually suffer starvation; the government can collect the land revenue; the peasantry do not have to borrow from the village moneylenders at a ruinous rate of interest and may even do something toward reducing the principal of their debts. But if the rains are scanty in any area or fail, not only do the fields get no direct water from heaven; the sources of irrigation dwindle too. Rivers fall; the village tanks are not replenished; the water table is lowered; wells dry up. So, too, if in Northern India, the rains are too full and make the rivers flood, as in 1950, seed may be washed out, cattle carried off, villages destroyed, and ruin come upon the peasantry and their land. Where there is irrigation from snow-fed streams, as in the Punjab, the case is not so desperate, for the mountain slopes always get a share of rain, which ultimately collects in the rivers. Elsewhere the inevitable result is poor crops or none at all. Agriculture stops; food is exhausted; there follows "distress," "scarcity," or "famine"; and relief must be brought in from outside. Such conditions have been reported since the third century B.C., just after India's historical records start; the case has not been different since. Today, under the political partition, rival national claims to irrigation water for the important agricultural sections of the Punjab have led to one of the most serious quarrels between India and Pakistan.

Though the subcontinent is an agricultural area—about 82 per cent of its crops are in food—it still does not raise all the food it eats. This is true even in a year when the rains are good. In pre-war and pre-partition times it imported from 1½ to 2½ million tons of rice annually from Burma; lack of that rice when the Japanese occupied Burma during the war was one of the causes of the Bengal famine of 1943. India is more dependent upon imports than Pakistan, and obtains food grains today under allotments from the Food and Agriculture Organization. Western Pakistan, however, is a wheat-growing surplus area, and in most years has a small amount to export.

Complicating the problem of feeding human beings is the presence of a large animal population. The subcontinent in 1945 had 170,-000,000 cows and 46,000,000 buffaloes. There are about 44,000,000 sheep and 56,000,000 goats and many camels (1,083,000), horses (1,838,000), and donkeys (1,918,000). Hindus do not eat the flesh of these, though Muslims (Mohammedans) eat meat when they can afford it. These many animals, therefore, do not relieve the country's food needs, except by providing dairy products. Even this last they do only scantily and in poor quality—hence Indians, who at all ages are fond of milk, on visiting the United States, exclaim at the abundance and the excellence of the milk everywhere on sale. Fishing is relatively undeveloped in the subcontinent and except in a few areas, such as Bengal, contributes little to food resources.

The chief food crops of the subcontinent in 1950–1951 were: rice, about 31.5 million tons; wheat, about 10.5 million tons; lesser crops of millet, maize, pulses, spices; about 6.4 million tons of sugar cane; oil-seeds, especially groundnuts (peanuts) at 3.5 million tons; also rape, mustard, sesame. Of commercial crops there were produced about 4.4 million bales (400 lbs. each) of cotton; and 7.8 million (400 lbs. each) of jute, almost all the best of the latter raised in Eastern Pakistan and constituting a virtual world monopoly; 0.4 million tons of tobacco; about 650 million pounds of tea. Both India and Pakistan produce much wool for export.

The bulk of the village population gets only the most meager living in terms of food, clothing, and shelter. Urban factory labor lives no better, possibly worse. Without seeing Indians in their villages, towns, and cities, it is difficult for a westerner to visualize the extent and effect of their poverty. And if the average American visitor wants to remain sensitive to the conditions in which the masses of the people live, it is well for him not to stay in the country long. Very quickly the want, the disease, the discomfort, the misery, become only accepted facts.

In 1946 the Goverment's Health Survey and Development Committee (Bhore Committee) reported the average individual diet figure to be 1750 calories a day (against a needed 2400 to 3000 calories), which was "ill balanced" as well as low and it estimated that 30 per cent of India's families were seriously undernourished. In prewar years, with food supply at "normal," the Director of the Indian Medical Service (Sir John Megaw in 1933) estimated that 41 per cent of the people were "poorly nourished," that is, endured continued semistarvation. The Government of India in 1952 said that its food deficit was 10 per cent.

For clothing a gauge may lie in the consumption of cotton textiles — almost all clothing in India and Pakistan is of cotton. The average for personal clothing and household purposes combined was about 13.5 yards per year in 1949–1950; in prewar years it was

about 16 yards; figures given for the world consumption of textiles
are 42 yards a person; for the United States 64 square yards of
cotton textiles alone.

Housing is equally inadequate. In the villages most dwellings are
made of mud and wattle or sun-dried brick, crowded together in an
irregular huddle, affording little protection from the winter cold,
the burning heat of summer, and the torrents of the rainy season.
The average floor space per person in the villages is impossible to
determine. In industrial urban areas surveys in 1938 showed it to be
less than 28 square feet in Bombay, about 43 square feet in Ahmedabad, about 24 square feet in Sholapur. Most urban workers with their families were living in one-room tenements; in 1931
in Bombay 74 per cent, in Karachi 58, in Kanpur (Cawnpore) 63;
in London at the same time it was 6.0 per cent. Often the quarters
were without a chimney or a window, with no lights or water supply, and no sanitary arrangements. Conditions can hardly be better now, since living costs have gone up more rapidly in intervening
years than wages, and the urban population has increased, while
little new housing has been erected. Every city, at least during the
present century, has had a large number of people with no housing
at all, who sleep each night in the open.

In typical village and urban dwellings furniture scarcely exists.
A house, or hut, has a fireplace consisting of a few bricks or stones
or molded clay set to form three sides of a rectangle over which a
pot or pan can be placed; it may also contain a few metal cooking
vessels and some primitive implements for farming or the pursuit of
a handicraft. That is likely to be all. Scavenging is a function of the
village dogs. With these basic handicaps to health go heavy incidence of disease and paucity of preventive and curative medicine.

The combined effect of poor diet, insufficient clothing, substandard
housing, lack of medical resources, is a high mortality rate. The 1941
Census of India gave a figure of 21.8 per 1000 (against 10.6 in the
United States), but some critical studies of the data by competent
demographers set it much higher, that is, at 31.2 per 1000. Life ex-
pectation at birth, according to actuarial calculations published in the
Indian Census Reports, averaged in 1941 31.8 years (it was estimated at about 26.7 in 1931), as against approximately 60 for whites
and 48 for Negroes in the United States (1929–1931). The brevity
and ills of life in India have often been held responsible for her preoccupation with religion, emphasis upon family organization, and

intense desire to have progeny and have it early in life, thus conducing to early marriage. In our time they look like an invitation to extremist remedies, such as communism or any other that claims to have a quick cure for social ills.

For some five millennia man in the Indian subcontinent has not merely held his own against the disadvantages which nature puts upon him, but has searched out and utilized means to maintain a life of high achievement in the arts of civilization. If on the spiral of history South Asia once was more accomplished in those arts than the West but now is less so, it may again reach a position of equality. That, at least, is the hope of many citizens of India and Pakistan. But the two young nations started life after a wearying struggle to achieve independence, and a destructive conflict between Hindus and Muslims, the ill effects of which still continue. With no time granted for recuperation, they have had to attack their basic living problems, build new sources of national strength, and assume international responsibilities. Their resources and energy have not yet been equal to the demands.

2. The Traditional Heritage

The principal motive forces for change in the subcontinent during the twentieth century have been nationalism, Hindu-Muslim antipathy or communalism, and modernization along secular lines free of religious motivation. Of these nationalism has been an affirmation of the stream of indigenous Indic civilization against foreign rule. Communalism has been the result of clash between the Indic civilization and the Islamic. The progress toward modernization has come from contact with the West during the period of British domination. Other motive forces of somewhat less importance have been those of language, caste, and regional rivalries. To a much less degree contrast of physical race has motivated social and political action. These various forces have all fought a kind of battle royal, with a bewildering sequence of unstable alliances among themselves. To understand these forces, appreciate their present manifestations, and assess them in respect to the future, it is necessary to look, however sketchily, at their origins in the subcontinent's traditional historic heritage and its legacy from Britain. We shall do so in this and the following chapter.

Civilization, centered in cities of the Indus valley, first appears in the subcontinent in the third millennium B.C. Starting then and coming down to modern times we can observe as a constantly recurring and decisive element in the history of India's civilization the intrusion of new forces from outside, their clash with those already in the country, and the slow process of resolving the disharmonies so created. The remaining unresolved disharmonies furnish problems of the present.

The longest standing clash in the subcontinent is that of non-Aryan with Aryan. This goes back to the first civilization there of which we have record. Archaeology has since the 1920's recovered a number of cultures from mounds in the hot and desiccated valley of the Indus and its tributaries, of which the most important, though not the oldest, is called "Harappa" after the place where it was first found. This was one of the great civilizations of antiquity. Its period has been established as the third and second millennia B.C. Well-excavated sites are Harappa in the southwestern Punjab and Mohenjo-daro and Chanhu-daro in Sind. Other sites are known from as far east and northeast as the Bikaner state in western Rajasthan and a village near Simla in the Himalayas and from as far south as in Kathiawar. The houses were built of brick in two or three stories, and copiously supplied with baths. Towns were well laid out; streets were straight; and there was an elaborate drainage system. The people used tools made of copper and bronze, as well as stone. They wore clothing of cotton. They had characteristic painted pottery, decorated with foliage, animal, and geometric motifs. They used a system of writing, which unfortunately we cannot read, though we have recovered many seals inscribed with it. Who the people of the Harappa culture were we do not know. The best guess, but it is only a guess, is that they were Dravidians, that is, speakers of the languages known as Dravidian, a people who were in India at that time and are now, and are known for three thousand years to have been, one of India's most important cultural groups. Certainly they were not Aryans (Indo-Europeans), the linguistic kinsmen of most European peoples, who seem to have entered India later.

This early Indus valley civilization contained many elements similar to elements in contemporary nearby Mesopotamian or Iranian cultures, such as the use of seals and of writing or among art motifs the representation of the human hero wrestling erect with one or two lions. It also contained many other items unparalleled in those cultures, yet echoed in later historic Indian civilization. Among the latter is the pipal tree, shown on seals and pottery as though in religious use; this is still sacred to Hindus, and is honored by Buddhists as that under which the Buddha sat when he won enlightenment. Various animals which are revered in later Hinduism are also common on Indus valley objects in what appears to be a religious environment, for example, the bull. There are figures of a god or man seated in yoga posture, as known in historic Hinduism for the past 2500 years; in one case the figure is flanked by rearing serpents, in another it is surrounded by a group of animals, both of which features recall current Hindu religious notions associated with the god Shiva. Many symbols commonly employed today appeared then, such as the *swastika* "emblem of well-being," widely used in India's three great native religions, Hinduism, Jainism, and Buddhism, and taken by the latter faith to China and elsewhere. There are evidences of phallic worship and mother goddess worship, both of which are extensive in Hinduism today. There is undoubtedly a large measure of continuity between the pre-Aryan Indus valley civilization and that of later Hindu India during historic times down to the present.

The Harappa culture seems to have continued to the sixteenth century B.C. Who destroyed it we do not know, though suspicion falls upon the Aryans, who entered India from the northwest probably at about 1500–1200 B.C. These Aryans were seminomadic, unlike the urbanized Harappa people. They spoke an archaic form of Sanskrit, which they introduced and maintained in India with modifications. Unfortunately, they have left us only literary records, namely, the four Vedas with ancillary texts, above all the Rig Veda, and the dominant interest of these works is the highly ritualistic Vedic religion with its numerous deities and elaborate fire sacrifice; other topics are treated only indirectly. They have left no remains of cities, burials, arts and crafts; what knowledge we have of their culture beyond religion is gleaned by inference.

The early Aryans record their warfare with the people who preceded them. They despised them for their darker color and false religion, and called them Dasa and Dasyu, as they did also the demonic enemies of their own gods. In the field they had the swift horse to help them—they may have introduced it into India. As social order they recognized three classes of Aryans—the Brahmans or priests, the Kshatriyas or rulers and warriors, the Vaishyas or commons—and a class of serfs called Shudras consisting of non-Aryans accepted on this humble level in the Aryan community. The fourfold structure of Vedic society afterwards became the framework into which the caste system was arbitrarily fitted. But it was not yet that system; in the three upper groups status was not yet rigidly fixed; society was mobile. From the time of their first invasion the Aryans have been steadily advancing into non-Aryan territory, whether by force of arms or peacefully, until now their languages occupy about three-fourths of the subcontinent.

Though the early Aryans had little of material culture when they arrived, the Aryan invasion was in many respects the most important thing that ever happened to India. It gave the subcontinent its great classical languages. It provided it with a priestly and learned class, the Brahmans, who hold a preëminent position today, even in South India, where Aryan speech does not prevail. Aryanism is in Hindu India the sign of the traditionally élite, and whoever can claim to be Aryan takes pride in doing so. In South India, where Aryanism is least strong, being mostly limited to the Brahman caste, the Dravidian elements in the population have in recent years used political means to express their resentment of Aryan domination. The Justice Party of the 1920's and 1930's made its campaigns on a platform of non-Brahmanism. Today the Dravidian elements are politically dominant and have imposed legal curbs upon the privileges and rights of Brahmans.

Historic indigenous Indian civilization was born out of the union of pre-Aryan and Aryan cultures. The process of fusion and growth to maturity had started by the sixth century B.C., after the Aryans were well established all over northern India. It seems to have risen in Bihar in the eastern part of the Aryan community, where Aryanization was still incomplete and society was headed by land-owning rulers who could not rightfully claim Aryan descent. This region was presumably then, as now, one of the most productive agricultural areas in India. In it, too, existed cities with a wealthy merchant class, which wanted a social position commensurate with its wealth, but could not claim it in Brahman-controlled Aryan society. The revolt appeared in both orthodox, that is, Brahmanical, and heterodox environments. In the orthodox, as shown in the speculative texts called Upanishads, the thinkers acknowledged the Vedas and the Vedic sacrifice as inspired and authoritative, but challenged priestly intellectual superiority based upon mere birth as Brahmans. Heterodox thinking rejected Vedic authority and was expressed most effectively in Buddhism and Jainism, whose founders (the Buddha and Mahavira) lived and preached in Bihar and nearby territory. These two faiths had wide patronage among the rising merchant class as well as the land-owning aristocracy.

For this period, that is, up to the fourth century B.C., our historical records of the Ganges valley are minimal, but from around the end of that century we begin to get fuller data. In about 321 B.C. a king named Chandragupta, belonging to a family called Maurya, established an empire with its capital in Pataliputra (modern Patna) in Bihar. His grandson, the great Asoka, who reigned probably from 274 to 237 B.C., had an empire covering the greater part of the subcontinent. He is one of modern India's most honored figures. A wheel symbolizing the Buddhist dogma, copied from a monument he erected, is now the emblem on the national flag.

Under the Mauryas and following dynasties, both in the north and the south, during a period of six centuries, Indian civilization was assuming its characteristic form. The greatest flowering took place just after that time under another great wide-ruling dynasty centered at Pataliputra known as the Gupta. This was founded 318/319 A.D. by another Chandragupta, and its greatness lasted until about 500 A.D. In the something over a millennium from the Upanishads to the close of the Gupta supremacy India developed the institution of caste, formulated its legal philosophy, gave classic character to its architecture, sculpture, painting, dance, music. It evolved the religion of Hinduism and the classic philosophies. All of this lives today, though with many variations resulting from historic experience.

After the Gupta brilliance, India entered her mediaeval period. The country was split politically into a number of small kingdoms; scholarship developed into scholasticism; religion was elaborated into a multitude of complex forms; philosophy, with some notable exceptions, turned from creation to commentary and dialectic; literature became less creative and more imitative and ornate. This period continued until at least the sixteenth century, and overlaps with the Muslim period.

The greatest achievements of characteristic Indian civilization are in religion and philosophy, and in this field first place possibly belongs to that form of monism known as *advaita* "non-dualism," described in the Upanishads, systematized by Badarayana, and brilliantly expounded by Shankara about 800 A.D. Second only to speculative thought is literature in India, exemplified in the great epics, the Mahabharata and the Ramayana, the Sanskrit drama, lyric poetry, and fiction. In sculpture, dancing, and music India has developed her own aesthetic theories, styles, and techniques. In architecture she erected some of the world's great monuments. As social organization she produced the caste system, which kept Hindu society together when disruptive foreign influences, such as Islam, entered the country. In science India has been preëminent in grammar; it was the European discovery at the end of the eighteenth century of Sanskrit grammatical achievements that led to the development of modern western linguistics. In mathematics, astronomy, and medicine she achieved less distinction. Her legal treatises are numerous, but she never fully separated civil from religious law. She was weak in the natural sciences, while in history she produced only the fewest of works.

Native Indian, that is Hindu, religious thought has viewed the world teleologically, as having no end in itself; the final end of man is other-worldly. While still preoccupied with the world and its affairs, his duty is to observe the rules of the group to which he belongs, his caste. But beyond that point, his effort is an individual one. Only when acting by himself can he accomplish his own greatest ends. Others cannot help him; they can never be more than strangers. In modern times there is a tendency in India to put less stress than in the past on the goal of final and complete salvation and to put more stress on group, that is social, responsibility, and to view that responsibility as one of producing social improvement.

One of the most interesting features of indigenous Indian civilization has been its ability to resist rival civilizations coming into conflict with it, though it may accept, modify, and assimilate elements drawn from them. This sort of clash has occurred three times—with the Hellenistic, the Islamic, and the European-Christian. The first of these took place during the formation of characteristic Indian civilization and was long ago finished. The other two are still in progress.

The Hellenistic civilization arose in the old Persian empire after Alexander's conquest and was a blend of Persian culture, at first with Greek, later with Roman. It used Greek science, literature, art, language, but Persian religion. Greek political institutions were a part of it, but did not flourish in Persia. About a century and a half after Alexander's invasion of the Punjab, at the time when the Maurya dynasty collapsed (180 B.C.), some Hellenized kings in Bactria (modern Afghanistan) penetrated Gandhara, the region of the present North-West Frontier Province. In the first century A.D. certain Central Asian peoples, named Kushana, of not very advanced culture, reached India by way of Bactria, having met Hellenism on the way and adopted it. They overran Gandhara, and went as far east as Mathura (between Delhi and Agra), which was then one of India's most important cities. There they established a capital, and from it extended their empire farther east. These various kings patronized both Indian and Hellenistic institutions. They used the Greek language in their courts, struck their coins in Greek on one side and an Indian language on the other, erected buildings and ordered much of their sculpture in Hellenistic style. But they also adopted much that was Indic. They were Buddhist in religion; they used Indian languages for literature; they employed the local Indian art of Mathura in sculpture. India eventually repudiated Hellenism in favor of her own civilization. Only the scholar finds vestiges of it there today.

The clash of traditional Indic civilization with Islamic began in 711 A.D., less than eighty years after the death of Muhammad, when Arabs invaded Sind to conquer it and the lower Punjab. At almost exactly the year 1000 Islamic penetration began from the kingdom of Ghazni in modern Afghanistan. From that time India was invaded by Muslim Turks, Afghans, Mughals. Muslims reached the Deccan and Bengal at the end of the twelfth century. The zenith of Islam in India was under the Mughal emperors in the sixteenth and seventeenth centuries. Every large part of India at some time or other fell under Muslim political control, but the central and southern parts of the country have had the least.

Islamic civilization came to India not only with military power but with the accumulated tradition of all Near Eastern culture. It had behind it the cosmopolitanism that flourished under the Caliphate and united the western Muslim world starting with Persia and stretching across the Near East, Asia Minor, and North Africa until it reached Spain. It had all the art and literature of Persia at its command. It was the heritor and developer of Greek astronomy, mathematics, and medicine. It had its own legal institutions and produced some of India's greatest governmental administrators, such as the Mughal emperor Akbar. Noble and beautiful buildings adorned its cities. Intensely and uncompromisingly monotheistic it was, but within that limitation it fostered philosophy. In India it promoted its own egalitarian social system, developed new schools of thought, and produced an extensive and often scintillating literature. At an Islamic court was cultivated the celebrated Mughal school of painting. The Muslims cherished their own music, which has come to dominate much of northern and northwestern India.

While the clash between Indic and Islamic civilizations was in progress, Europeanism entered, gained political power, and in so doing clashed with its two great predecessors.

In the framework of cultural history as sketched above, race, language, and religion have been dynamic forces and we should note the basic facts about them.

The subcontinent contains today representatives of two of the major human races, namely, the mongoloid or yellow-skinned, and the caucasoid or white-skinned. The mongoloids live only on the northern and eastern edges of the subcontinent, and include the Gurkhas of Nepal, whom the British used to recruit as soldiers; the people in the states of Sikkim and Bhutan, in the eastern Himalayas; many tribes living in the Assam Hills; some of the people of Kashmir; and a few groups scattered along the base of the Himalayas. The common physical type of Bengal may also contain a mongoloid element. The caucasoids, as a group are darker than those of Europe, but otherwise they are "Whites." They are of two varieties. One is tall, often blue- or gray-eyed, lightish in skin color, and is found among the Pathans of the North-West Frontier Province, the Kashmiris, whose women are celebrated for their beauty, the Punjabis, including the Sikhs, and occasionally elsewhere in India. Like the mongoloid this type seems to be a late arrival in the country, having been preceded by the other type of caucasoid.

This latter is the characteristic physical type of India. It is short and generally slender, though in the better nourished portions of the population it may acquire a thick cushion of fat. It is darker of skin than the first variety of caucasoid, frequently a deep black; and for this reason it has sometimes been defined as a separate human type and called "Hindu" man.

Color difference has not in general been the basis of social prejudice in India. Speaking more broadly, race, in the sense of distinction based upon physical, bodily, characteristics, such as skin color, facial structure, or other, though possibly a criterion of social differentiation among the Aryans during the Vedic period, is now almost negligible in India. Certain groups living in remote areas on a low economic level have in traditional Sanskrit literature been mentioned with fear and loathing. Some are still mentioned slightingly. But the population of India and Pakistan is not seriously divided into separate self-conscious groups differentiated by such criteria. Gradations in color have an aesthetic significance for Indians and Pakistanis, fairness being desirable—somewhat as is the case with those Americans who prefer blondes—but they do not constitute a basis for political, civil, or social discrimination. Nor do the distinctions of indigenous physical types in the subcontinent correlate with distinctons of language, religion, occupation, social status, or any other cultural phenomenon.

But perhaps because Indians and Pakistanis do not harbor prejudice based upon physical differences, they are particularly sensitive

to white western racial intolerance. Resentment of British color prejudice contributed importantly to the formation of nationalism. It now
has an international significance. To Indians and Pakistanis the widespread western phenomenon of racism appears baseless and unreason-
able. They do not comprehend the common attitude of many white
Americans toward the Negro. They cannot understand why citizens
of India and Pakistan, on emigrating to South Africa, Canada, or the
United States, should have been and in some places should still be
subjected to discriminatory laws of entry or denied citizenship or
deprived of normal human rights primarily because of difference in
skin color. Removal of racial discrimination is for both India and
Pakistan a major point of foreign policy.

Language difference has been recorded in the literature of India as
a source of group antipathy since about the middle of the first
millennium B.C. At that time speakers of "standard" Sanskrit expressed scorn for those whose pronunciation was inferior, for example,
in sounding *l* for *r*. This corresponds to the strong linguistic consciousness and high development of scientific language study in ancient
India. Linguistically, the people of India and Pakistan are today
distributed among five speech groups. In the descending order of
number of speakers, these are Aryan, Dravidian, Munda, Tibeto-
Chinese, and Khasi (in Assam). The best, that is, most arable, regions are occupied by Aryans and Dravidians; speakers of the other
languages and some speakers of Dravidian occupy the less desirable
areas, which are on the fringes of the subcontinent or in the interior
hills.

The Munda languages may have been the first of the five groups to
reach India, perhaps coming in from the East. They are now restricted to hilly and inferior areas in Bengal, Bihar, Orissa, and
Madhya Pradesh (Central Provinces). They consist today of so-
called "tribal" groups, with a comparatively low economic culture.
They may nevertheless have been a substratum of the population in
areas where speakers of other languages are now in full possession.
There is today a strongly self-conscious movement among them as
Adibasis ("first inhabitants") which seeks to establish their equality
with the economically more advanced peoples of India.

The Dravidian languages constitute the second most important
group in the subcontinent. They were certainly there before the
Aryan, and may once have occupied nearly all the country. They
dominate South India today below an irregular line starting south of

Goa on the west coast, running roughly northeast to skirt the eastern side of Berar, and then about east-southeast to the Bay of Bengal. Small scattered preliterate groups speaking Dravidian tongues are found in some areas where Aryan speech prevails.

The most important Dravidian tongues are four which have well-developed literatures. These are Tamil, covering most of the lower part of the Madras state and some adjacent territory in Mysore and Travancore; Telugu, spoken chiefly in the Hyderabad state in the Deccan and in the northern part of the Madras state; Kanara (or Kannada or Kanarese), prevalent chiefly in the state of Mysore but overflowing into adjacent states; and Malayalam, used in Travancore and Cochin and in the southwestern part of Madras.

The Dravidians, whether or not they created the Harappa culture, have long had a high cilivization. Though most of their literature is secondary to Aryan Sanskrit literature, they also possess an independent and ancient literary tradition going back a century before the Christian era, and have a pride in their peculiar cultural achievements.

The largest and most important language group in India is the Aryan, to which our own European languages are cousins. To the Indian branch of Aryan belongs Sanskrit, the chief classical language of Hindu India, in which are expressed its intellectual canons. As the common language of culture, Sanskrit was in ancient and mediaeval times the tongue through which the learned of all parts of the country communicated with one another, whether their native speeches were Aryan or Dravidian. In this way it was the cement that bound together diverse linguistic groups in a cultural unity, and, though the Aryan language complex is an immigrant into India, we call the country's culture Aryan.

The preëminence of Sanskrit as a medium of educated communication throughout India was impaired by the Muslims as they spread over the country. The languages they honored were Arabic as the vehicle of religion and Persian as the tongue of palace, courts, and polite letters. In the period of their power the position of Sanskrit declined. The English, in the nineteenth century, made their own tongue the main subject of instruction in Indian high schools and colleges and the preferred official language.

Modern Aryan languages in India are many. The most widely used has been for some centuries a group of dialects broadly called Hindi, which is native in the important state of Uttar Pradesh (formerly called United Provinces) and regions west and south. It has several spoken varieties; one of them under the name of Hindustani serves as a lingua franca over northern and central India and even in a very spotty fashion in south India. Hindustani has two literary forms, of which one is known as Hindi, in a narrow use of the term, and the other is called Urdu. The next most numerously spoken Aryan language of India is Bengali. Others are Marathi, spoken east and south of Bombay City, and in nearby portions of Madhya Pradesh and Hyderabad; Gujarati, spoken north of Bombay City; Punjabi; Sindhi; Rajasthani; Balochi, used in Baluchistan; Pashtu, spoken on the northwest frontier; Bihari; Oriya, the chief language of Orissa; Pahari, spoken in the Himalayas; Kashmiri; Assamese. Out of the various kinds of language diversity have grown a variety of social and political conflicts in modern times.

By far the most effective force in separating Indian communities from one another and so producing national disunity has been religion. At the same time religion, that is, in the case of Hinduism, has contributed to the formation, growth, and power of nationalism.

Hinduism is the most numerously followed religion of India. At the last census (1941) of undivided India, Hindus numbered 255,000-000 (the corrected figure after adding Hindu "tribals," that is, adherents belonging to preliterate "backward" groups, would be about 270,000,000). This faith, as now practiced, contains elements drawn from all known periods of Indian life, including the pre-Aryan. It is a complex of vegetation and fertility cults, sun cults, and hero cults, mostly derived from non-Aryan sources but blended with Aryan ideas and practices, and to a greater or less degree transfigured by Aryan philosophic speculation. It countenances every shade of intellectual belief from the crudest animism to the most profoundly metaphysical monism, and it does so by taking a relative, but realistic, view of human intellectual capacity. All but the smallest fraction of mankind, it feels, is incapable of comprehending pure and absolute truth. The rest can only approach it according to their limited intellectual and spiritual capacity. With the latter, the relative degree of truth to which it is possible for a man to attain is the truth for him and all that it is reasonable to expect him to hold.

In its most intellectual and spiritual form Hinduism recognizes the absolute under the terms Atman or Brahman, eternal, unbound by time, space, and causality, consisting of pure existence, consciousness, and bliss. Realization of absolute truth is hard; the most esteemed help on the way is practice of the Yoga technique of meditation.

To men of lesser capacity Hinduism operates as sectarian religion, and contains cults centering about the god Shiva, his wife Parvati, who is the universal Mother, their sons Ganesha (Ganesa) who removes obstacles and is the patron of success, and Karttikeya, god of war, and some ancillary gods; or about Vishnu, his wives, especially Lakshmi, the goddess of prosperity, and himself in various incarnations. Among these last, one of the most important is Krishna, the bucolic hero of the land near Mathura (Muttra) beside the river Yamuna or Jumna (Jamna) and lover of the milkmaids, who are interpreted as symbolic of human souls. It was he who, just before the epic battle of the Mahabharata, addressing Arjuna, general of the forces of righteousness, recited his teachings in the well-loved mystic poem called Bhagavad Gita ("Song of the Blessed One"). Another incarnation is Rama, hero of the great epic Ramayana, whose wife Sita was abducted to Ceylon by a demon Ravana. Rama, with the aid of animal allies, led by the monkey general Hanuman, killed Ravana and rescued Sita. She is the Hindu pattern of wifehood, and he of kingship. The "Rule of Rama" is the mythical golden age, for whose return pious Hindus pray.

On its lowest levels Hinduism admits worship of spirits and godlings of the forest, rivers, mountains, disease, and much else. It fosters many holy men or ascetics, conspicuous for their bodily mortifications. Vows and pilgrimages are a part of its practice, taking devotees to the sacred rivers, mountains, and other shrines of India, of which the most renowned is the city of Banaras (Benares) on the Ganges. At these the pilgrims gain an auspicious view, if only by the eye of faith, of the great being or beings honored at the place—as in other spheres people conceive that they are benefited if they can only so much as see the bodily form of a great leader like Gandhi or Nehru. Hinduism makes wide use of images, which the intellectually perceptive recognize as symbols, but the unsophisticated may take for deity itself. It is a faith that is highly imaginative and has inspired a rich art. Its ethics center around the principle of Ahinsa, noninjury of living creatures, especially the cow, which it holds sacred.

The characteristics of so amorphous a faith are hard to define. It has no formal creed. But there are two almost invariable requirements. One is acceptance as revealed literature of the mass of ancient texts known collectively as the Veda and including the four Vedas— Rig, Sama, Yajur, and Atharva—coming from the earliest Aryan

times in India, and a number of other somewhat later texts subsidiary to these, of which the philosophic treatises called Upanishads
are intellectually the most important. It gives almost as great venera-
tion to certain still later works dealing with religious and civil law
and practice and known as the Shastras and to the two long epic
poems mentioned above (Mahabharata and Ramayana), and somewhat less to a still later body of religious works known by the term
Purana ("Ancient Text").

The other requirement is the acceptance of the caste system as the
structure of society. Every Hindu is in traditional theory born to a
caste, in which he must remain for life, and he is bound to live by its
rules, subject to severe consequences for failure. A caste is a hereditary, endogamous group, which has a name of its own and some
special traits of occupation, cult, or custom, giving it a separate
place in the system. A man must take his wife from his caste—there
are a few well-defined exceptions—usually can eat only with caste
fellows, and is ranked in the social scale by the nature of the traditional customs of his caste. No individual can in accepted theory become a Hindu and enter a caste, though under certain conditions a
group may. Hence Hinduism is a non-proselyting faith.

Caste stratifies Hindus into more than two thousand mutually exclusive groups, most of which, however, have limited geographical
extent, so that no more than fifty to a couple of hundred may exist in
any single locality. At the top of the caste hierarchy are the Brahmans, whose various castes include about 6.4 per cent of the Hindus;
at the bottom are the Untouchables, known also as the Scheduled
Castes, Exterior Castes, Paraiyas, Fifths, and by Gandhi, *Harijan*
("God's folk"), forming about 21 per cent. The Brahmans define
social position, officiate in religious ceremonies, have custody of
sacred lore, and enjoy marked privileges.

The Hindus associate the caste system with the four classes into
which Vedic society was divided three thousand years ago, and a fifth
class developed since. In the three upper groups the boys undergo
an initiation ceremony at which they are invested with a sacred cord,
and hence are "twice born," but the boys of the fourth, non-Aryan,
Shudra (*Sudra*) group, descended from pre-Aryan aboriginal peoples
made into serfs, have no second birth. Nevertheless, in South India,
the position of Shudras is in general good. Orthodox Hindus consider
that every caste—which they call a "subcaste"—belongs to one of
these four major groups, which they call the "castes."

But below even these four main groups are now, and have been for at least eighteen hundred years, the Untouchables, whom orthodox Hindus regard as without caste and call Panchamas ("Fifths"). Actually they, too, are subdivided into castes, with their own hierarchical gradations. They do most degrading work, and for centuries, if not millennia, have suffered humiliating disabilities, such as denial of the use of village wells or limitation of approach to members of higher castes. Among them are leather-workers, scavengers, and others pursuing unclean occupations. They, like the Shudras, are descended from non-Aryans, but being accepted more recently by Aryan society are lower in the economic scale, weaker than the Shudras, and tolerated only on more shameful terms. Their case has been quite different from that of certain other non-Aryans who entered India as conquerors and afterwards, by reason of their military and political position, were brought into the Hindu community in a noble status. Many Rajput (Kshatriya) families of today are such descendants of Central Asians who won kingdom and position by force of arms. Brahmans have conveniently found them a genealogy leading back to the Sun or the Moon, from which all Rajputs are traditionally sprung.

The lower castes continually struggle to gain higher rank, for the hierarchy of the caste system, though immutable in theory, is variable in practice. If a caste which has been too degraded to have Brahman priests can bribe or otherwise persuade Brahmans to officiate at its ceremonies, it achieves thereby a victory and elevates its status. The rank of castes is not settled by law, only by social convention. A caste, or section of a caste, therefore, may in one way or another come to consider its origin nobler than it once did, and in successive censuses may move, on its own nomination, from a lower one of the five major groups into a higher; only the limits of what public opinion will countenance can check the advance. This aspect of the human will to rise has a corollary in that every caste knows of at least one other which it considers lower than itself.

Though nearly every caste has in orthodox Hindu theory a traditional occupation, it frequently happens that some or even most of its members may not follow it. This is especially true in urban communities. Brahmans, for example, may be lawyers, messengers, clerks, cooks. Some ruling princes may not be Kshatriyas, but members of herdsmen or Brahman or merchant or other castes.

The sanction for caste lies in the Hindu belief in the joint doctrine of Rebirth and Karma ("Act"). When a person dies, as we say, the Hindu thinks that he merely passes from one state of existence to another. This process continues indefinitely until a rare individual, by realizing the truth about the identity of the human soul with the Absolute Soul (Brahman), succeeds in saving himself from further rebirth to attain nirvana in association with Brahman. But while still in the cycle of rebirth every creature lives in a state which has been determined by his past actions in previous existences. Correspondingly, what a human being is doing now determines the state he will have in his next existence. Everyone, therefore, is living in exactly the state which he deserves in consequence of his previous actions. If he is born in a high caste, it is because he has lived righteously. If he belongs to a low caste, he is suffering now for previous misdeeds. But let not the high caste man be complacent; if he is a sinner in this life, or even only negligent of duty, he will pay a penalty in future lives. And let not the low caste man despair. He has the hope, if he endures with fortitude and virtue, of enjoying a happier state in the next birth.

Caste, as an institution under the intellectual leadership of the Brahmans, gave Hinduism in the past the toughness to withstand social attack. It is uncongenial to a democratic west, but it has given a framework to traditional Hindu society for twenty-five hundred years. Undeniable as is its unfairness to the lowly, it has had advantages as well; for example, caste councils institute and enforce much of minor law and order.

Gandhi and many other Hindus have denounced as sin the imposition of exaggerated disabilities upon the lower castes; it was not the aim of the eternal powers, they have held, to inflict such pain upon living beings. So, too, conditions of life in the world today are not adapted to the preservation of many established caste customs. Rival religions to Hinduism, which deny the validity of caste, especially Islam and Christianity, welcome the depressed as converts and ease their social and economic lot. Finally, the Untouchables themselves have grown conscious of their potential strength as a political group, and have formed political parties. Since they numbered one-eighth of undivided India's population (48,813,000) in 1941 their prospective vote under any system of universal adult suffrage is an important consideration in politics.

Within the caste the traditional unit has been the "joint family," which consists of a man, his wife (or wives), and all his descendants except the married females, living in a common household, the earnings of each member being in some measure the property of all. When the patriarch dies, the eldest son may assume the headship, or the sons may separate, dividing the father's inherited property among themselves. This system has largely broken down in modern India as the economic structure has been changing.

Other ancient indigenous religions of India are Buddhism, less than half a million strong in its homeland in 1941, and Jainism, which had about a million and a half. Both of these faiths developed in the sixth-fifth century B.C., had a steady growth in succeeding centuries, with a great access of power, but have been in decline since the Muslims struck them in the centuries from 1000 A.D. on. At the latter time their followers were being reabsorbed in Hinduism. These religions taught the ethical principle of Ahinsa (noninjury of living beings), and perhaps popularized that doctrine so that it came to be adopted by Hinduism as well. Though Buddhism and Jainism have so small a following in India today, and Jainism, unlike Buddhism, does not exist outside, each of them has produced a voluminous literature and an important art.

The imported religion Islam (Mohammedanism) had in 1941 in the then undivided country a following of about 94,447,000, approximately one-third of all the world's Muslims. Like Judaism and Christianity it originated among the Semitic peoples, and like its sister religions it is monotheistic, dogmatic, iconoclastic, and aggressive. But, though it demands credal conformity, it has its "two and seventy jarring sects," and a major differentiation between the Sunnites, who are generally considered orthodox because they accept the traditional Muslim law, and the Shiites, whose center is in Persia. About one Indian Muslim in eleven or twelve is a Shiah. The Muslim religion is the dominant feature of Islamic civilization. Before partition the Muslims were the majority group in the provinces of Bengal, the Punjab, Sind, the North-West Frontier, Baluchistan. The first criterion in drawing the dividing line in 1947 was to separate from the rest of India, as far as feasible, and constitute as the new nation Pakistan, contiguous areas in which the population was predominantly Muslim. There are also a number of the old Indian States in which the Muslims were the largest part of the population; of these the most important was Kashmir, where, however, the ruling family was Hindu. There were also Indian States in which Hindus were the most numerous but the ruling family Muslim, such as Hyderabad, the premier state of India.

Sikhism, about 5,700,000 strong in 1941, is a compromise religion between Hinduism and Islam. It was founded in the northeastern Punjab in the fifteenth century by Nanak. It has a simple dogma accompanied by a rigorous discipline of life, is monotheistic, and rejects the use of images. It reverences a holy book known as the *Granth Sahib* and the memory of its Gurus (teachers), several of whom were sternly persecuted by the Muslims. In recent decades it has been approaching Hinduism. The Sikhs have increased rapidly in the past sixty years—they numbered only 1,853,000 in 1881. The reason lies partly in their standard of living, which is better than that of Hindus and Muslims, partly in their better social practices— they permit widow remarriage and profess to deny caste—and partly in their acceptance of proselytes. Most of them are cultivators, though many are soldiers. Two-thirds of the community were living in the Punjab at the time of partition and the line put some of them in India and some in Pakistan. In the disorders following partition the most bloody conflict was between Sikhs and Muslims.

Zoroastrianism exists in India among the Parsis, a community of about 115,000, of whom around half live in Bombay. These were originally Persians who began to leave their native land in the eighth century under pressure from the Arabs. On coming to India, they settled in Gujarat, north of Bombay, and stayed there until the seventeenth century, when they moved south. The Parsis are a wealthy urban community, which has an importance far beyond its size. Much of India's biggest business, particularly in air travel, steel, and other industries, is in Parsi hands.

Christianity came to India early; legend, unconfirmable, says that the apostle Thomas atoned for his doubt by becoming a missionary to that land. By the fourth or fifth century a community of Nestorian (Syrian) Christians existed at Cochin far down the western coast, and still survives, though now the greater part of it is affiliated with the Church of Rome. Roman Catholicism came to western India with the Portuguese, who established themselves at Goa in 1510. In the year 1542 St. Francis Xavier went to Portuguese India to preach. The Inquisition was established at Goa in 1560. Protestant missions entered south India in the seventeenth century. They became vigorous in Bengal in the eighteenth century, at first against British opposition, which was removed later, so that in the nineteenth century they expanded rapidly. The total Christian population according to the 1941 Census was about 6,317,000 (the corrected figure to include Christian "tribals," that is, converted preliterates belonging to tribes not assimilated to Hindu culture, would be 7,400,000), of whom about 60 per cent live in South India.

The Jews, who are only about 23,000 in number, are also considered to have been in Cochin in the fourth or fifth century A.D., and a community still exists there, though most Indian Jews live today in the large modern cities, especially Bombay.

The religions practiced by "tribals" outside the orbits of Hinduism, Islam, Buddhism, or Christianity are characterized as "primitive" forms of spirit or nature worship. These aboriginal groups live in hilly regions inside the country, speak Munda or Dravidian languages, and in 1941 numbered about 8,791,000. They are economically the most backward of India's peoples and the most helpless and inarticulate. The government has treated them essentially as wards and under the Constitution of the Republic of India the policy is to be continued for a period of years.

All religious groups in the subcontinent have been acutely self-conscious, and all minority religions have viewed themselves as being in greater or less competition with Hinduism. Sikhism, in addition, contrasted itself sharply with Islam. The greatest social and political conflict in pre-partition India was that between Hindus and Muslims.

3. Effects of British Rule

The chief preparation of India and Pakistan for modernization has come from the subcontinent's association with Britain. This gave India political unity, administrative efficiency, inner economic coherence, a fairly modern system of education, a public health service, and an acquaintance with western industrialism, scientific research, technical accomplishment, and social thinking. With the aid of these, India had by 1947 progressed further into modern life than any other large or medium-sized Asian nation except Japan.

All this came about not so much by intent of the British as incidentally. The British purpose in coming to India was the simple one of conducting profitable foreign trade, which under the mercantilist economic theory then current in Europe should be pursued as a monopoly subject to state regulation. It was, therefore, appropriate that under pressure of circumstances European merchants journeying to India should be supported by arms, whether to check their European rivals, or to defend themselves from the Arab traders in the Indian Ocean, or to maintain their interests against local powers in India.

The English interest in India crystallized on December 31, 1600, when the London East India Company received a charter from Queen Elizabeth. The first voyages were to Sumatra, Java, and other islands east of India, but trade began with India after several Englishmen had called to make "contacts" at the court of the Mughal emperor Jahangir—Captain William Hawkins in 1609, William Edwards in 1615, and Sir Thomas Roe as ambassador of James I in 1615. The English got permission to open trading posts called "factories" at several ports in the Gulf of Cambay, now no longer important, and at Ahmedabad. During the century they established other factories, especially at Madras, Calcutta, and Bombay, which last had come to England in 1661 as a small and unesteemed island included in the wedding portion of Catherine of Braganza on her marriage to Charles II. The vicissitudes of the Company were many, leading to reorganization, but business expanded, the number of merchants was multiplied, and the size of the armed forces increased. Thus was the British Indian Empire conceived.

It was born in the eighteenth century. After the death of the last great Mughal emperor Aurangzeb in 1707, the Mughal power disintegrated, though a series of successors held nominal authority in Delhi until 1858. Other Indian regimes arose, including the Marathas in western and central India and Muslim dynasties in the south. Local rulers who wanted to widen their holdings or defend themselves against Indian rivals or foreign intruders drew the Europeans into their quarrels, desiring their superior military equipment, while Britain and France, fighting in India the same wars which they were waging in Europe and North America, made alliances with Indian potentates. In this way European holdings and responsibility expanded. The British broke the French power partly by battle and partly by treaty terms, which sometimes reversed field successes. In so doing they gained wide territory and then found themselves obliged to administer it.

The weakness of the Mughal authority was demonstrated in 1757, when Robert Clive in the strange battle of Plassey, following skillful intrigue and with the aid of treachery on the other side, won the great province of Bengal. In 1765, with the formal consent of the Mughal emperor in Delhi, the British East India Company assumed the revenue collection and administration of Bengal. As Englishmen acquired more political authority in India, they also secured more opportunity for corruption, dishonesty in dealings with the Company, graft in supplying Indian princes, and oppression of Indians. Many became fabulously rich. Such conditions under Clive showed the British Parliament the great importance of India as a source of wealth which should belong to the Crown but was being diverted into private possession, and it began to deal more strictly with the Company, regulating its affairs more thoroughly and limiting its powers.

Warren Hastings, who ruled from 1772 to 1785, constructed the framework of the Empire. He tightened the administrative machine and by his conquests in north and south and his diplomacy made the name of Britain respected everywhere in the subcontinent. The conquests were extended by Richard Wellesley Lord Mornington (later

Marquis Wellesley), Governor General 1798–1805, who won the rest
of South India and shook the Maratha power so that it was afterwards easily destroyed. In 1842–1844 the British took Sind following
their disastrous First Afghan War (1838–1842), which had been inspired by fear of Russian expansion in Central Asia. In campaigns
during 1845–1849 they annihilated the Sikh kingdom in the Punjab,
and in 1856 they annexed Oudh, now a part of Uttar Pradesh. Little
remained to round out the Indian Empire but to consolidate gains
and fill in a few corners, and this the British did after the Sepoy
Mutiny of 1857. By the India Act of 1858, Parliament transferred
the British holdings in title and law as well as in fact from the old
trading Company to the Crown. In 1877 the last symbol was put like
a finial on the imperial structure when Queen Victoria was proclaimed
Empress of India. The English who had obsequiously knocked at
India's side door at the beginning of the seventeenth century, happy
to do only a little buying and selling, had stepped inside and remained to take over India itself, ruling the occupants with a strong
hand and maintaining a monopolistic control over all outside relations.

In the eighteenth century, British dealings with Indians were stern
and direct. Troublesome rulers and men of wealth were mulcted of
immense sums of money and ruined, or their lands seized, or in some
cases themselves executed on grounds that today appear inadequate.
From the imperialistic point of view these methods could be condoned
as necessary for Empire building, and to Warren Hastings, the most
severely blamed and the defendant in one of England's most noted
trials, more than to any other man were due the decisive British conquests. The more ruthless form of imperialism that existed under him
began to pass away with his successor, Lord Cornwallis (of York-
town), who was Governor General from 1786 to 1793. From then on,
British policy allowed India a government that increasingly concerned
itself with the welfare of the country. It remained an imperialism,
but it gradually acquired rigorous standards of honest administration
and by degrees became more and more concerned with India's agriculture, education, public health, industry, and in the 1920's a protective tariff, and inclined to look upon India's financial problem
as distinct from Britain's. By the beginning of the twentieth century
the Government of India was often in sharp disagreement with the
home government.

In surveying British control we may start with political and ad-

ministrative policies. These were framed primarily with the twofold
purpose of promoting profitable trade and collecting adequate revenue
to operate the civil and military establishments. The basic need was
that the country be secure both from internal disorder and external
aggression, such as was the state in the eighteenth century which had
compelled European merchants to arm and had damaged trade by
keeping the country in that anarchic condition described by classical
Hindu political theorists as "the way of the fishes."

The first step was to reform and strengthen the Company's administration, and this was begun in 1773 when Parliament in Lord
North's "Regulating Act" asserted its supervisory rights. British
power then lay in three "Presidencies"—Bengal, Madras, Bombay.
The Bengal Presidency was now made the chief and its Governor
(then Warren Hastings) was made Governor General. Calcutta was
the seat of government and remained so until the change to Delhi
which was provided for in 1911. In 1784 Parliament passed Pitt's
"India Act" whereby it vested all political power and the power to
recall any British official from India in a Board of Control appointed
by the Crown, but left commercial patronage and commercial administration to the Company's Court of Directors. By Lord North's
act Parliament was to renew the Company's charter for only twenty
years at a time, and before each renewal was to subject the administration of India to a parliamentary inquiry; by Pitt's act it
made provision for substantial reform in the administration.

Lord Cornwallis, who went to India to inaugurate reforms under
the latter act, made one of the first objects of his governorship the
purification of the civil service. The old methods of the Company were
discarded, and appointees to administrative positions were paid adequate, in fact large, salaries; corruption, jobbery, and private enrichment were sternly discouraged. Officers were at first nominated
under the old Company system of patronage but from 1853 they were
selected on the basis of competitive examinations. Thus there came
into being the élite Indian Civil Service, a socially elect corps of
picked officers, almost universally capable and honest, which probably gave India the most just and efficient administration it has
ever known. Under Lord Cornwallis it was the practice to restrict
admission to the British; minor posts were filled by hundreds, literally
thousands, of Indians. It was not until 1833 that the Service was
thrown open to Indians at all, and then only with many limitations,
excluding them from the upper grades, to which they were finally ad-

mitted in 1854. The framework of the Service still remains the framework of both the Indian and the Pakistani administrative systems, though now scarcely a British officer remains in either nation. Its ideals still exist, though admittedly in both India and Pakistan they are conspicuously impaired.

During the nineteenth century Parliament steadily encroached upon the prerogatives of the Company. In 1813 it abolished the monopoly of trade; in 1831 it asserted authority over all Indian territories owned by the Company; and in 1833 it enacted a demand that all laws made in India should be laid before it. It was then, too, that it abolished the Company's right to trade at all, though the Company continued to exist and influence legislation until it was dissolved in 1858, after the Mutiny.

By this time, too, Mughal authority was only a fiction, for the power of the Mughals had long since departed. The Company had at first nominally operated under it, though the real source of power was Parliament, and through that body the British electorate. Parliament, therefore, destroyed even the fiction. The India Act of 1858 created in the British Cabinet the position of Secretary of State for India, with full control over India. To the Secretary of State was made responsible the Governor General (Viceroy), and to the latter alone was responsible, until late in the period of British rule, the provincial governments and through them every government officer in India.

In assuming larger powers over India during the days of the East India Company, Parliament granted to its agents in India the right of making many changes to assist in the better execution of the British purposes. The law was codified, with recognition being given to the Indian (both Hindu and Muslim) systems as well as to the British. A police system was established, and public education was instituted. After the Mutiny, Parliament made other reforms. It defined the status of the Indian Princely States and guaranteed their autonomy subject to certain restrictions. It provided for local District Boards and subordinate bodies in 1883–1885 to take an interest in local education, sanitation, famine relief, and roads, and extended the power of Municipal Boards. It reorganized the army to make the land safer for the British occupation and to preclude another Sepoy Mutiny. It devised a plan of defense for the northwest frontier and the seacoast. The total result of all these various reforms was in the direction of internal peace and safety from invasion.

Under Britain India gained inner unity. It had a single rule everywhere unchallenged, which brought the whole subcontinent for the only time in its 2500 years of known history to the traditional ideal of living "under one royal parasol." This rule, again for the first time in the subcontinent's history, was strictly secular, favoring no religion. As united, India consisted in the nineteenth and twentieth centuries of many units, diverse in political character and often of mutually contradictory political aims, yet all were unified at the center. All owed common allegiance to the British Crown; all respected its representatives and its courts, police, army, and administration. Even the conflicting social groups in the population, which were never really homogenized but only shaken together in unstable union like oil and vinegar, were formally synthesized at the highest level of government and usually at that level were decently civil to one another.

Again, throughout all parts of British India and generally in the princely states as well, law and order and the processes of justice came to be good. On the lower police levels there was always much petty oppression and corruption, not dissimilar in spirit from that often reported of our own American municipal police, but on the upper levels administration was efficient and, with only rare exceptions, free of abuses.

The means used by Britain to hold India included a good deal of the "divide and rule" philosophy, whether by design, as nationalists used to charge, or because of the inner nature of imperialism operating automatically and unconsciously. Large regions, namely the Indian princely states, were allowed to lag politically behind the other parts, that is, the provinces comprising "British India," so that the two kinds of political units stood side by side physically but philosophically were in contradiction. Large social divisions of the population, especially the Muslims, were permitted and in effect encouraged to develop and express their already existing fear and hostility toward the Hindu majority and to stand apart as a divisive group.

For a century and a quarter after Hastings no legislative function of any sort lay with the Indian people or any part of them acting through their elected representatives. Indian legislative reform proceeded slowly by stages which at the beginning were minute and infrequent. The principal early ones were as follows.

In 1833 Parliament added a Law Member to the Governor General's Council, and so differentiated the Council's legislative functions from the executive. Thus it inadvertently created the institution that afterwards grew into the Central Legislative Assembly—the thought of which latter body would doubtless have horrified the authors of the 1833 action. In 1861 Parliament enacted a statute enabling the Governor General to nominate to his Council for advisory assistance in framing legislation not less than six or more than twelve Indians. Again the proposers of the statute did not foresee the future growth of the Council into anything resembling a parliament, nor the growth of similarly designed Councils in the Bombay and Madras Presidencies into provincial representative legislative bodies.

This latter revolutionary outcome started under Lord Dufferin, Governor General 1884–1886. At that time middle-class opinion was expressing itself strongly enough to produce in 1885 the Indian National Congress. Dufferin announced, of course with the authorization of the Secretary of State for India in London, that it was his wish "to give a still wider share in the administration of public affairs to such Indian gentlemen as by their influence, their acquirements, and the confidence they inspire in their fellow-countrymen are marked out as fitted to assist with their counsels the responsible rulers of the country." During the next Governor Generalship (Lord Lansdowne's) the Act of 1892 was passed directing the Governor General and the Governors of the provinces to nominate the non-official members of the Councils after consulting important bodies in India. In theory and in law this was not election by those bodies, but it was equivalent to election in fact, for their recommendations were accepted. At this time the Councils were granted the right to question the government and discuss the budget, important concessions, for they made clear that the Councils were more than merely advisory.

The development of representative institutions from this time on is closely associated with the growth of nationalism. By successive demands Indians won concessions through the "Morley-Minto Reforms" of 1909, the "Montagu-Chelmsford Reforms" of 1919, the Constitution of 1935, and the Indian Independence Act of 1947. In the end Britain gave nationalism its full demand, not from generosity, as is frequently stated, so much as from recognizing that government of India as a British dependency was no longer either possible or desirable under the greatly changed conditions that followed World War II. The constitution and administrative machinery which Britain had provided gave to India and Pakistan when they attained nationhood an operating political structure with which they were able to carry on government and start an attack upon many of their unsolved problems.

During the British occupation notable changes occurred in Indian society and economic life. An obvious basic fact is growth in population. It has been estimated by W. H. Moreland that in 1600, during the reign of Akbar, the country had 100 million inhabitants. It is further estimated that by 1750 the population had increased to 130 million. When the first complete census of India was taken in 1881 (there was a partial and less satisfactory census in 1872), the area corresponding approximately to the present nations of India and Pakistan had more than 250 million. In 1941 the same area had a little less than 390 million, showing an increment of about 56 per cent in sixty years. The increase came from a lowering of the mortality rate through elimination of internal warfare, curb of banditry, control of famine, and check of disease. With these went increase of agricultural production, both food crops and commercial crops.

In furthering trade, the Government of India gave the subcontinent much that is today economically important. One of the largest items is the railway system, which was begun about the middle of the nineteenth century. Besides opening up India economically, the railways had a strategic purpose. A good deal of the latter kind of mileage, economically unproductive and expensive to maintain, was constructed along the vulnerable northwest frontier, now lying in Pakistan. The economic railways connected the agricultural areas with the inland urban centers and the seaports, promoted export and import trade, helped to mitigate the ravages of famine, and provided work for more than 800,000 persons. They are the greatest single agency available in the subcontinent today for further economic expansion.

Other kinds of economic development which took place during the period of British occupation include, in the way of agricultural aids, first, expansion of the irrigation system, especially in the Punjab and Sind. Extensive areas were opened to new settlement and cultivation through large projects for storing and utilizing the waters of the Indus and its tributaries. The government fostered agricultural experimentation and animal husbandry, and extended credit to agriculturists through credit coöperatives and otherwise. Forestry research was modestly fostered under the British control. Some roadbuilding took place, of which a part, as in the case of the railways, was for strategic, rather than economic, purposes. A banking system was developed under government control.

The most fundamental change in the economic structure of India was that in agriculture; this has seriously affected the village and, therefore, the basic social structure. The country's economy for as far back in the past as we have records has been based upon its villages. Though statistical information does not exist from before the successive censuses starting in 1872, it can scarcely be doubted that somewhere around 85 to 90 per cent of the population has always consisted of village inhabitants. These were of two sorts: agriculturists, who cultivated the surrounding land, and the various kinds of artisans, such as weavers, blacksmiths, potters, oil-pressers, and other nonagriculturists, who provided the village with services. The village was, therefore, practically a self-sufficient community. It raised its own food, supplied most of its other needs by its own products, and imported only a few commodities, such as salt or metal. Agriculturists, artisans, local officials and functionaries, and the Brahman priests lived an interdependent life, based upon transfer in kind. The village paid the governing authority a tax or landrent, again almost always in kind, consisting of a portion of the annual crops, and this constituted the bulk of the state's revenue. It also usually furnished labor to the overlord. Land was used by families on a hereditary basis; the artisans, again, inherited their crafts and their position in the community. Land when transmitted from one generation to another was often subdivided, frequently ending up, after several stages of inheritance, in uneconomic fragments which would in time, by some form of redistribution, be assembled again in larger tracts. Then division and subdivision would occur again. The process was iterative and cyclical. Within the village most of the functions of government lay in the hands of a council of village elders. Petty rulers passed part of their returns from the village to higher rulers, and they to others, and so to the top, at whatever number of levels it might be removed from the village.

Living conditions in the villages were far from idyllic, but at least they had shaken down to a pattern, which might be interrupted by pestilence, crop failure followed by famine, and war, yet gave the villages modest food reserves for a little resilience under minor misfortune. Within the relative stability of such life society was defined by the caste system, which gave every person status from birth often accompanied by inherited and nontransferable specialization of occupation.

The village or agrarian community was the state's chief source of income. For the British, as for their predecessors, the collection of the land revenue was the most important feature of administration. The method had been to make a periodic revenue assessment and "settlement," but when the British assumed the collection in Bengal, administration was in chaos and collection was inadequate. The British desired the land revenue to be paid in money, not in kind. For this purpose they established new types of land ownership. Under Lord Cornwallis in 1793 they instituted the *zamindari* system, by which they converted the old tax farmers and revenue collectors into landlords, called *zamindars,* who were given proprietary rights in the land including sale and purchase, while the agriculturists were made tenants, their old hereditary rights were ignored, and they were left helpless before the landlords. The latter, unable to carry the legal burdens imposed by new judicial processes, in many cases sold their rights to businessmen of one sort or another, who became absentee landlords. Thus both the peasantry and the resident tax collectors lost ownership.

Cornwallis, in establishing this system, permanently fixed the assessment on the landlords at £3 million annually. This was a seriout mistake, because as the country's economy expanded, it came about that the landlords could get increased rent from the peasants, until in the last period of the British control the total amount was reaching figures of from £12 million to £20 million, yet the government's portion remained the same. The difference went to support a series of intervening renters or speculators.

In some other parts of India (notably in Madras under Sir Thomas Munro, 1820–1827) another system called *ryotwari* was employed. By it the peasant (*ryot*) dealt with the government not through the old commune or through a newly created landlord class, but individually and directly. However, his tax also was now collected in money. The ryot had rights of private ownership, could sell or lease his land, and could be evicted or sold out for nonpayment of taxes.

Under both systems the village economy was changed from one of self-reliance based upon exchanges in kind to a money economy, which stimulated the planting of cash as well as subsistence crops, and the individual inhabitants of the village lost that measure of security which they had enjoyed in the commune. The emphasis now placed on money in all parts of British India permitted the rise of a moneylender class which could get control of the land under the revised terms of ownership.

Further, village artisans lost employment as foreign machine manufactures displaced their handicraft wares. When European nations first engaged in trade with India, they came for pepper and spices, and also undertook commerce in the handicraft manufactures of the land. Often, their ships came out chiefly in ballast since there was little market in the East for European goods. In India they had to purchase their homeward cargoes of raw and finished products, especially the wonderfully hand-woven cotton fabrics, with hard Spanish dollars and silver bullion brought from Europe or with products brought to India from other parts of Asia. India was at that time an exporter of manufactured goods. But during the latter part of the eighteenth century the situation changed. The cotton and silk textiles of India competed with the growing textile industry of Europe, especially that of Britain, which latter dreaded a rival and was seeking a larger market. A profitable business grew up of exporting textiles to India. Before long definite efforts were made to discourage the Indian textile industries. More important, the machine-made goods of the West undersold the handmade goods of the Orient, and the handicrafts of necessity declined. India became a great consuming nation. Thousands of her skilled artisans were ruined and a source of wealth was taken from the people. Large numbers of landless agriculturists and unemployed weavers, therefore, had no recourse but to fall back upon the land as laborers.

All these changes led to impoverishment of the villagers, destruction of their independence, instability of their social system. In the opinion of many economic historians they lowered the standard of living. The great increase of national wealth during the British period did not raise the level of individual consumption, they maintain; it was more than absorbed by the increase of population living at the subsistence level, and the end result was that India merely harbored more people living in greater misery than before.

To take up the increase in population and provide it a living, new forms of productive employment were needed. In another Asian country, Japan, the population more than doubled between 1870 (35 million) and 1940 (73 million) but the increase was absorbed in the cities, where a large industrial growth was in progress. In India no parallel development took place. The reason was in part that capital in India was shy of investment in large modern industry and preferred the unproductive fields of land speculation, buying and selling of agricultural products, and other forms of entrepreneur activity. It was also partly due to the fact that in the nineteenth century the British managing agencies in India, operating with British capital, functioned in many economic fields including banking, mines, jute factories, tea and coffee plantations, and others, and were able to check Indian enterprise. It was also due in part to governmental discouragement. The government did not exploit natural resources for the country's benefit, and there were no protective tariffs for infant industry until the 1920's. On the contrary, after the destruction of India's handicrafts by the flood of cheap British manufactures in the nineteenth century, when India developed a cotton textile industry, all Indian textile factory products were until the year 1926 subject to a countervailing excise duty to equalize the market for Lancashire products. Currency was manipulated also to British advantage. It was only with difficulty that the subcontinent built up a heavy steel industry at Jamshedpur in Bihar and at Asansol in Bengal, its jute manufacturing mills near Calcutta, its cotton spinning and weaving industry located in a number of cities, its sugar mills, cement works, paper factories. The failure to develop industry during the British period is a serious drawback to the subcontinent today, when the total number of factory workers is only around two to two and a half million.

A system of public education was introduced in India by the British on a decision made by the Governor General Lord William Bentinck in 1835. It was afterwards modified and extended, and as so altered provides the present framework for public education in both India and Pakistan. Being a predominantly agricultural area, India did not have public education in pre-British times nor was private education general among the population. A limited number of people could read and write, and they were likely to belong to just a few social groups; among Hindus these would be certain castes; among Muslims administrators, merchants, divines. Instruction might be given at home or in schools conducted by Brahmans or mullahs, and was mostly confined to religious subjects. With Hindus law, medicine, mathematics, geography, grammar, the sciences of metals, elephants, horses, or others, the arts—all fields—were considered to have a religious sanction and so were fit subjects of instruction. With Muslims, subjects other than religion, philosophy, law, might be left to guilds as unworthy of a place in the universities, which were meant for educating divines. This situation in both cases tended to freeze the content of any science and perpetuate it from century to century in a traditional form with only minor changes. Hence, for example, in modern India and Pakistan traditional medicine, whether Hindu (Ayurvedic) or Muslim (Yunani or Unani), uses textbooks composed in mediaeval times, does not practice such an innovation as dissection, is unaware of antisepsis, and employs a pharmacopoeia unaffected by any scientific research.

The British on accepting the duties of government had to face the problem of education. The first moves to introduce western learning were made privately in several centers by missionaries and by a certain agnostic watchmaker in Calcutta named David Hare, whose college came to be the core of the University of Calcutta, now the premier institution in India. The principal aim then was to promote higher education among the élite groups. When pressure was put upon the government to inaugurate a public system there was a controversy between those Europeans who were students of Oriental learning and wanted to use traditional material for literary and cultural content and those other Europeans, like the missionaries and T. B. Macaulay, and some Indians, like the social and religious reformer Ram Mohan Roy (1774–1833), who wanted to employ the western alone. In England, after the Reform Bill of 1832, the Whigs, then in power, sided with the missionaries and Macaulay, who wrote a notorious minute in 1835 that was decisive.

The decision was finally made in India on the practical ground of training personnel for government clerkships and similar low-level service. For this purpose the English language, as the language of government, was considered to be of overwhelming importance. It was made the medium of instruction and the principal subject of study. Other western subjects were included with it, though natural sciences were recognized only sparingly. Classical languages—Sanskrit, Arabic, Persian—were discouraged but were afterwards taught and in time acquired an honorable place among the offerings, but always as elective subjects secondary to English. The neglect of the traditional languages, literature, thought, art, was a great disadvantage for India. Students received no introduction to their own cultural heritage, and the English cultural material which they were offered was so remote from their experience that they could not understand and profit from it. They came out of college culturally impoverished.

Public elementary education, already preceded by private missionary enterprise, was instituted following a dispatch of Sir Charles Wood in 1854, according to which it was to be given in the local vernaculars. The government, besides maintaining its own schools, provided financial assistance to private schools which met its standards. There was always a disproportionately large amount of higher education in the system.

On the higher level graduate ("post-graduate" in Indian terminology) and professional courses were duly added, though to the present time students wishing advanced work who can afford the expense tend to go abroad, particularly to Britain.

The results in raising literacy during the British period were not outstanding. The country has been too poor to give education to any large number of pupils and most families cannot afford the economic burden of sending their boys to school when they might be working. Estimates made by Kingsley Davis on the basis of sample figures in the 1941 Census give 15.1 per cent of the population aged ten and above as literate (27.4 per cent of the males, 6.9 per cent of the females).

The educational system, though a small thing in relation to India's educational problem, nevertheless introduced some western science, technology, history, philosophy, and political, social, and economic ideas. It gave India enough acquaintance with modern scientific achievement to appreciate its usefulness and enough teaching of it to be the basis for enlarged offerings as instructional personnel and financial support may become available. It expounded to India the democratic political and social philosophies of the West, and gave it a good deal of an international viewpoint. It provided the country in English a language of educated communication, such as it had not had since the Muslims in their spread had shattered the importance of Sanskrit.

The public health system of India initiated under the British has been an important factor in the lowering of the mortality rate and the increase of the population. Sometimes it has had to do so against religious opposition, as in administering smallpox vaccine, which, being made from the sacred cow, is liable in the eyes of fanatical Hindus to involve sacrilege. The greatest victory of the service in dealing with epidemic diseases has been in reducing the incidence of bubonic plague. Little, unfortunately, has been done in providing adequate sanitation for large cities and nothing for the villages. Though the public health service of India under the British was far from sufficient, it furnished a practical working basis for the present services in India and Pakistan.

Though the British policy while in control of India made the immediate British hold during the nineteenth century easier and brought that economic profit which had been the first and always remained the dominant motive in British relations with the subcontinent, it did not produce in India the desire to stay within the Empire. Perhaps no form of imperialism could have achieved so paradoxical a result. Rather, the policy both aroused the demand for self-government and involuntarily provided nationalism with many of the instruments it used to satisfy the demand. It also produced a desire in India for commercial relations with other nations, and the volume of British trade with India in terms of percentage declined during the twentieth century. What Britain now gets from India and Pakistan she gets through good will. In this situation it must be said that the British have been amazingly adaptable. British business representives now say "Sir" without self-consciousness to the kind of Indians from whom forty years ago their predecessors would have demanded obsequiousness.

Throughout the subcontinent one of the most striking of general effects during the British period has been the accelerating secularization of life. With both Hindus and Muslims religion and magic are contracting into narrower and more sharply defined boundaries. A traveler making occasional visits during the past half century can observe this fact when he comes to a traditional pilgrimage point such as Allahabad or Banaras (Benares). The latter city used to support its municipal budget by a pilgrim tax of one anna (equivalent now to a United States cent and a quarter) a head, which was included in the price of all railway tickets to its stations. The number of pilgrims had been materially reduced by 1948 from the figures of twenty years before, the Banaras railway stations were receiving but a fraction of their former throngs, and the pilgrim tax had become insufficient for the city's needs. Food restriction and the need to use a rationing card in the place where issued have reduced pilgrim traffic, but the people also appear to be less interested. We may think that they see less profit for themselves in visiting and bathing at the holy spots. Brahman priests at pilgrimage points in various parts of India—north, south, east—confirm this impression. They complain that their business has fallen off in the past decade. Fewer members of the families for which their families have stood vicar during centuries have been arriving and paying fees for their services. Within the cities Brahmans are called upon less frequently for prayers and ceremonies in times of illness and misfortune. Brahmans add that in the cities witchcraft has come to hold fewer terrors for the populace, magicians are less patronized, and their own antidotes are less in demand. Muslims say that charm-workers have fewer customers than fifty or even ten years ago. In 1948 and 1950 urban temples and shrines seemed less frequented than in 1922 or 1928 or 1935. Contrariwise, the number of apothecary shops, drugstores, professional signboards of homeopathic, Hindu ayurvedic, and Muslim yunani physicians seemed to have multiplied in the same period. It is probable that most of the diagnosis, prognosis, and medication dispensed by these practitioners and in these shops is useless if not actually injurious, but the interesting point is that people are more and more relying upon physical means to cure physical ills rather than upon deities, devils, demons, and magic devices. All these remarks apply to cities and towns; there is no reason to think that any great change has taken place in the villages.

Another aspect of secularization appears in the weakening of Brahman prestige. That "god on earth" has come during the past three decades to suffer restrictions in Madras, once his firmest stronghold, where the number of seats in colleges open to his sons is less than the number of them who wish college education. Lower castes who control the legislature have lost their fear of the formerly privileged Brahmans, and allow them only their numerical proportion of public advantages. In the Maratha country in and near Poona anti-Brahmanism has long existed; after Gandhi's assassination in 1948 by a fanatical Brahman from that area there were violent attacks upon the houses and persons of Brahmans in many villages. All over India the Brahman has to face competition from every caste down to the untouchables in seeking posts that a century ago would have seemed his by rightful monopoly. The ridicule of the poor and not too bright Brahman appearing scatteredly throughout Indian fiction for over fifteen hundred years now has a somewhat more serious tone. His sacrosanct position is hardly conceded anywhere without an argument. Much of the change in attitude is due to Brahmans themselves; Nehru and many others repudiate the doctrine of position by birth and have encouraged the process of social leveling.

Certain features of the caste system have come to be ignored in a number of quarters. One of these features is limitation of occupation. For example, merchants, who in ancient India hardly aspired to political power—except with Jains and Buddhists—during the British period, under the influence of the British example, became eager politicians and ardent nationalists. Caste systems too have changed. Physical contact between members of different castes, formerly forbidden by caste regulations, is now a commonplace. In railroad trains and busses high and low sit side by side without a qualm; in factories they work beside or with one another; they are comrades in labor unions; these situations did not exist in the agrarian society where caste developed and are not covered by the rules. Interdining between castes is another commonplace among the socially élite in cities; to some extent it exists now in towns; it is said even to be appearing in villages. Some persons who in 1922 strictly avoided it were practicing it in 1948, quite unaware that their mores had changed.

Marriages across caste lines, which fifty years ago raised a public scandal in the Hindu community, are now common enough not to produce newspaper comment. Participants frequently seem to have no difficulty with either family or with caste members. Castes which regarded it as a disgrace for a girl to menstruate without being married are not seriously disgruntled in conforming to the law concerning age of consent (sixteen years for girls, eighteen for boys) enacted in 1930. Untouchability is now "abolished" by the Constitution of India. In Cochin at a Hindu-controlled Sanskrit school in 1948 an untouchable was teaching Sanskrit to Brahman boys. In Trivandrum at a Hindu girls' orphanage, operated by Hindus, Brahman, Shudra, and untouchable girls slept in the same dormitory, played and worked together, ate in the same small room, sitting intermingled and being served from common dishes with food prepared in the same kitchen, all directly contrary to traditional rules. Discrimination did not exist until time of marriage, when the girls were found husbands in their own caste groups. The association with untouchables did not impair the Brahman girls' eligibility. Throughout India now there are numerous other instances of similar relaxation of caste requirements.

Such changes must not be assumed to mean that the caste system is withering, though some good Hindus think it is. In Uttar Pradesh in 1950 there were Hindus who predicted that the system would be finished in fifteen years; in Bengal a Brahman said it would last only ten years; in Mysore another set its limit at twenty years. These were hardly the judgments of sociologists and should not be taken to indicate more than skepticism about some features of the institution. Caste provides the social structure for some 270 million people, and it is not likely to vanish, even if that were desirable, in such a brief time. It is merely being modified in what, except for marriage, seem to be superficial features. What the future of the system will be it is not possible to foresee. Gandhi, who was one of the most influential of Indians in inspiring the recent reforms, believed strongly in caste and did not advocate its abolition; he only wanted it humanized.

In education secularization appears in the fact that the Hindu and Muslim classical languages—Sanskrit, Arabic, Persian—and the literatures composed in them have attracted ever fewer students in the past five years. The fairly distinguished position which those subjects had achieved in the public education system by the late nineteenth century and continued to hold for some decades has now contracted disastrously in the eyes of Sanskrit, Arabic, and Persian scholars. Instead students flock to modern natural sciences and technological subjects. It is a question whether this neglect of traditional culture is to the two nations' best interests.

Secularization is embodied in the new 1950 Constitution of India. This develops the principle that state and religion should be separate, and thus implements the secular motivation of the Indian National Congress. Congress was organized to promote secular ends, aimed to represent all Indian communities, and though it has sometimes been led by strongly partisan communalists and religious enthusiasts, has always returned to the secular position. Secularism of government is being attacked today in India by Hindu communal groups, but the highest echelon of government supports it faithfully. Speaking before the All-India Congress Committee on July 13, 1951, Prime Minister Nehru said concerning the secular character of the State, "On this subject there can be no compromise of any kind; we must be prepared to stand or fall by it." The secular state was a platform of the Congress Party in the 1951–1952 general elections, wherein it won a sweeping victory.

The status of political secularism is not yet clear in Pakistan.

The statement of principles adopted by the Pakistan Constituent Assembly for guidance in framing the Constitution declares that Pakistan is to be an Islamic state. But the nation's spokesmen, who are also the heads of the Muslim League, say that this does not mean that Pakistan is to be a religious state. The state, they assert, will be secular; it will be Islamic in that it accepts Islamic ideals of social justice. These leaders of Pakistan have indeed promoted secular ends in building their new state. It is uncertain how the apparent contradiction will be resolved.

4. The Will To Be Free

Nationalism was India's expression of confidence that it could match in the present its greatness of the past. The immediate provocation and most of the specific aims came from living under British rule. The techniques of revolt were partly shaped by western patterns, but in their most effective forms by traditional Hindu ideas.

The early organizations nurturing nationalism were mostly religious; one, the Indian National Congress, which ultimately had almost a monopoly in furthering it, was secular. For some decades the movement was strictly a middle-class phenomenon, promoted by intellectuals, manufacturers, entrepreneurs, newspaper owners and editors, lawyers, religious reformers and revivalists, and other professional persons. It remained so until Gandhi won it mass support in 1920. The purpose in its early phase was to replace British control of the country with middle-class Indian control. The issues it agitated were, first, that of political structure; second, those of economic relations between India and Britain; and, third, certain social questions. The aristocracy of the country, which consisted of the Indian princes ruling the Indian (native) States and the great landlords, almost to a man opposed it. Peasants, other villagers, and industrial workers, when they came to support the movement, sometimes did so because of economic discontent and sometimes on religious grounds.

Indian nationalism was primarily supported by Hindus, that is, the nearly two-thirds of the total population living by the Hindu way of life. It drew only slightly from the minority communities, of which the largest was the Muslim, comprising something less than one-fourth of the population. The will of India at first to be a self-governing dominion within the British Empire, and later to be an independent nation, was the will of Hindu India. Though the Hindu religion, in the narrower sense, or Hinduism, in the broader cultural sense, provided scarcely an issue which Indian nationalism contested with the British imperialism, it did the more basic job of defining the group which struggled to win self-rule.

Before identifying elements of the historic culture that supported nationalism, we may first note a few features of modern India which often used to be cited as blocking national unity; some of these still operate to prevent India and Pakistan from attaining full national strength.

One of these lay in the political structure; many students and government officers believed that the autocratic rulers of the Indian States would never consent to an intimate political association with the democratizing provinces of British India. The Indian States were 562 in number, comprised about 45 per cent of undivided India's area, and in 1941 contained a little more than one-fourth of the population (93 million out of 389). Mapmakers in Britain and India used to show British India in pink and the Indian States in yellow, and the two colors were mixed in a patternless jumble like a New England country flower garden gone wild. In the outcome the Indian States furnished no serious obstruction to national independence. They were weaker than had been supposed; nationalism took them over in its stride.

The social institution of caste was often named as a sure preventive of any unified nationalistic action, and in the first decade of the twentieth century Sir Herbert Hope Risley, a celebrated civil servant and anthropologist, predicted that political divisions would follow caste lines. In general this has not been the case. The Indian National Congress, which was the efficient organ of nationalism, drew from all castes. Though the lower caste groups were often suspicious of Congress, it generally succeeded in retaining them; at the most critical junctures it was able to do so because of dramatic gestures toward social reform made by Gandhi, who knew that the Hindu community needed the support of its lowest segments if India was to win national independence.

The large number of languages was also cited as a hindrance to nationalism, and the separatist effect of language continues to this day to be an internal plague for both India and Pakistan. But the language divisions turned out to be a less serious handicap in the struggle for independence than they had seemed, because English had become the common speech of the educated and as such was a tool for nationalism.

Another aspect of Indian life which was expected to thwart nationalism was religious rivalry. Its effect in setting Muslims and Hindus against each other has already been mentioned and will be discussed in later chapters dealing with communalism and partition. But though religion in this way served as a brake on nationalism it also provided, through the dynamic quality of native Indian faiths, the principal driving power. It gives the adherents to native Indian Hindu culture a distinctive body of belief and practice and in consequence a special kind of social cohesion which facilitates the growth of nationalist sentiment. This is aided, to a marked degree, by the literature of Hinduism, especially the great epics, the Mahabharata and the Ramayana, and their literary successors, the Puranas, read by the learned, heard in recitation by the illiterate. In the latter are found the stories of Rama, the national ideal of manhood and kingship, and his wife Sita, the ideal of womanhood; of the five Pandavas, who waged the war of righteousness against their wicked cousins; of Krishna, god become man, who was charioteer to the Pandavas' greatest general Arjuna and taught him the Bhagavad Gita; of all the human beings who most affect the Hindu imagination. These heroes and heroines are of the soil of India itself; their lives moved in India; their names are associated with India's mountains, rivers, forests, and cities. Their tales are told with Indian phraseology and with Indian figures of speech. Their hold upon the people's mind is primary and unrivaled.

Hence the religious element in Hindu culture became the heart of Indian nationality, and so various reform sects of Hinduism preaching against actively proselytizing Islam and Christianity promoted a religious nationalism. Hence, too, Gandhi, the most influential political leader of the land in our times, was first of all a man of religion. The life of sainthood which he embodied was a national ideal; the book which he quoted most often and with the most effect was the Bhagavad Gita.

It used to be said that nationalism in India could draw no strength from a national historical sense; for there are few works of history in India's abundant literature, and most of these make little distinction between myth and fact. But this judgment must be modified. Important for nurturing nationalism was the fact that in the late nineteenth and the twentieth centuries a historical sense was growing in India and growing in a way to flatter the national self-esteem. Archaeological excavation and study revealed to Indians the extent, quality, and age of their ancient civilization, and its influence upon the rest of Asia. National imagination was stimulated by discoveries which showed that ancient India had a culture in the Indus valley rivaling those of Mesopotamia and Egypt and in special points surpassing them. Increased knowledge of Asian history contributed to national pride. Indians were stirred when they learned that their religions, literature, languages, art, law, had migrated to central, eastern, and southeastern Asia, to help build civilization there.

In other cultural fields the Hindu ego was being enlarged. A number of Indians were winning intellectual successes in the West, of whom perhaps the most appealing to Hindu imagination was Swami Vivekananda (born Narendranath Datta, 1862–1902) at the Parliament of Religions held in Chicago during the World's Fair of 1892–1893. There in a moment the vigor and brilliance of his mind and corresponding qualities of presence and eloquence raised him from complete obscurity to a position of dominance over the whole Parliament, and brought India a special prestige in America. It made Vivekananda a legendary figure in India as the Hindu who could equal and excel in intellect the thinkers of the otherwise dominant West. Later there were Indian scientists, J. C. Bose and C. V. Raman, mathematicians, such as Ramanujan, literary artists, such as Rabindranath Tagore, who received recognition of the highest order in the West.

When to the national self-assurance so generated was added in the latter decades of the nineteenth century the achievements of orientals in modern warfare, culminating in the Japanese victory over Russia in 1904–1905, Indians began to acquire confidence that they could compete militarily with Europeans. They came to hope that perhaps in some new epoch of history their nation might again have a place with the world's greatest.

Two sections of India were the principal seats of nationalist activity during the nineteenth century. These were Bengal in the east, and Poona and the nearby Maratha country in the west. In the twentieth century other areas of activity were the Punjab, Gujarat, and South India.

In Bengal the immediate source of nationalism lay in an intellectual renaissance, springing partly from the introduction of new ideas from the West and partly from a revival of indigenous Bengali literature. It was in Bengal that western education had first taken hold. There was located Calcutta, the chief European city of India and the most important channel for the influx of western ideas into

India. During the nineteenth century Bengal effervesced with literary activity, which got special point from the aspirations of the Hindu Bengalis to win equality with the Muslims who had ruled them before the British came, and with the British who were ruling them then. Bengal was intellectually the most advanced portion of India; the Bengalis were the most sensitive to white arrogance and the most articulate to express their resentment. Among many authors the most influential was Bankim Chandra Chatterji (1838–1894), who voiced the sentimental attachment that was growing up among Hindus for India as the mystic Mother threatened by non-Hindu aggression and needing the defense of her sons. From one of his novels (*Ananda Math*) comes the song *Bande Mataram* "I worship the Mother," which has an anti-Muslim motivation in its context, but until superseded recently by Rabindranath Tagore's *Jana-gana-mana* was the anthem of Indian nationalism, and as such was given an anti-British application. Pride of race was stirred by the writings of Bankim and similar, though lesser, authors, and a purpose was evolved which rapidly took form as Hindu nationalism.

Whereas in Bengal nationalism arose largely from intellectual stirrings and expressed itself chiefly in speech and writing, in Poona and the Maratha country it derived from religious dogmatism coupled with the suppressed ambition of a warlike people, and its expression was marked from the beginning by violence.

The Marathas were from the seventeenth to the nineteenth century one of India's most martial peoples. They were the most important foes of the crumbling Mughal empire, and they have never since lost their anti-Muslim zeal. Their first great leader Sivaji (1627–1680) harassed the Muslim kingdoms, and became the acknowledged champion of Hinduism; for he patronized Brahmans, honored the gods, and protected cows. When the Mughal empire started to break up at the death of Aurangzeb (1707), the Marathas began to sweep over western, central, and northern India, overthrowing Muslim and Hindu alike, and establishing their own dynasties, which ruled some of the most important Indian States (Baroda, Indore, Gwalior). The central authority of the Maratha states during the eighteenth century was at Poona, and they constituted a loose confederacy which the British finally shattered in 1818. Poona then became the radiation point of Maratha frustration.

Here there came into prominence during the 1890's a fiery Brahman named Bal Gangadhar Tilak (1856–1920) who in the 1900's was the dominant figure in the Indian National Congress. His first interest was the preservation of the Hindu religion, which he saw doubly imperiled, on the one hand by westernized Indians preaching social change and collaborating with the even more subversive Government which enacted such religiously dangerous innovations as an Age of Consent Bill (1890), and on the other hand by foreigners who themselves engaged in sin and defied Hinduism by eating the flesh of the sacred cow. Second to religious grievances were certain economic complaints which he championed. During the famine of 1896 he tried to launch a "No-Rent" campaign among the impoverished peasants, urging them to withhold from the Government the land rent (tax). He published a newspaper which advocated violence as a means of political protest, and political murder followed. Political violence still has a home in the Maratha country. It was from there that Gandhi's assassin came, who acted in protest against Gandhi's program of peace with Muslims.

Of a different character was Tilak's caste-fellow, Gopal Krishna Gokhale (1866–1915), also from Poona. Tilak had emphasized the ceremonial side of Hinduism; Gokhale's interest was in the social values of his religion and the wider application of its ethics to life. Where Tilak was provocative and conservative, Gokhale was persuasive and liberal. He represented the tolerant, expansive, compromising side of Hinduism. He waged a long fight with the Government for social ends, rather than political. He welcomed instruction from the West on social problems, and was especially an advocate of general popular education, which he felt was necessary for the progress of India. He founded the "Servants of India Society," a constructive social agency still active in India, to work for the improvement of all Indians, without restriction of caste, race, or creed. He came to believe that India would obtain the necessary social changes only if Indians themselves had a greater share in legislating and administering, and here was the basis for his political propaganda. To him, more than to anyone else of his generation, Indian nationalism was indebted for forward-looking purpose. While Tilak gave passion and fighting vigor to nationalism in its early stages, Gokhale gave it secular objectives and statesmanship.

In the Punjab nationalism developed among the Sikhs, who had been renowned as unwavering supporters of the British. Though the British had destroyed the Sikh kingdom in the 1840's they had in the next decade, at the time of the Mutiny, clashed with the

Mughals, who for over two centuries had been the Sikhs' oppressors and enemies. Punjab nationalism arose partly because of discrimination against Indians in other parts of the British Empire, partly in consequence of economic dislocations, as when in 1907 the Government's policies concerning irrigation canals were compelling the peasants to make economic readjustments, and partly in consequence of religious disputes among the Sikhs themselves, accompanied by bloodshed and death, in which the Government became involved.

Gujarat, in the west of India, where Gandhi long had his home, became vigorously and actively nationalist only in 1928. There nationalism was inspired partly by the presence of Gandhi, partly by economic distress of the peasants, partly by disaffection of the mill owners in Ahmedabad, the largest city of the region, who wanted the Indian cotton-goods market for their products.

In southern India nationalism was also of comparatively recent growth. In part it was due to sectional desires of linguistic groups, especially the Telugu in the Andhra region, for separation from the larger province of Madras. It was even more largely due to the desires of the non-Brahmans to get the government of the provinces away from the Brahmans and into their own hands.

In the beginning the various nationalist organizations were weak and mutually antipathetic. Few of them were primarily political. There were religious societies which, as a corollary to their main purpose of establishing true doctrine, engaged in activities with nationalist implications. There were social reform societies, like Gokhale's Servants of India Society, which were bound to have nationalist tendencies. There were commercial bodies with interests that led to nationalism as their natural expression. After the granting of the Constitution in 1919, which provided for partly elected legislative bodies, certain of the parties came to be principally political in purpose.

Of those organizations which proceeded to nationalism through religion, two, though now negligible, were politically influential in their time. These were the occult-slanted Theosophical Society and the revivalist Arya Samaj. It was evident, according to Theosophical reasoning, that the Hindus were unexcelled in religion, and, since religion is the highest phase of human activity, they were unexcelled as a people. The logical conclusion was that they should be subject to no other people, but should have political freedom. The chief leader of the Theosophical Society during this century was Mrs.

Annie Besant (1847–1933), who believed in self-rule for a "Commonwealth of India" as a member of the British Empire. In 1916 she founded the all-India Home Rule League to promote it, which cooperated with the Indian National Congress and lasted until the 1920's. She was president of the Congress in 1917.

The Arya Samaj, which was strong chiefly in northern and northwestern India, looked upon all existing forms of native Indian religions as left-handed corruptions of a pure faith taught in a mythically distant past and preserved in the Rig and other Vedas. This forsaken religion it aimed to revive. The founder of the Arya Samaj was Pandit Dayanand Sarasvati (1825–1888), who after some years of preaching organized his society in 1875, meaning to save India for Hinduism from the encroachments of Islam and Christianity, and to lead Hinduism back from the "left-hand" path to the "right-hand." His methods were combative and sophistical, but he had a social program against the rigidity of caste, child marriage, enforced widowhood, the seclusion of women. He aggressively promoted "cow protection," which through his inflammatory propaganda came to be a constant source of trouble between Hindus and Muslims. He had a method of interpreting Vedic texts by which he found mentioned in them all the scientific discoveries and technological inventions of his own day, thereby proving to his own satisfaction that modern civilization was only a deterioration from the perfect civilization of the ancient Hindu seers. The natural conclusion was that India should revert to the glorious past, and to do so she must first become self-governing, free of all non-Hindu elements. The great political leader of this society in the twentieth century was Lajpat Rai (1865–1928). The Arya Samaj was especially strong in the Punjab, where before the first World War it provided nationalism with many recruits. In the interval between the wars it contributed to the hostility between Hindus and Muslims.

With a somewhat different twist to events, the Theosophical Society, or the Arya Samaj, or the Servants of India Society, or some one of several other organizations not primarily political in purpose might have been captured by the politicians and turned into a political body. Instead each became increasingly less political during the 1920's and 1930's and transferred its political support to the Indian National Congress, which had become the unrivaled spokesman of nationalism.

The Indian National Congress, also commonly known as Congress, was founded in Bombay during Christmas week, 1885, by Allan Octavian Hume (1829–1912), a few other Europeans, and some Indians who had westernized sociological notions. It had no religious motivation; rather, its philosophy was secular. Its purpose was to discuss social reform. The first presidential address by W. C. Bonnerjee contained expressions of gratitude to Britain for the good government she had given India, the railways, the new education from the West. The second president, Dadabhai Naoroji (1825–1917), a celebrated man in modern Indian annals, spoke feelingly of "the blessings of British rule," which he characterized as "numberless," and stated his belief that events showed that "the people of England were sincere in the declaration made more than a half century ago that India was a sacred charge entrusted to their care by Providence, and that they were bound to administer it for the good of India, to the glory of their own name, and the satisfaction of God."

The change of Congress to an actively nationalist attitude was due, primarily, to the disappointment of Indians in not finding its reasonably presented proposals more sympathetically considered by the Government. It objected to the "home charges," which consisted of payments on public debt owed in London, certain expenses of administration, and pensions; it complained of unduly large military expenditure, of the failure to separate the judicial and executive branches of government, of the lack of equal opportunity for Indians as officers in the army, of the neglect of general primary education. By 1900 it was severely questioning the sincerity of the British professions it had accepted so enthusiastically in 1885. In 1904 a "radical" or "left" element began to struggle with the conservatives for dominance of Congress, being weary of the failure of the moderates to achieve results by their methods of persuasion. In 1907, under the pressure of continued grievances, including the partition of Bengal during the Governor Generalship of Lord Curzon, the Congress split for a few years between the extremists led by Tilak and the old-fashioned moderates. The next year it adopted a "creed" calling for political rights. From then on it never ceased to be a political body first and a social reform body second.

After the first World War Congress attained a commanding position among nationalists under the leadership of Gandhi. In 1916 the "radicals" gained control, and it came to stand for reform by revolution (though without violence) rather than by constitutional evolution. After Gandhi went to jail in 1922 there followed a period of uncertainty and confusion, largely because of dissension among Indian politicians as to what course they should pursue in connection with the constitution of 1919. By 1929 Congress was again united and extremely popular. It led a fight against the Simon Commission which had been appointed by the British Government in 1927 to devise constitutional reform. It adopted a goal of full self-government at the end of 1929 and set the next January 26 as Independence Day, which since then it, and now the Republic of India, has celebrated annually. It persisted in its campaign during the second World War, though harried and declared illegal by the Churchill government. After the war it emerged again as the leading Indian political party and rightfully takes the credit for winning independence.

The growth of nationalist sentiment and activity in the nineteenth and early twentieth centuries is marked, as if with milestones, by a series of crises, developing from a longer or shorter series of political, economic, or social experiences.

The first serious expressions came at about the time of the Indian Mutiny (1857–1858). Those Indians who already felt that they had an inherent right to share in governing India were shocked by the brutal vengeance which the British inflicted upon the vanquished mutineers. After the Mutiny, in spite of a general British policy of consideration for the persons of Indians, there continued to be ruthless lapses into militaristic violence, each of which easily undid in the minds of Indians the effect laboriously achieved through many preceding years of moderation.

The means used to quell the Mutiny had revolted and alienated the Indian press, which professed to see a potential helper in Russia, then advancing in Central Asia. At about this time came economic difficulties also. There was a crash in Indian cotton in 1865, following the temporary boom during the American Civil War, and in 1866 there was a severe famine, which brought widespread discontent. The press was violent in criticism of the Government on this matter too.

Following the Mutiny there also arose an acute racial problem between British and Indians, which had scarcely existed before it. The mutineers had inflicted atrocities upon Europeans, including women, as at Cawnpore (Kanpur), and this fact aroused in the whites a hatred of Indians. They described their former enemies as cowardly, weak, treacherous, bestial, and symbolized those qualities by the darkness of the Indian skin. A "Mutiny Complex" arose among European women fearful of rape, a mental state prevalent until well into the twentieth century. The Indians came to distrust the whites as brutal, bullying, arrogant. The British now disdained intermarriage, which in the eighteenth and early nineteenth centuries had been frequent, and looked down upon the Anglo-Indians (formerly called Eurasians), who were sprung from mixed unions. They had many exclusive clubs which denied membership to Indians; they considered India only a temporary camping spot where they were making a living, and spoke of Britain as "home," to which they meant to retire as soon as it was possible to do so. They sent their children back to Britain to school. Some would remain in India as long as thirty years without learning to speak any Indian language. Almost all took advantage of their prerogatives as the ruling group to exercise social discrimination in railway trains and other public places. From about 1917 on, these features were curbed but they were never fully eliminated until 1947. The extreme form of anti-Indianism was sometimes openly expressed and usually implicit in the utterances of prominent Britons, to the effect that the Indians were of a different and inferior "race," were a "conquered people," and were unworthy of self-rule and treatment as social equals. A problem of group relationship was created, considered by some observers like the late C. F. Andrews to be the most important element in hardening nationalist sentiment.

The racial antipathy first came to a point in 1883 when the "Ilbert Bill" was introduced. At this time the Indians who had entered the Indian Civil Service when the higher ranks were opened to them in 1854 were reaching senior grades, and those in judicial service were due to attain posts where, if the right had not been denied them as Indians, they would have had the status to try Europeans. Indians resented the restriction, and the bill was aimed to remove it. The Europeans protested heatedly; Indian feeling also was intense. The Government finally withdrew the bill and substituted another granting European defendants the right of trial by jury of which 50 per cent should be European. Indians, however, received no such corresponding right.

The next events to strike the popular imagination came in 1896–1900. At that time fierce famines, some of the severest on record, swept large sections of central and northern India. It was then that Tilak and his followers, feeling that the Government was dilatory in relieving the peasants, organized a "No-Rent" campaign. It had no marked success, but it was dramatic, and it introduced into modern India a weapon that the peasants had used in pre-British times and were to employ later under nationalist leadership. Accompanying this famine was an epidemic of plague, and the Government, in segregating patients so as to control the disease and in disinfecting and evacuating houses, was not tactful in handling ignorant and suspicious Indians, with the result that India had its first political murder in modern times, when two British officers were killed at Poona in 1897. The introduction of violence into the political struggle made a profound impression upon the public.

In 1899 Lord Curzon (1859–1925) became Governor General (Viceroy), ruling until 1905. He was a man of commanding intelligence, tremendous industry, strong will, and great courage. It is probably true that no other Viceroy ever accomplished so much of material benefit to India. It is also probably true that no other ever so severely lacerated the feelings of Indians. Two of his actions were sufficiently unpopular to become symbols to the educated classes. One of these was his Universities Act (1904), by which he greatly improved those institutions, but did so at the price of ruthlessly overriding Indian feeling. The trouble lay in the fact that he reduced the number of members of the various Senates, the ruling bodies of the universities, and at the same time increased the number of members nominated by the chancellors of the universities, who were always the governors of the provinces in which the universities were located. In this way the Government-nominated members came to be in the majority. The Bengalis greatly resented this action in its application to the Calcutta University. This had become to them the emblem of their intellectual life and cultural renaissance, and they opposed the act violently on the ground that the Government was taking over control of the university out of hostility to the vigorous and independent Bengali intellectual development that was showing marked nationalist tendencies.

The second of Lord Curzon's inflammatory actions was the "Partition of Bengal," announced in the year 1905. At that time the Bengal Presidency contained not only the two Bengals now belonging to India and Pakistan, but also the area included in the present states of Bihar and Orissa and had a population of about 78 million people, far too many for efficient administration. To give relief Lord Curzon decreed that the eastern part of the province, containing nearly one-third of the population, should be cut off and combined with Assam as a separate province called Eastern Bengal and Assam, an arrangement which administrative experts recommended as the most efficient way of handling the problem. But the Hindu Bengalis regarded the scheme as destroying their ethnic integrity. The line of division went through a linguistic entity, and they took it as intended to divide them and remove their effective solidarity.

The Muslims in India, and especially those in Bengal, welcomed the change, for the new province, which contained most of the present Eastern Pakistan as well as all of Assam, was predominantly of their faith and would be taken out from under potential Hindu control. This feature especially incensed the Hindu portion of the Presidency. Protests of many sorts were made; all India took an interest in the fight. Bomb outrages were perpetrated beginning with 1906, after the Earl of Minto had succeeded Lord Curzon. Terrorism accompanied them, consisting of robbery by armed gangs for political purposes, and other forms of violence; a revolutionary movement was the result. Meanwhile Muslims in 1906, to protect their interests, had organized the Muslim League, which afterwards became the organ of Muslim political aspirations and eventually accomplished the partition of India.

At last in 1911, after six years, while still another Viceroy (Lord Hardinge) was in office, the King-Emperor himself announced that the partition of Bengal was nullified and Bengal was reunited. In 1912 a different partition of Bengal following linguistic boundaries was put into effect, which took away Bihar and Orissa and made them into a new province, which in 1935 was itself separated into two provinces. The British had pleased no one—the Muslims, the Hindus, themselves.

The Partition of Bengal brought the Indian National Congress unequivocally into politics in 1908. Before, it had been little more than a society for social reform; afterwards its primary object was to advance Indian self-rule. It was also the occasion for the first use of the economic boycott or *Swadeshi* ("[buy] home goods") movement, a weapon later used by Gandhi in his long-continuing campaign for *khaddar*, that is, home-spun and home-woven cotton cloth.

Under Minto a new departure was made in Indian political structure. He and Lord Morley, Secretary of State for India, formulated the Indian Councils Act of 1909, known as the "Morley-Minto Reforms," which established Executive Councils in other provinces than the (then) presidencies of Bombay and Madras, greatly enlarged the imperial (Governor General's) and provincial Legislative Councils, and provided that nearly all the nonofficial members should be elected—by a narrowly circumscribed electorate—leaving the Government only a small nominated official majority in the imperial Legislative Council, while nonofficial majorities were created in the provincial Legislative Councils. This was a step toward self-rule which in retrospect seems comparatively slight but when announced was impressive.

The Indian Councils Act, however, had another feature which inaugurated political communalism. While the proposals for reform were being considered, Minto received a deputation of Indian Muslims headed by the Agha Khan, which asked that the Indian Muslim community be given separate electoral representation. Minto promptly acceded to the principle and the Reforms when enacted instituted it as a system. Thus began a corroding process that thereafter ate its way steadily into public life.

Lord Morley denied that he ever looked forward to parliamentary institutions in India; like other Britons of his time he thought them unsuitable to the country. He had no hope of gaining the good will of irreconcilable extremists who had "fantastic dreams that some day they will drive us out of India." Rather his hope was to win as willing coöperators the reasonable proponents of self-rule who only sought a larger part in the government. He did not foresee that the Councils he had fashioned would be the means used later for making parliamentary experiments. Though the Reforms did not seem to shake British autocratic rule, since ultimate power rested with the Governor General in (Executive) Council and the Governors of the provinces, who could do as they wished without being bound by the opinions of the Legislative Councils, it was, nevertheless, portentous that they could discuss many subjects, ask questions, and criticize. It was inescapable that they would also want the accompanying power of action.

But hardly had India reflected upon these reforms, when the country received another shock. King George V and Queen Mary had come to India in December 1911, to be crowned as Emperor and Empress of India at Delhi. On this visit the King-Emperor made two announcements. One, calculated to be conciliatory, was that the Partition of Bengal was to be reversed. The other, which proved remarkably provocative, was that the capital was to be transferred from

Calcutta to Delhi, the old seat of the Mughals. There were certain advantages to be gained from setting the capital in a more central and more historic spot, but the people of Bengal viewed the matter differently. They saw a close connection between the subjects of the two announcements. They felt that the removal of the capital from their province was intended to diminish the importance of Bengal and to punish it for its successful contumacy in opposing the Bengal Partition. All the good will created by the Morley-Minto Reforms vanished; Bengal never forgave her demotion.

Shortly after this, national feeling burst out in the Punjab. In May 1914, a shipload of 351 Sikhs and 21 Punjabi Muslims recruited in Hongkong, Shanghai, Moji, and Tokyo, was denied admission into Canada under the immigration laws and all the prospective immigrants were returned to India, where they arrived at the end of September. These in their disappointment saw precisely two things—that they were British subjects; that they had been denied entrance to a part of the British Empire. Here, they felt, was racial discrimination, and if that had to exist within the Empire, then they did not want India to remain in it. When they landed in Calcutta, 300 of the Sikhs tried to march on the city, were turned back forcibly with 18 deaths, then scattered throughout northern India, making their way to the Punjab, preaching hatred and violence, and strengthening the hand of the already existing Ghadr (mutiny) party there, which had been organized in America in 1913. Many were arrested and tried; twenty-eight were hanged; a number of others were transported. Other Sikhs were returned to India from various British dominions to a total number of about 8000, and they all fomented discontent.

Political terrorism was now rife, supplemented by robbery with occasional murder to raise money for alleged political use, especially in Bengal. There is no reason to believe that the Indian National Congress instigated any of this terrorism, though members of the Congress may have participated.

During the period from 1906 to 1914 Indians had increasingly felt that the British Dominions were unfair to Indians living within their borders. The chief region then concerned was South Africa, especially Natal. Indian immigrants had been coming there from 1860 to work as indentured laborers. So long as these were serving their terms, they were a welcome convenience to the whites, but when the terms were at an end and they became free, they constituted a menace, for their lower standard of living made them competitors endangering the economic security of their former masters. The European community used many weapons to curb the Indians, such as the imposition of a heavy poll tax, limitation of residence on "sanitary" grounds, restriction of travel within the various South African colonies, denial of franchise, hindrance of trading, imposition of educational tests. In 1906 the "Black Act" was enacted, by which all Asiatics, male and female, were to register and take out a certificate, accompanied by fingerprints and detailed personal information ordinarily required of no civilians except criminals. Failure in any respect to comply with the law was punishable by fine, imprisonment, or deportation. The despairing Indians found a leader in Mohandas Karamchand Gandhi, who had gone to South Africa as a lawyer, and under him they waged a long struggle against the governments of the various colonies, and finally against the South African Union. The weapon they used was that of non-violent resistance—the use of violence would have been hopeless—and at last in 1914 they seemed successful, though actually they were not, and the contest has continued periodically ever since.

India had watched the struggle with a twofold interest. It had, for one thing, been moved at seeing Indians subjected to racial discrimination. It had, for another, been thrilled to see the development of a successful means for offering resistance. The Indian imagination was kindled; Gandhi, author of the new weapon, became a name of power in his homeland. Neither he nor anyone else suspected the important part he was soon to play there.

During the first World War, Britain had two problems to solve in India. One was to check the strong and rising antagonism to British rule; the other was to get men and money from India for use against the enemy. The British did not complain that India failed them. Recruitments were many; funds were raised to equip the troops; both the Congress and the Muslim League supported the war effort; the princes were loyal; the people as a whole gave their support, making the cause of their foreign rulers their own. Yet at the same time the anti-British agitation did not cease in Bengal and the Punjab. The Congress hoped that Britain, in identifying her war role as the defense of democracy, would inaugurate democratic institutions in India, and wanted action accordingly.

While the war continued, two policies appeared as Britain's joint program for controlling India. One was persuasive, leading to constitutional liberalization. The other was repressive, directed against extreme nationalism.

The persuasive policy was initiated by the celebrated announcement of Edwin Samuel Montagu, Secretary of State for India, made in Parliament on August 20, 1917, when he said that His Majesty's government would provide for ". . . the increasing association of Indians in every branch of Indian administration, and for the gradual development of self-governing institutions, with a view to the progressive realization of responsible government in British India as an integral part of the Empire." This was a definite promise, though undated for fulfillment, and Parliament followed it up by passing the Government of India Act of 1919 ("Montagu-Chelmsford Reforms"), giving India a constitution with a new system of government more liberalized than that which it then had under the 1909 constitution or than anything that would have been imaginable three decades before in the early years of the Indian National Congress. Yet now it fell far short of nationalist demands. British and Indians alike regarded it as temporary, to precede a transition to further self-government.

Under the 1919 Constitution decentralization of authority was instituted. The natural tendency of the strong autocratic British power in India was toward centralization, and this the nationalists had attacked. Now the division of function between the central and the provincial governments of British India was more sharply drawn, and many subjects of administration were assigned to the provinces. The central government retained control of certain matters like defense and customs; the provinces got control of law and order, certain classes of revenue, education, agriculture, public health.

The central government consisted of the Governor General (the Viceroy) with his appointive Executive Council, an upper legislative chamber called the Council of State with a life of five years, and finally a lower chamber called the Legislative Assembly with a life of three years. In each chamber there was a large number of seats filled by government nomination—27 out of 60 in the upper, 40 out of 146 in the lower. There was also a Chamber of Princes, where these rulers could meet—with due pomp and ceremony and flashing of jewels—and talk but take no legislative action. There were then ten "Governor's Provinces," including Burma, which afterwards in 1937 was separated from India by the 1935 Constitution, while at that same time two new provinces, Sind and Orissa, were created.

Each had an appointive Governor with his Executive Council, and a legislature. The Governor General and the provincial governors were not responsible to the legislative bodies but to the British Parliament. There were also five Chief Commissioner's Provinces without legislatures, covering a very small portion of the whole of British India.

In the Governor's Provinces government was by a system called "dyarchy." Some subjects considered to be of first importance, such as law and order, the land revenue, canals, finance, were "reserved" for control by the Governor in Council, who was responsible to the British Parliament, and others considered to be of second importance, such as education, agriculture, public health, were "transferred" to the Legislative Councils for control by the Governor through ministers responsible to the Councils and thus to the Indian electorate. In the case of the central government all subjects could be treated by the Legislative Assembly except the Army—which had claim to a sum not liable to discussion or refusal by any body in India—but a final power of veto and another of "certification" rested with the Governor General in Council (the Governor of a province had similar rights), which he could employ to enact legislation refused by the Legislative Assembly and Council of State but in his opinion vital. This self-contradictory system, which gave representation but denied responsibility, was difficult to make function and was not acceptable to most nationalists. The Constitution of 1919 was the target against which nationalism directed its attack, and as it did so it gained the strength it needed for its ultimate victory.

Elections were held by the very limited electorate, and on February 9, 1921, the new governmental machine began to operate, when the Duke of Connaught, acting in the name of the King-Emperor, opened with pageant and pomp the Chamber of Princes, the Council of State, and the Legislative Assembly.

But all the Indian nationalist good will necessary to make the liberalized scheme effective had been killed by the second, the repressive, policy. This was epitomized in the two Rowlatt Acts (1918), named after the English justice who framed them. These were to crush the extensive terrorism then existing, and they provided for summary procedure. There were to be secret trials before three judges, without the right of counsel, jury, and appeal even from sentences of death, and suspects could be interned without trial. The nationalists were enraged. Parliament would not dare, they claimed, to impose such measures in England; in India the Government meant to use them not only against criminals but against any political agitator it might wish to quiet; they were designed, they said, not to preserve law and order but to repress anti-British sentiment. Riots followed, and violence. One act was never passed, and when the other was enacted neither the nationalists nor the Government foresaw that it would be too unpopular ever to be employed. These Acts, however, further fomented anti-British feeling, particularly in Bengal, where they were primarily meant to be used.

While the resentment against the Rowlatt Acts was at its height, the Muslim community adopted an anti-Government attitude over the *Khilafat* (Caliphate) question. This concerned the temporal power of the Caliph, or spiritual ruler of Islam, which position vested in the Sultan of Turkey. Many Muslims in India considered the destruction of the Turkish Empire after the war by the Treaty of Sèvres (1920) and the extinction of the Sultan's position as Caliph to be part of a general conspiracy among the Allied Christian nations to dismember Muslim unity and scotch pan-Islamism. The Muslims, who had been hard to arouse in the interests of nationalism, who under their leaders had favored the partition of Bengal which had inflamed the Hindus, whose chief organ of expression, the All-India Muslim League, was generally in opposition to the Indian National Congress, who in 1916 had extracted from an unwilling Congress the Lucknow Pact conceding their separate electorate and giving it specified weightage, were now at the prompting of the Ali brothers (Mohammed and Shaukat) at last falling into line with the Congress against Britain. The Khilafat movement was entirely hollow; even the Turks, after their republic was established, repudiated it; but it increased the number of Britain's enemies in India.

For Gandhi seized upon that discontent as a means of uniting the mutually hostile Hindu and Muslim communities against the British. He openly espoused the Khilafat movement, and got the Congress to do so as well. This mixture of oil and water could not endure, but the excited agitation of nationalism kept the two in apparent union for a brief period. Gandhi led the joint forces in demonstrations meant by him to be non-violent and to consist of protest by *hartal,* that is, cessation of business activity, but not all those connected with his cause were sufficiently convinced that his method was sound to abstain from violence. There were riots and bloodshed; the country was in a state of tension.

The scene of the most dramatic episode was in the Punjab. There agitation had led to disorder; the situation was complicated by the third Afghan war; and the civil Government had felt constrained to call out the military in some regions. At the city of Amritsar in that province, the center of the Sikh community, five Englishmen had been killed and an Englishwoman injured, and there had been other bloodshed. Leaders were deported and assemblage was strictly prohibited. But on April 13, 1919, a crowd variously estimated at from 6,000 to 12,000 disregarding the order, had assembled inside the city in a garden known as Jallianwala Bagh where it was listening to speeches. It was here that the fatal event occurred.

The Jallianwala Bagh was a small square of perhaps four or five acres, surrounded solidly by the bare unpierced sides of brick houses and high walls, prohibiting any egress except by one narrow opening, which was also the entrance. The ground inside was level but for a slight elevation just at the left of the entrance. About halfway down the left-hand side near the wall was a large well, perhaps twenty feet in diameter, the only bit of cover in the entire garden.

General Reginald Dyer, the officer in command, acting on his own responsibility, though the civil administration was in charge, hastened there with fifty infantry to control the situation. When he arrived he marched his soldiers through the entrance, deployed them on the low eminence beside it, and with no word or signal to the crowd ordered them to open fire. "The targets," he said afterwards, were "good." There was no escape; the walls were too high to scale; those who leaped into the well only exchanged the bullet for the water. After ten minutes, when 1650 rounds had been fired and the ammunition was exhausted, he marched his men out, leaving the dead and dying without attention. The casualties, according to the Government report issued after long delay, were 379 killed and 1200 wounded; nonofficial estimates set them higher.

There is no doubt that in consequence of the third Afghan war then in progress and the proximity of the Punjab to the frontier passes, the situation from a military point of view was dangerous, and General Dyer claimed that, "It was no longer a question of merely dispersing the crowd, but one of producing a sufficient moral effect, from a military point of view, not merely on those who were present, but more especially throughout the Punjab. There could be no question of undue severity." A "moral effect" was indeed produced throughout all India, but not of a sort which he had foreseen. Amritsar became for India a symbol, and the Jallianwala Bagh is now a public memorial to her sons who died there.

Events following the Amritsar tragedy accentuated the ill feeling. Martial law was proclaimed two days later throughout the affected districts. The section of the street where the Englishwoman had been attacked was roped off, and for eight days all Indians who wanted to pass along it had to do so by crawling. Floggings in public were frequent; roll calls were enforced upon students; arrests were many; weapons of war were turned against villages.

The British were slow in calling General Dyer to account for his handling of the situation, and when they did so, Indians felt that the case had been unduly postponed and the investigation instituted unwillingly. He was finally censured in a dispatch from the British Government to the Government of India, but any effect this action might have had in mollifying Indian sentiment was obviated by the fact that a large sum of money was raised by public subscription among Europeans in India and England and presented to General Dyer with a sword of honor as the "Saviour of the Punjab." In 1924, when the matter was aired in England in a libel suit against Sir Sankaran Nair, a distinguished Indian lawyer, presiding justice McCardie in his opinion absolved General Dyer of blame, and again Indian sentiment was inflamed; nor could the Labour Government, then in power, counteract the feeling by its conciliatory statement that the learned judge was not in full possession of the facts.

There was another effect of the Amritsar affair which General Dyer had not foreseen, and that was the influence upon public opinion throughout the world, and more precisely in England. At a time when the esteem of other nations had come to be an object of great concern to every country, and Britain was beginning to feel the advisability of a "good press" in Europe and America, the harshness at Amritsar did more in a day in the West to discredit her occupation of India than could have been effected by a century of economic wrong and a decade of nationalist propaganda. In England itself it shook the confidence of many people in the imperialism that held India, and divided public opinion on future policy. The proponents of firmness and imperialistic self-assurance were ever afterwards periodically balked by the doubters, and the treatment of India continued to fluctuate between conciliation and repression, first trying to soothe nationalism with concessions, then irritating it with severity.

It was to the accompaniment of Amritsar that Britain presented India with her new constitution. Its provisions, far more liberal than those of 1909, sure of a welcome reception in an India that had not yet known the Punjab terrorism, now were rejected. India was not satisfied with a scheme that gave the new legislatures control over only relatively unimportant subjects and reserved the most important for final decision by the Governor General and the Governors of the provinces, that allowed the Government the right to nominate large numbers of members to these legislatures, and above all that withheld from India all control of the army, which was responsible only to London. Amritsar had made her want the power to protect herself from her own instrument of defense. It was a decisive dramatic climax to sixty years of accelerating nationalist activity that made firm the will of India to be a fully self-governing nation. If any single event can be said to have destroyed the possibility that Britain might hold India, it was Amritsar. From this time on, under the leadership of Gandhi, sometimes as field commander of the nationalist struggle, sometimes as strategist in the planning room, India marched toward her goal of self-rule, which was later to be conceived as full independence. She had made that fixed resolve which for Hindus is the first and essential step in accomplishing any sacrificial purpose.

5. The Leader of Revolt

India today considers Gandhi the author of her independence. He had her confidence more than any other of her leaders; he organized the resistance to the imperialist government; he swayed to his will politicians who had no belief in his mystical theories; he is the Master whom all public figures profess to follow. His saintly life won for him the courtesy title of Mahatma, "the Great-Souled," and his warmth, humor, kindliness, and wisdom gained him the devotion of India's masses as their personal refuge. This they acknowledged by another title *Bapu* or *Bapuji*, "Father," which was affectionately applied during his lifetime and after his death was used by the Government of India on a commemorative stamp. The night he died Jawaharlal Nehru in a moving broadcast said, ". . . the light has gone out of our lives and there is darkness everywhere." His death rites were celebrated in every corner of India and wherever Indians lived abroad. His ashes were minutely divided and sent to all parts of the country to be scattered in the rivers and lakes and so to be mingled with that sacred water by which the whole land lives. No man in these times, if ever, has commanded so much affection in India, nor has anyone's death been so deeply grieved. He was to his countrymen patriot and prophet in one; after he died it was a fear of his closest associates that he might be translated into a deity.

Mohandas Karamchand Gandhi was born in 1869. His father was an officer in a small seaside state in the peninsula of Kathiawar, about 300 miles north of Bombay. His education was fragmentary, but had its climax when he went to England, where he studied law and was admitted to the bar. On his return to India he spent several years in an unsuccessful effort to launch a practice, then suddenly went to South Africa on business. He at once became interested in the social problems of the Indians living there, who suffered from

severe disabilities imposed by the whites, and he led a long struggle in their behalf, which in 1914 had at last, but misleadingly, seemed
to be successful.

When the first World War broke out, he returned to India, at first
helped the Government in recruiting, then was disappointed by the
Government's indifference to Indian rights as he conceived them,
and was horrified by the Amritsar tragedy in 1919. From that time
on he was the unrelenting opponent of British imperialism in India.
He led the Indian National Congress in the Civil Disobedience, or
mass Non-coöperation, Movement in 1920–1922, and ultimately went
to jail. In 1924, following an operation for appendicitis, he was released. For several years afterwards he had relatively little part in
politics, but in 1928, when the appointment of the Simon Commission on Indian constitutional reform had aroused India, he again
took the lead in the Congress. In 1930 he organized and directed a
second Civil Disobedience Movement, which lasted formally until
1934, and at the beginning of the campaign he dramatized this political protest by organizing and leading a march from his ashram
(retreat) at Sabarmati to the sea to manufacture salt in violation
of the government monopoly and tax. In May of that year he was
again arrested. He was released in 1931 to go to London for the
Second Round Table Conference on constitutional reform. Within
a few days' time after his return to India, he was once more thrown
into jail. While in prison in September 1932, he entered upon a "fast
unto death" against Prime Minister Ramsay MacDonald's award of
separate electorates to the depressed classes, and gained his objective. He remained in prison until May 1933, when on the first day
of a three weeks' fast meant for his own and his followers' purification he was released. He did not at this time take direct control of
Congress again, instead he remained in the background, but his was
the dominant voice in Congress affairs.

When the second World War broke out, he still did not assume
the leadership of Congress, but in September 1940, Congress began
another campaign of Civil Disobedience—this time on an "individual," not a mass, basis—which he led. He was the consultant of
Congress negotiators concerning the British War Cabinet's proposals of March 1942, known as the "Cripps Offer," which Congress
rejected. On August 9, 1942, the day after Congress passed its "Quit
India" resolution, he was again put in jail, and was held until May 6,
1944, when, seriously ill, he was released. He was after this time the

chief figure on the Congress side in the negotiations between it, the Muslim League, and the British Government, leading finally to the grant of independence and the partition of India in August 1947. In the riots between Hindus and Muslims preceding this double event he endeavored to restore harmony and peace, especially by visiting the worst disturbed areas in Bengal, and after the event, when killings and other violence took place in both India and Pakistan, he pled for mutual tolerance. In January 1948, he engaged in a fast for the cessation of communal hostility, and, many people also believe, to persuade the Government of India to pay to Pakistan sums due it, according to agreement, from the balances of the Government of undivided India. A few days later, on January 30, 1948, he was assassinated by a fanatical champion of orthodox Hinduism.

Like many another great man, Gandhi had an easy simplicity. Spare of body, thin of leg and arm, with shaven head, his features plain, even ugly, wearing no clothes but a simple white lower garment that set off strongly the dark brown of his skin, seated cross-legged on the low platform of a bare, whitewashed hall, lecturing in monotonous tones to middle-aged peasants on fertilizers and animal husbandry; or sitting in his tiny workroom before a spinning wheel, which he would turn with one hand while he fed the cotton with the other, its scratchy whir now rasping across the conversation, now jarring as with irregular and irritating frequency the thread would break and the turning stop—he was not a personally impressive figure. Nor did he try to be; farmer and weaver he called himself. And he denied that he was worthy of the title Mahatma.

A biographer trying to appraise Gandhi's character can find a wealth of significant detail in the revelations he makes of his sex life and his statements concerning sex problems, in his love of abasing himself as a scavenger, and in his guilt feeling for comparatively trivial lapses from his standards, in his early fear of ghosts, of the dark, and of other bugaboos, in his susceptibility as a young man to social disapproval. One can easily relate these to the vows of celibacy, the self-mortification through fasts, the renunciation of wordly pleasures, which he imposed upon himself and the inmates of his retreat. Or, again, one may see a connection between his youthful experiences with whites, when his all too sensitive spirit was injured by their arrogance, and his difficulty in later life in coming to an understanding with British officials. So, too, one may study closely the inconsistencies in his personality, as when he re-

cruited for the British army, though he was an avowed opponent
of even the mildest violence, let alone the bloodshed a soldier must
cause; or as when in 1920 he stated in an open letter to the Englishmen in India that the unarmed Indians must adopt the weapon of
non-violence because of "our incapacity to fight in open and honorable battle," though at other times he spoke constantly of non-violence
as the only weapon he could ever conscientiously advocate.

Gandhi was first of all a religious genius. Every kind of human
activity, social, political, commercial, or other, he felt should spring
from a religious motive; no sanctions were valid except those of religion. The religion that he professed was undeviatingly Hinduism,
yet that type of Hinduism which tolerates all shades of opinion in
others. He said, "Personally I do not regard any of the great religions of the world as false," and he frequently spoke in the highest terms of the Sermon on the Mount. What he asked was that he
might draw from other faiths provided he did not have to submit
to proselytism. Thus there was much in his personal belief that has
parallels in western creeds along with much that has not, as when
with his monotheism and belief in mystical realization of God he clung
staunchly to the doctrines of Rebirth, of Karma that determines the
conditions of rebirth, of caste that allots a man his proper status in
life, of protection for the sacred cow, that "poem of pity," wherein
man recognizes his eternal kinship with the animal creation.

His great strength in religion lay on the practical side, in applied
ethics. There, too, he was profoundly Hindu and humanitarian. The
vows of those who came to live in his retreat, always known as
Ashram, included truthfulness; *ahinsa,* that is, noninjury of living
creatures, whether by word, deed, or thought; celibacy; restraint of
the desire for savory food; non-thieving, carried to the extreme of
not owning more than one can use; patronage of one's native industries to the exclusion of foreign; fearlessness; amelioration of the
lot of the Untouchables; the use of native Indian languages for education; the wearing of homespun cloth. Their combined purpose was
to work the regeneration of India, a return to the assumed moral
purity of its pristine rural state; for his Utopia was a return to a
golden, if mythical, past.

In the application of these principles he long labored with an unswerving intensity and he contributed much to India's social improvement. The campaign he waged against untouchability, which
reached its climax in his "fast unto death," September, 1932, was

the most spectacular of the many efforts made by Indians in that direction and should be regarded as the most influential force in producing in India's present Constitution the clause which says "untouchability is abolished." He was deeply concerned with the conditions of India's peasantry. Cottage spinning and weaving, advocated by him, have, where tried, at times been mildly helpful in temporarily alleviating rural economic misery. He was not, it happened, very sophisticated in respect of exploitation of labor in modern industry, but took an ideal mid-Victorian attitude on relations of employer and employees. Subsidiary items of his program, such as prohibition of alcohol and narcotics, are today parts of the local law, in one form or another, of many large states in India.

Some phases of this program seemed strange to non-Indians, for example, patronage of home industries to the degree which he advocated. If you live in Madras, and "a man comes from Bombay and offers you wares, you are not justified in supporting the Bombay merchant so long as you have got a merchant at your very door, born and bred in Madras." The quality of the goods offered does not signify. "In your village you are bound to support your village barber to the exclusion of the finished barber who may come to you from Madras."

The underlying basis of Gandhi's social and political program was simple. "My uniform experience," says he in his autobiography, "has convinced me that there is no other God than Truth. And if every page of these chapters does not proclaim that the only means for the realization of Truth is Ahinsa, I shall deem all my pains in writing these chapters to have been in vain." And again, "To see the universal and all-pervading Spirit of Truth face to face one must be able to love the meanest of creatures as oneself. And a man who aspires after that cannot afford to keep out of any field of life. That is why my devotion to truth has drawn me into the field of politics; and I can say without the slightest hesitation and yet in all humility that those who say that religion has nothing to do with politics do not know what religion means."

The application of these principles was as follows. India, and for that matter the world at large, was in bondage to evil as the result of departure from the pure teachings of religion. In India the disease, he said, showed itself in many symptoms, of which subservience to a foreign power was only one; others of major importance were the Hindu-Muslim antipathy, the social crime of untouchability, the poverty of the masses. The cure was to be spiritual regeneration, religious reform, and, if this were accomplished, all the unhappy features of modern Indian life would automatically vanish. What remained, then, was to determine what things were false and what were true, and it was here that "non-violence," that is, non-injury of other creatures, came into association with truth. Says the Sanskrit, *ahinsa paramo dharmah* ("non-violence is the highest religion"), adding that on this point the Scriptures, though frequently at variance in other respects, are unanimous. Gandhi agreed fully when he remarked, "I am fascinated by the law of love. It is the philosopher's stone for me. I know Ahinsa alone can provide a remedy for our ills."

It was the preoccupation with Ahinsa that was primarily responsible for Indians' esteem for Gandhi. It was not so much his acceptance of bare poverty, weighty as that was—others who had done so had not the same popularity; and one who has not accepted such poverty, Jawaharlal Nehru, has been second only to him in the affections of India. Neither was it his individual political, social, and economic views, with which large numbers of his ardent admirers were in greater or less disagreement. Nor was it finally the mere fact that he was sincerely devoted to religion, for so were many other Indians. But it was his precise interpretation of the essence of religion that won response from his fellow countrymen, and the fact that he provided a channel for action in keeping with traditional Hindu ideals. The Hindu really believes in the doctrine of Ahinsa, though through poverty, custom, lack of imagination, or mere human frailty he may often fail to practice it, and in making an idol of Mahatma Gandhi he revealed his own deepest self.

Being a man of strong feelings and deep concern for life about him, Gandhi was no slavish logician. The doctrine of noninjury as enunciated by him should lead to an absolute refusal to harm any creature for the sake of one's own interest, and this is the conclusion of that doctrine in Buddhist and Jain scripture. Gandhi, more practical, drove monkeys from his retreat in Sabarmati, though only after painful soul-searching, and had a suffering calf destroyed.

That India trusted Gandhi was due, next to his promulgation of Ahinsa, to the completeness of his ascetic and religious life. If nothing else would have gripped the imagination of Indians, his fasts and his hunger strikes would, being ancient and honored Indian practices. Similarly the habit of silence, which he observed every Monday, is true to the equally ancient Hindu notion that a sage seeking truth can find it only through concentrated silent meditation: a common Sanskrit word for "silence" is *mauna,* which means literally "quality of an ascetic" (*muni*). At the same time Gandhi did not strain the intellect of the masses with ideas that were difficult to comprehend or were revolutionary of the Hindu tradition. He accepted the old dogmas in principle; he wanted only to modify them. Lacking the freedom of the artist that so often arouses distrust in the general public, he had the self-confident strength of the puritan. He spoke to the people simply, forcefully, and on issues of prime importance, while his sincerity was coupled with a personal charm that made his propagandizing a work of genius.

So much freedom from conservatism and traditional prejudice was offensive to strict orthodox upper-caste Hinduism. Throughout his career Gandhi was subject to denunciation from such elements. At various times and in different parts of India he was met on his travels with open hostility and sometimes violence from those who disapproved of him. It was one such person, belonging to disaffected orthodoxy, who finally assassinated him.

Possibly the greatest contribution which Gandhi gave to nationalism, greater even than his convincing justification of its aims, was a philosophy of resistance on which he developed a practical technique of revolution. This was his political mass use of non-violence. Though this abstract principle had an ancient and honorable tradition in India, it had never before been applied there on a concrete national scale to achieve a broad political end. He persuaded Congress to adopt it, in spite of misgivings and disbelief among many Congressmen. To see how it operated we may look at a simple, uncomplicated average case of a sort that attracted no special notice in the press when it occurred but shows non-violent resistance in typical application.

At Jubbulpore early in January 1932, Congress sympathizers attempted a parade and, when ordered by police to disperse, merely halted, squatted on the roadway, filling it from edge to edge, and refused to move. The police charged and beat them with *lathis,* which are wooden staves, six to eight feet in length, shod at one end with metal. The demonstrators offered no resistance, but submitted to the beating without retaliation, and, still without offering violence, let themselves be bundled off by the hundreds to jail. In 1920–1922 and again in 1930–1932 scenes of this sort were common all over India. Often a demonstration would be preceded by a closing of shops for a one or more days' cessation of business. Arrests were inevitable and so numerous that the Government had to set up many special detention camps and confinement quarters to care for the prisoners. It was a form of conflict that left the victorious government embarrassed and shamefaced. Though non-violent resistance seemed to fail in each single case, in the end it produced an atmosphere in which the government appeared to act illogically, inhumanly, indefensibly.

Gandhi's method differed from any used by his nationalist predecessors. Some of these proceeded secularly and opportunistically, with no consciously rationalized philosophy of resistance, merely employing argument and debate. Most early Congressmen were of this sort. They were for change through constitutional means, by "evolution rather than revolution," and their method was to use persuasion upon the British in the hope that well-reasoned claims would meet with success. This was the method of Gokhale; it was still the method used by the Indian Moderates or Liberals, such as Sir Tej Bahadur Sapru, Mr. Srinivasa Sastri, and Dr. Mukund Ramrao Jayakar, as recently as 1945. It never got effective response from the British. Such men had the respect of thoughtful Indians for their patriotism, honesty, and political sagacity, but the masses rarely if ever heard of them, had no confidence in their method, and never gave them popular support.

Some others of Gandhi's predecessors invoked a religious sanction, but not that of religion in its compassionate, non-violent mood. Rather, it was that of religion when it uncompromisingly strikes down an opponent with physical force. The most noteworthy of these was B. G. Tilak. The god of Tilak and his school was no more shocked by violence than was Jesus, when he said "I came not to send peace, but a sword." The precise means of attacking the infidel foreigner they borrowed from Russian terrorists, who had adopted the pistol and the bomb, and the bomb was greeted by Tilak as an "amulet" for India. There followed a long list of political murders and attempted murders in eastern, western, and northern India down to the time of Gandhi's assassination in January 1948. With this violence became associated, especially in Bengal, worship of the Mother Goddess, under the locally popular form of Kali, who is to be appeased by blood, and the victims of assassination were her sacrifices. The Mother Goddess is perhaps the oldest of all existing cults in India, being known to us from the Harappa culture in the third millennium B.C., and in her service young political radicals often showed a marked degree of physical courage and selfless religious devotion.

Political murder also added unto itself robbery with the purpose of securing funds for prosecuting nationalist aims. Such terrorism gave the government its chief grounds for refusing to negotiate with the nationalists. Though the Indian National Congress as a whole did not endorse this violence, many of its members were sympathetic and condoned it. Even during Gandhi's period of leadership, after every such murder there was discussion in the Congress, and usually a resolution was passed which deplored the use of violence but at the same time lauded the perpetrator for his patriotic motive. These equivocal pronouncements show that even in the years of Gandhi's leadership violence had not been repudiated by most Congressmen on moral grounds but lay just under the surface of the revolutionary movement. On many occasions when Gandhi's non-violent campaign seemed futile, Congressmen pressed for the use of violence.

Gandhi's method of non-violent resistance was not the same as passive resistance, which it was often called in the West. He himself repudiated the latter term. The resisters were not merely to submit and suffer; this would have been negative. Rather, they were to take positive action against their injurers. The action, however, was to be without the use of physical force, and was to employ only that of the spirit. The method was an outgrowth of Gandhi's own philosophy, and was a fusion of ideas derived from various sources, Tolstoi, Jesus in the Sermon on the Mount, and above all certain tenets of Hinduism. His total philosophy, being meant to accomplish the regeneration of the individual in a state organized to promote spiritual values, advocated an individual and national life of simplicity and self-denial. It included a theory of rulership by rulers who do the minimum of ruling. It demanded abstention from violence toward all human beings, and a corresponding practice toward them of invariable loving-kindness. The word which Gandhi used for his method was Satyagraha, a compound of two Sanskrit words—*satya* "truth" and *agraha,* "steadfast grasping"—the two meaning "stubborn adherence to Truth." Gandhi translated it freely as "Soul-Force." He taught that in a "battle of righteousness" it was self-contradictory to employ violence, which was the antithesis of Truth; the only proper, and in the end the only effective, weapon was the power of righteousness inherent in the cause.

The conduct of the struggle was to be fundamentally in the hand of God. The method is one for the weak who are being oppressed by the strong. "Only when the combatant feels quite helpless," said Gandhi, "only when he has come to the extreme point of weakness and finds utter darkness all around him, only then God comes to the rescue. God helps, when a man feels humbler than the very dust under his feet. Only to the weak and helpless is the divine succor vouchsafed."

To Gandhi and his followers, the important elements in practicing Satyagraha were the following: faith in God, a just cause, helplessness, a pure and humble heart. The leaders of such a campaign must begin by purifying themselves. Their intention must be single; they must "adopt poverty, follow truth, cultivate fearlessness"; they "have to observe perfect chastity," and besides denying sex must abstain from all other pleasures of the flesh; they may, perhaps, fast. None of their energy is to be dissipated in ends other than the main one. When the leaders are prepared, the community must observe the same vows and take a solemn oath not to submit to the injustice against which they are protesting; rather they must endure all penalties for refusal. They must, however, bear no hatred against the legislators, the police, the jailers, who oppress them. They must fill their hearts with warm love for these opponents. In the struggle they will suffer; let them be glad to do so. The suffering purifies their own souls, and at the same time becomes a force which mystically operates to their advantage, softening the hearts of their oppressors. With their love, too, they suffuse their opponents until at last a counter-love is generated in the once hard hearts. If the community endures unflinchingly, it must eventually triumph. But it triumphs, not by humiliating the opponents, but by bringing to them such a love that they will see that their own happiness as well as that of the community exercising Soul-Force is best served by granting justice. The solution, in theory, will come as a free and joyous gift. Thus Truth shall conquer.

That many of Gandhi's associates never believed in this method with the conviction that was Gandhi's is certain. Some openly opposed it and asked for measures of violence. Some others frankly admitted that they adhered to non-violence only because they lacked arms. Many political leaders regarded Satyagraha not as a means of practicing religion but as an opportune way of getting a mass of people to act in disciplined unity for a political end. They had no faith in mystical direction by God and the attainment of victory through the inherent power of Truth. Many, too, among the masses whom Gandhi persuaded to use Satyagraha did so from opportunism rather than conviction. The bloody wholesale killings at the time of partition showed this and were the great disillusionment of Gandhi's life. To the end he preached Satyagraha, but in those last months in Delhi, when with hardly intelligible words he spoke his thoughts in his evening prayer-meetings, the old fire and confidence seemed to be gone.

The opportunists, however, were not the only ones who marched behind Gandhi. There were close associates who did share his philosophy, and so did, in a simple way, many of the uneducated masses. For his method drew from an ancient and honored metaphysic in India that concerns the very nature of truth. In quite early times truth (*satya*) became invested with magic power. In the Rig Veda Truth is identical with the cosmic order, and whatever conforms to it is right and belongs to the created and organized universe, while anything violating it is Untruth and is of the region of chaos where demons dwell. Every creature, man or god, has in Vedic thought his function in the universe, and for him Truth consists in fulfilling that function.

This idea underlies the later Hindu doctrine that the different castes ideally have different specific fixed functions, and their members should fulfill those alone, refraining from others. "Better," says the Bhagavad Gita, "to do one's own duty poorly than another's duty well." In this connection there existed in ancient India the concept of a ceremonial Act of Truth (*satyakriya*), which was a solemn asseveration of the complete perfection with which the declarer fulfilled his duty in the cosmic scheme. If in this respect his conduct was flawless, he had attained Truth itself, he had reached his highest goal, achieved his summum bonum. He had become one with the universe, and in becoming one had acquired a special power in it, even over it, for it was himself. He could by the formal asseveration of his Truth execute the Truth Act by which he could work what we would call miracles.

Many are the stories of Hindu, Buddhist, and Jain literature illustrating this theme. Righteous kings, pious ascetics, future world Saviors, faithful wives, a wide range of other types, accomplish marvellous results. The Truth Act is not confined to persons whose life work conforms to normal social ethics. In the world are persons born to pursue an antisocial calling, which is however needed in the cosmic blend like the drop of bitters in a cocktail, and one of them too may win the power if he follows his calling with 100 per cent perfection. In the case of Gandhi's Satyagraha, the justice of the cause and the completeness of adherence to it were similarly to provide a basis for magical—or mystical—accomplishment. The age-old Hindu confidence that Truth will prevail, so vividly dramatized in Gandhi's Satyagraha campaigns, is now illustrated in India's national motto adopted since independence, *Satyam eva jayate,* which in Sanskrit means "Truth alone is victorious."

Another element in Gandhi's Satyagraha that had analogues in ancient India was persistence in enduring suffering for the sake of righteousness. This means not merely to undergo asceticism for achieving spiritual perfection. That feature did indeed enter in. But there was also submission to injury from one's opponent or the infliction of self-injury in his name that is a part of Satyagraha and is also of ancient status in India. There is a custom in India known as sitting dharna, that is, of sitting in obstruction before the housedoor of one who has injured you. This especially includes fasting, which may be continued unto death if the grievance is not redressed. The custom of threatening suicide by starvation or some other means to obtain a just demand is a powerful weapon, with a peculiar efficacy lying in the belief that if the faster should die, his death would be a sin, punishable by Heaven, charged to the account of the person against whom the fast was directed.

When Gandhi entered upon his fasts for social and political ends he was utilizing this powerful means of coercion. His opponents must in many cases have feared the consequences upon their own other-worldly future. But whether they did or not, the Hindu public saw in the fast an affirmation of just purpose, certified by Gandhi's sincere willingness to starve to death if necessary, and a corresponding presumptive evil on the part of the opposition. If Gandhi had died in one of his fasts, those against whom the fast was directed would probably have been ruined both politically and socially. In the theory of Satyagraha there is an added element, also abundantly attested in Indian legend, which translated Gandhi's practice from the level of sitting dharna to a higher sphere. This is the idea that disinterested love for an antagonist, persisting in the face of fierce assault, will accomplish conversion.

In Satyagraha Gandhi adapted these various long-established notions to use by a group. This was a contribution of genius. With the use of Satyagraha planned by capable leaders and directed in action by trained lieutenants called "volunteers," Gandhi transformed nationalist political protest from a middle-class agitation to a mass movement. Though the agricultural and industrial masses had little if any comprehension of the political ends involved, they supported the campaign because of its religious content and the hope of remedying immediately and concretely their present economic distress. They were induced in consequence to make a political alliance with the professional and business bourgeoisie.

There was also a practical point that had nothing to do with religion. Indians could not hope to resist the British by force of arms. Gandhi himself, as we saw above, acknowledged this as a contributory reason for adopting Satyagraha. Similarly in 1942, when the Japanese had overrun Burma and seemed poised to invade India, and the British seemed to Indians powerless against them, Gandhi urged the British to quit India and let the Indians face the Japanese with Satyagraha as their defense. It would be, he maintained, a weapon for the weaponless against which arms could not compete.

After Gandhi introduced Satyagraha in India, a number of campaigns were conducted successfully with its aid. In 1917 the peasants in the Champaran district in Bihar persisted in refusing to plant three-twentieths of their acreage in the, to them, hated and unprofitable indigo for the sake of the landowning planters until finally a commission appointed by the Government affirmed the justice of their contention. Another instance was at Khaira (Kaira, Kheda) in Gujarat in 1918, when Gandhi led the peasants in a struggle to have a subnormal crop declared low enough to justify suspension of taxation for the year. Another celebrated case took place in 1928 in the Bardoli taluq (small administrative unit) in Gujarat, where reassessment of land for purposes of taxation was undertaken by the Government. The new assessments were considered by the peasants to be too high. They refused to pay and were ejected from their homes; their lands were sold for a song at auction; there were fines, beatings, jail sentences. The peasants stubbornly continued their refusal, yet refrained from violence. At last the Government had to appoint a new commission, which reported in general in their favor.

Gandhi's method of resistance obviously put mysticism into the nationalist struggle. To him British rule was wrong, as was the rule of any people over another; it was, in his word, "satanic." Whatever may have been the constitutional and economic issues of imperialism, they were in his eyes less than this issue of religion. But further, from the viewpoint of nationalism struggling against imperialism, his method was justified. It won mass support, when no other method had been able to do so, and by doing so contributed materially to final success.

In his own major purpose Gandhi failed. His aim was the religious regeneration of India and Indians. As success for nationalism became step by step more likely, the politicians slipped out more and more from his control. They had no faith in the ultimate value of his religious purpose, as he had none in the ultimate worth of any purely secular end. He had said that he made a religious use of politics; many a politician of the time, if frank, would have admitted that he, in his turn, was making a political use of religion. Gandhi's own principle of non-violence went into the discard at the same time as did India's political subservience to Britain. He is venerated today by word wherever the voice of the politician is heard in the land; the wearing of homespun khaddar which he advocated is the mark of the Congressman holding or seeking public office; but his own dearest principle lies unused in either foreign or domestic national action.

Even more, though Gandhi abhorred Hindu-Muslim communalism and Partition, he nevertheless contributed to them. He could not in his time have become the political leader of the majority group in India, fortified by mass support, without being religious. He could not be religious without being Hindu. He could not be Hindu without being suspect to the Muslim community.

His economic preachings were palliative, not curative. The future building up of India is not possible merely in his terms of village cottage industry, home spinning and weaving. Industrial expansion he viewed unsympathetically. Nor did he understand the relation of labor's troubles to national well-being. His message was one from the past, an ancient and great India reasserting itself. Some other leader with a different outlook, a philosophy of modernism, was needed to direct India's life in the middle of the twentieth century.

6. The Winning of Independence

After the Amritsar Massacre in April 1919 there was no going back for nationalism. Its purpose hardened; the people were in a mood to support it; a leader was at hand with a practical method of revolt. The industrialists had been encouraging a boycott of British manufactures in favor of *swadeshi,* "home-made" goods, especially textiles, which constituted India's greatest industry. This gave Indian industry a stake in nationalism and predisposed it to underwrite the nation-wide agitation that was soon to commence under Gandhi and the Congress.

At this time India's young labor movement was instigating industrial strikes and so helping to create disturbances which handicapped the Government in maintaining law and order. Peasant movements were active against landlords and had the sympathetic interest of political personages, among whom was the young Jawaharlal Nehru. Both kinds of movements were ready to hand for the uses of nationalism. Muslims, too, were for the time being available to help because of their discontent over the Khilafat issue.

Nationalists were divided as to the best way to treat the new Constitution of 1919. Some favored full coöperation, accepting in good faith Parliament's statement that it was only experimental and after ten years would be superseded by another with terms dependent upon the condition, necessities, and powers of India at that time. Others were in favor of complete boycott. Still others preferred partial non-coöperation. Congress after consideration chose first the method of full non-coöperation, under the direction of Gandhi, in a movement which started in 1920.

Non-coöperation was with Gandhi founded upon religion. To get back to the assumed pristine righteousness of India existing before materialism had corrupted the land and debased the Indian soul, it was essential, he taught, to throw off the evil of the present, to "non-coöperate" with it, and this meant, as far as India was concerned, to "non-coöperate" with the British Government. It, more than anything else, represented Satan and Satanism, and the abolition of the "Satanic" British rule was an inescapable prelude to spiritual regeneration.

Led by Gandhi, Indians boycotted the first elections under the new Constitution, forsook the courts, deserted the Government colleges, and refrained from buying European imports, especially cotton goods, which they hoped to replace with handmade Indian cloth that would provide work for many starving Indians. Many prominent Indians, including the poet Rabindranath Tagore, resigned British titles, though Tagore himself thought the Non-coöperation Movement too narrow in its practical program to accomplish results of permanent value. Civil disobedience, as by not paying taxes, was to be the climax if the British did not yield. During 1921 most of the Congress leaders were thrown in jail. The campaign, for the first time in the history of nationalism, succeeded in getting outside the cities and reaching the countryside and the villagers. From then on nationalism used the agrarian problem as a major issue.

As the movement spread, many of Gandhi's followers, thinking non-violence had now served its purpose, wanted to use physical force. The government had fixed gathering-points for Europeans in case a revolution broke out; all military precautions had been taken. The nationalists awaited only the word of Gandhi to proclaim full Civil Disobedience and so inaugurate an uprising. This he was to give unless the volunteers who had been arrested were released from prison and the imperialist repression stopped. Both Indians and British expected that word at any moment.

But it never came. And the reason it did not come was a religious one. Gandhi was in earnest when he said that the first requisite for the individual citizen and the nation was the self-control to observe ahinsa, "non-violence." As his movement came more and more to draw in those whose basic motive was political, not religious, he became disillusioned. There were attacks in rural districts on the licensed liquor shops, and he was glad of the hatred shown for strong drink, but he abhorred the violence. When riots occurred in Bombay at the time of the Prince of Wales' visit in 1921, he deplored the bloodshed. Finally, a notorious affair at Chauri Chaura (February 4, 1922) in the United Provinces, where a mob led by non-coöperator "volunteers" burnt and beat to death twenty-two Indian policemen, convinced him that civil disobedience could not be put into effect without an accompaniment of bloodshed occasioned by his own followers. He would not run the moral risk, no matter what the prospect of political success. He felt that he had been warned from heaven; he withheld his word; the crisis passed. His supporters in their turn were disillusioned and discouraged by losing the opportunity to strike; the high pitch of revolutionary enthusiasm quickly fell. Gandhi was sent to jail, after a dramatic trial in which he stated that in believing India had accepted non-violence he had made a "Himalayan blunder."

But non-coöperation, as directed by Gandhi, had achieved certain striking results for nationalism. It had shown that Indians could unite—much to the surprise of Indians and British alike—that nationalism could get mass support, and that there lay in "non-violent resistance" a weapon of tremendous possibilities. It also prompted respect among the British, and induced a greater spirit of conciliation. At the same time it spurred the government to seek allies among the princes through the Chamber of Princes, among the Untouchables by appointing representatives for them in the Legislative Councils, among the business interests by granting tariffs and other concessions, among the Muslims by observing communal representation in making administrative appointments.

Out of the Non-coöperation Movement was born the Swaraj party, which under Chitta Ranjan Das (1870–1925) of Bengal for several years held the center of the nationalist stage. Das's method was that of partial non-coöperation and was aimed at the fundamental weakness of the system of "dyarchy" established by the new constitution. His party was to capture as many as possible of the elective seats in the legislative bodies, where the elected representatives were to make their demands. If these were met, well and good; but it was self-evident that they would be refused, and then the representatives were to "non-coöperate" by opposing all Government measures. The scheme was foolproof, for the legislative bodies were not finally responsible for the government; the responsibility rested with the British-appointed governors, who had the power to enact by certification any legislation they thought necessary which was refused by the councils.

The Swarajists were successful in some of the provincial Legislative Councils, thus compelling the Government to certify measures repudiated by the people's elected representatives. In the central Legislative Assembly, the Swarajists, in combination with members

of other parties, in 1924 succeeded in throwing out important parts
of the budget, but the upper chamber, known as the Council of
State, where the majority of seats were occupied by Government
nominees and official members, restored it, saving the Government's
face. So, too, the Legislative Assembly in 1925, at the challenge of
the Secretary of State for India, once adopted by a vote of 72 to 45
a constitutional program moved by Pandit Motilal Nehru, father of
Jawaharlal Nehru, but the upper chamber again saved the Government's position by rejecting it. The Swaraj party added to the
lesson of the Non-coöperation Movement by teaching India the
effectiveness of parliamentary procedure as a weapon for nationalism.

During the years following Gandhi's imprisonment in 1922 other
matters of note occurred. In 1923, to balance the budget, the Government proposed to double the tax on salt. The nationalists directed
a campaign against this measure in the Legislative Assembly and
defeated it, but the Governor General restored the proposed tax by
his power of certification. Further, terrorism broke out again in
Bengal and in 1925 a repressive ordinance was promulgated, along
the lines of the Rowlatt Act, and under it many persons were
arrested, some of whom were not released until as late as 1928. The
nationalists were later in 1930, under Gandhi, to use the salt tax as
the object of one of their most dramatic demonstrations; and in
1931 the Government was to turn again to ruling by ordinance.

In the Panjab the Government in the early 1920's became involved
in a struggle between the aggressive revivalist puritanical reform
division of the Sikhs known as Akalis and certain other elements of
that community which were in possession of rich Sikh temples. The
Akalis demanded that the shrines be turned over to them as the only
true Sikhs, and charged the incumbents with licentious living, ir-
religion, and misuse of temple funds. The Mahants (abbots) of the
shrines refused, and the Akalis marched, non-violently, to take possession. At one shrine the Mahant had in 1921 organized a massacre
of Akalis; at others there were lesser but more prolonged disturbances. It was impossible for the Government to remain outside the
struggle and in taking part it was automatically committed to support the Mahants, who were in legal possession but were morally
wrong. Just then in 1923 one of the Sikh princes, ruler of the state
of Nabha, was forced by the Government to abdicate for malad-
ministration. The Akalis looked upon the Government's action as a
blow to the Sikh community, demanded the restoration of the prince,

and endeavored to hold religious exercises in a great demonstration at a shrine within the borders of the Nabha state. Five hundred Sikhs in February 1924 marched there and were met at the border by troops and dispersed with rifle fire, many being killed. Successive pilgrimages followed every two weeks, and the pilgrims were arrested, until no less than 14,000 had gone to jail. At last, in 1926, matters were adjusted. The Akalis got most of their demands, though the deposed prince was not restored and in 1928 was even stripped of his title. Since that time, the Akalis have been the effective arm of Sikh nationalism, which since shortly before Partition has agitated for a separate nation to be known as Sikhistan.

Still further in the 1920's anti-Indian legislation in Kenya, British East Africa, created intense indignation in India. In 1927 the Government of India protested to the home Government in London, and there was much nonofficial agitation in India. This intra-Empire discrimination against Indians fed the nationalist rancor against white rule.

Meanwhile, the temporary alliance between Hindus and Muslims had broken down. In 1921–1922 a backward and fanatical Muslim group known as the Moplahs (Mappila), living along the southwest (Malabar) coast of India, periodically notorious since 1836 for violent anti-Hindu activity, undertook to convert Hindus forcibly, with the result that the Government had to intervene. This affair ended the Hindu-Muslim alliance except for the association of a handful of political leaders. When Congress organized a boycott against the Prince of Wales in 1921, communal riots occurred in connection with it. From time to time local hostilities broke out between the two communities in other parts of India. Casualties ran into the thousands.

In southern India the non-Brahman elements of the Hindu community were becoming actively hostile toward the Brahmans, and the Justice party representing the non-Brahmans captured power. It, with the somewhat older Liberal party, leaned toward the British hold, and was providing a diversion from the Congress nationalists.

In 1927 the fire of nationalism blazed up again. The immediate occasion was the appointment by the British Government of an Indian Statutory Commission headed by Sir John Simon to propose the next stages in constitutional reform that had been foreshadowed in the Government of India Act of 1919. When the personnel of the commission, seven in number, was announced, India experienced a great disappointment. For not a single Indian had been included, and India took the omission as an insult.

The British Government was unwilling to enlarge the Simon Commission by appointing any Indian members. The commission itself later invited advice from Indians and asked the various Legislative Councils to appoint commissions to meet with it, but this did not mollify the nationalists and two of the eleven legislative bodies refused the invitation. The Simon Commission found its official welcome from the Government offset by general popular suspicion, hartals, strikes, frequent boycott, monster meetings of protest, and other unfavorable demonstrations, including attempted violence.

Violence was, indeed, common, especially in the Punjab. At a demonstration in Lahore the elderly nationalist leader, Lajpat Rai, was beaten by the police, and a few weeks later died. His physician diagnosed his illness as heart trouble, but many nationalists ascribed it to the beating, and the young English lieutenant of police who had been in charge at the scene of the beating was murdered as an act of reprisal. In April 1929, bombs were thrown into the central Legislative Assembly in Delhi while it was in session.

When the Indian National Congress met during Christmas week, 1928, Gandhi, now back in politics with full vigor, announced that unless the wishes of Congress were met by January 1, 1930, he would call upon India to resist Britain by the use of general civil disobedience, that is, nonpayment of taxes and other forms of resistance. As the year passed, the threat gained evident sympathy among Indians and appeared to disturb the Government. The nationalist demand was for two things: first, full home rule, either with complete independence or with Dominion Status; second a Round Table Conference to frame a new constitution, at which Indian nationalist interests should have their due representation.

The British response came when the Governor General Lord Irwin (later Lord Halifax and British ambassador to the United States) made an official declaration on October 31, 1929, in which he first referred to the celebrated pronouncement by E. S. Montagu in 1917 designating full responsible government as India's constitutional goal, and then went on to say that it was "implicit in the declaration of 1917 that the natural issue of India's constitutional progress as there contemplated is the attainment of Dominion Status." He announced that after publication of the Simon Commission's report, a Round Table Conference of British and Indian leaders of all interested groups, including the Indian States, would be called to make constitutional proposals to Parliament. Later he invited Gandhi and some other Indian leaders to confer with him and discuss the membership of the Conference.

The meeting of the Governor General with Gandhi and other Indian political leaders, held December 23, 1929, was fruitless, chiefly because Gandhi and Pandit Motilal Nehru, the Congress representatives, demanded that Dominion Status be granted immediately, and that the proposed Round Table Conference in London have no duty except to frame a constitution bringing it into effect. This was more than the British would concede. The Indian Liberals and most of the minority groups, however, seemed in favor of entering the Round Table Conference, and working out a scheme in coöperation with the princes and the British.

Among the Congress nationalists there was a sudden crystallization of opinion in favor of complete independence which became a slogan under the Hindi term Purna Swaraj. This fact became evident at the meeting of Congress immediately after Gandhi's conversation with the Governor General, and a momentous resolution was adopted declaring for it.

This time Civil Disobedience was begun with an attack on the salt tax. This was an ancient levy coming from long before British times, and while the amount of money it took from the individual was not great, it was still a burden upon the poor. The fight in 1923 against the doubling of it had shown that it was a good target for popular antipathy. Gandhi organized a march of protesting nationalists from his Ashram at Sabarmati, near the city of Ahmedabad, to Dandi, a tiny fishing village, 165 miles distant on the lower east coast of the Gulf of Cambay, there to manufacture salt from the sea water in defiance of the government monopoly. The party started on March 12, 1930, consisting of Gandhi and seventy companions. Along the way there were demonstrations, followers grew in numbers, and the publicity throughout the world was enormous. Gandhi reached the sea, went through the motions of dipping up water to evaporate in the sun, and made a crude and unpalatable salt. The intrinsic economic value of the product was nothing; the symbolic political value was incalculable.

The second non-coöperation movement, like the first, was meant to boycott government schools and administrative organs, liquor shops, opium, and foreign cloth, which last was to be displaced by

homespun cotton *khaddar* or *khadi*. It was supplemented by local refusal to pay taxes, terrorism (in Bengal), and something close to
mutiny in Peshawar.

On May 5, 1930, Gandhi was arrested and interned, to be held
without trial indefinitely; his chief followers had already been
arrested or soon were; and between that time and the end of January
1931, when he was released, somewhere between 40,000 and 60,000
Indian political offenders were held for greater or less periods in jails
and detention camps. In many parts of the country Congress was
declared an illegal body. But the demonstrations did not stop. One
of the most striking features was the emergence of women in great
numbers to take part in the struggle. Labor, with its red flag, joined
the Congress, especially in Bombay. Through it all, Gandhi admonished the resisters to abstain from violence.

The first Round Table Conference met in London in the autumn
of 1930, consisting of representatives of British and Indian interests
nominated by the Government. The King opened it; the Indian
princes appeared in great splendor; the Muslims and other minorities
were represented; the Indian Liberals were present. Only the Congress members were absent. They were in jail. The Conference held
its sessions, and recommended a general scheme of government, consisting of a Federal India, to be loosely organized at the British-con-
trolled center and to allow for divergent systems of administration
in the autocratic Indian States and the partly democratic British
India, with most matters of importance being left to the internal
control of the provinces and States as constituent members of the
federation. But no one considered the proposals final; everybody
knew that without the coöperation of the Congress no scheme could
be successful. As soon as the Conference was over, the Indian Liberals
hurried back to India to persuade Gandhi.

In due time it became evident that a second Conference would be
necessary, and Gandhi was released from jail that he might discuss
participation with Lord Irwin. On March 4, 1931, the two negotiated
the Irwin-Gandhi truce; the civil disobedience campaign was suspended (another frustrating experience for nationalism, as had been
the suspension of the first Civil Disobedience movement in 1922,
and a puzzle to leaders like Jawaharlal Nehru); political prisoners
were released; and negotiations were undertaken about arrangements.

Gandhi was for long undecided whether or not to go. The chief
doubt came from his realization that the various Indian elements

would not present a solid front, and he was concerned above all about the attitude of the Muslims. At almost the last minute, after considerable changing of his mind back and forth, he decided to go. He insisted, however, upon being the Congress' sole representative.

The result again was failure. The demands of the Congress were not acceptable to the British; for they wanted military, financial, and political safeguards extending over a non-delimited transition period, and this the Congress, represented by Gandhi, considered inadmissible. Aside from that fact, the Conference was doomed to wreck on the rock of communal discord. Before it came to a close, the representatives of the various minority communities—Muslims, Europeans, Anglo-Indians, Indian Christians, and Depressed Classes (Untouchables)—made a pact directed against Congress and the residual majority which the Congress represented. The minorities wanted separate electorates and separate representation; Congress wished a single general electorate. Gandhi unwillingly conceded that the proposal should apply in principle to the Muslims, but could not agree on the number and proportion of representatives, and he refused to consider it at all for the Untouchables. In the end the Conference was adjourned with unfinished business to be transacted by committees in India.

Just as the Second Round Table Conference was coming to a close with failure certain, the Government of India issued the first of a series of repressive ordinances. This was an anti-terrorist measure for Bengal, where violent political crime had occurred. It was promulgated on November 30, 1931, and gave the Government the power to commandeer property, impound bank accounts, conscript specified classes of the population for maintaining law and order, impose collective fines on areas where certain crimes were committed, make arrests without warrants, hold secret trials by special tribunals, try an accused in his absence, give sentences of death or transportation; and the findings were to be subject to no appeal. Other ordinances of a character more or less like this were afterwards published for other parts of the country.

During December 1931, a No-Rent campaign moved with great force, and its leader, Jawaharlal Nehru, was arrested on December 26. The agitation on the North-West Frontier increased, and Abdul Ghaffar Khan, leader of the Red-Shirts, a Muslim party sympathetic to Congress, was arrested on December 24. Gandhi, returning from the Second Round Table Conference, landed in Bombay on December 29, and within a week, on January 4, 1932, was again taken into custody. On the same day the late Vallabhbhai Patel, then president of the Congress, was arrested. The arrest of others followed by the hundreds and thousands. On April 24, Congress, already outlawed, was to hold a meeting in Delhi. As the delegates prepared to assemble, the Government arrested at different points 369 of them, including the poetess, the late Mrs. Sarojini Naidu, acting president of the Congress, afterwards Governor of the United Provinces (1948–1949), who was on the point of boarding her train in Bombay. It was officially stated by Sir Samuel Hoare, Secretary of State for India, in the House of Commons, on June 27, 1932, that the number of political convictions under the ordinary law and the ordinances up to June 1, totaled 48,576.

At the time when Sir Samuel gave these figures, he made two announcements which further exacerbated public opinion in India. The first was that the method of Round Table discussion for constructing a new constitution would be discontinued. The other was that the ordinances, which would have expired at the beginning of July, would be renewed.

On August 16, Ramsay MacDonald, the Prime Minister, announced the Government's proposal for solving the communal question, which was to divide the electorate into twelve separate constituencies, thus extending the political communalism which Congress was opposing. Gandhi had foreseen that the Government would separate the Depressed Classes from the General (Hindu) constituency, and on September 20, in protest, began a "fast unto death." Eventually he carried his point. To nationalism his success was highly important, for he prevented an open fissure in the Hindu body politic, which was the field of nationalist activity.

With the cessation in 1934 of the second Civil Disobedience campaign, the Congress entered upon a period of confusion. The campaign collapsed partly because Gandhi withdrew in August 1934 into private, or at least semiprivate, life; partly because the large contributors of funds to the Congress were discouraged by the domination of Gandhi and his, to them, idealistic and impractical program of non-violent resistance; partly because there was disagreement inside the ranks of Congress between an economically and socially conservative old guard, with which, on the whole, Gandhi coöperated, and a liberally minded left element, of which the chief spokesman was Jawaharlal Nehru. The latter came in time to be flanked by an ultra-radical violence-minded wing, led by Subhas Chandra Bose (1897–1945). This was not allied to the Communist party in India, which at that time was outlawed, but was motivated rather by Fascist ideology.

Liberal, or socialist, movements were developing in India during those years. The largest of these was among the peasants, whose various organizations came to center in the All-India Kisan Sabha ("Peasants' Association"). This in 1938 claimed over a half a million members, and both Congress and the Communists endeavored to get control of it. Trade unions also expanded, though not to such numbers; in 1938 the All-India Trade Union Congress claimed 325,000. The left elements in Congress in 1934 had created the Congress Socialist Party, which confined its membership to members of Congress, and endeavored to win Congress to a program of organizing Indian society on socialist lines. In 1936 Nehru and his associates succeeded in getting Congress to commit itself to an agrarian program.

In that same year Congress had to decide whether to coöperate with the Government of India in working the new Constitution of 1935, which by that time had been adopted over the head of the Congress, just as in Britain it had met at every point the bitter opposition of Conservatives of the die-hard school, especially Winston Churchill, who could not brook any abridgment of Britain's imperialism in India and publicly ridiculed Gandhi as a "half-naked fakir."

The new constitution had two main features. One was the grant of autonomy to the eleven principal provinces known as "Governor's provinces" through ministries fully responsible to elected legislatures (the remaining parts of British India known as "Commissioner's provinces" had no legislature or ministries). The other was a provision for federation of the Indian States and the provinces of British India. The first was put in operation in 1937 after elections. The second was never utilized, since the parties to the proposed Federation could not agree on specific terms. The new constitution also contained a series of "safeguards" for British military, financial, and political interests, which were thoroughly distasteful to the nationalists.

Congress contested the elections and won a sweeping victory, gaining approximately 70 per cent of the vote cast, a majority of the legislative seats in seven of the eleven Governor's provinces, and a plurality in another. The problem for Congress was then whether to accept ministerial offices, since, by the Constitution, the Governors of the provinces had powers of vetoing and certifying legislation. Eventually a "gentleman's agreement" was reached by which the Governors were to retain the rights but not to exercise them, and Congress then established ministries. Congress was now supreme; its membership was announced by Jawaharlal Nehru at the beginning of 1938 to be 3,000,000 (it had been only 600,000 in 1936), of whom, however, only 100,000, or about 3.3 per cent, were Muslims.

The Congress ministries (1937–1939) moved effectively to improve educational and public health conditions, but were slow to act on agrarian reform and the demands of labor. They alienated the Muslims and so helped set the stage for a growth of the Muslim League during the war and the promotion of communalism.

Congress opposed the new Constitution's scheme of Federation between the provinces of British India, which were developing democratic institutions, and the princely Indian States, which were ruled autocratically and were not obliged by the Constitution to liberalize themselves. The latter were to have a representation proportionately far greater than would have corresponded to their population. The rulers of the States were lukewarm to federation, fearing the spread within their borders of representative institutions. The Federation was never effected, and to the end of the British authority the government of India at the center was conducted under the Constitution of 1919.

During the second World War, the conflict between Indian nationalism and British imperialism reached a new climax. Indian nationalism was ready to support democracy against totalitarianism, but there was a proviso, sometimes openly expressed, always implicit. This was stated to be that the struggle should actually be for the maintenance and promotion of democratic ideals, not for the gratification of national rivalries. If Britain were really fighting for "freedom," then, in the eyes of leaders like Gandhi, Nehru, and many others, the logical accompaniment would be that India should have freedom. Indians used the slogan "freedom is indivisible" to mean that freedom should not in logic have geographical or color limitations.

Not long before the outbreak of hostilities, the British Parliament adopted an act by which, in time of war, the central Government of India, functioning under the Governor General, could suspend many

provisions of the Constitution of 1935 concerning provincial autonomy. Congress, in consequence, acting through its "high command,"
instructed its representatives in the central Legislative Assembly not
to attend the forthcoming session of that body. When war came on
September 1, 1939, the Governor General, without consulting the
Legislative Assembly, at once declared India automatically a belliger-
ent. At the same time he suspended political reform for the duration
of the war. In these steps he was legally correct but tactically at
woeful fault, since India was humiliated and her good will toward
the British cause was chilled.

From this time on the Government of India and Congress engaged
in a wearying and profitless exchange. Congress professed itself willing to support the war if India were given self-rule or promised it
definitely at the end of the war. The Government would not commit
itself. In October 1939, the Congress high command ordered the
ministries to resign in the seven of India's eleven provinces where
Congress had control. Consequently, in these provinces, the governors
assumed administrative and legislative powers.

The Muslim League, which had been growing stronger during the
time while the Congress ministries were in office, was demanding
equality of power and position with the Congress. When the Congress ministries resigned, the League celebrated "Deliverance Day."
Early in 1940 the Viceroy gave M. A. Jinnah, leader of the League,
assurance that any new constitution would have to receive the approval of the large minorities. The Government wished to retain the
Muslim ministries in the three provinces where it had a majority and
in a fourth where it had been able to form a new ministry with the
aid of other minorities, and it succeeded in doing so. The delicate
position of the British in their diplomatic relations wth the Islamic
Near East was an additional incentive to placate the Indian Muslims.
The Congress reply was to elect (for the second time) as president
a prominent Muslim scholar and astute politician, Maulana Abul
Kalam, called "Azad" (Free), and in so showing its all-Indian,
rather than communal Hindu, character, make a bid for Muslim
support.

In March 1940, at its annual session, Congress again decided not
to support the war effort, declaring that Great Britain was fighting
a war for imperialist ends, threatened to launch a Civil Disobedience
campaign in the near future, and demanded an immediate declaration of Indian independence and the summoning of a Constituent

Assembly, based on universal adult suffrage, to frame a new constitution.

When the Muslim League met at Lahore that same month it demanded two things: independence of India and partition of the country into separate Hindu and Muslim States. The latter constituted adoption as a political goal, without use of the name, of "Pakistan," which term was already in vogue among Muslims.

About this time (July 1940) Subhash Chandra Bose was arrested for sedition, and was to be tried in February 1941. The day before the trial, however, he disappeared, later to appear in the Axis countries and still later to collaborate in Southeast Asia with the Japanese as Neta ("Leader, Duce, Führer") of the "Indian National Army" and head of a puppet Indian government in exile.

After the fall of France, Congress, thinking that probably Britain would now be willing to end the deadlock in India, voted to coöperate in the prosecution of the war, provided a National Government was established at the center which would be responsible to the legislature. Gandhi at this point ceased coöperating with Congress, because Congress, in intimating that it would support the war, had abrogated his principle of non-violence.

The British Government declined the Congress offer, on the grounds, first, that the Indian political parties were not agreed on political goals, and second, that in time of war it was impracticable to reform the constitution. The Muslim League also opposed the Congress plan.

In September 1940, Congress decided to withdraw its conditional offer to coöperate with the Government, called Gandhi back to leadership, and under his direction began a campaign of limited Civil Disobedience or Satyagraha. This was to be by individuals, not by mass movement, and was to be "symbolic." Prominent Congressmen, selected by Gandhi, would court arrest by making antiwar statements in public, previously notifying the police. In this way large numbers of the most prominent leaders, including Nehru, were arrested and sentenced. By May 1941, the number held for such offenses was over 14,000.

While relations between the Government and Congress were blocked, relations between the Government and the Muslim League were also deteriorating. In July 1941, the Viceroy enlarged his Executive Council by creating five new posts, thus making a total of twelve, of whom seven were Indians, and an eighth was to be an

Indian when a then imminent replacement was made. The Viceroy also appointed a National Defense Council of thirty members, including the four Muslim premiers of the provinces where representative ministries still functioned. Congress, of course, derived no satisfaction from these developments, and the Muslim League was equally aroused. Jinnah, as Leader of the League, compelled the three Muslim premiers of provinces where the League was in control to resign their appointments in the Defense Council, and continued to demand creation of Pakistan.

In August, when the "Atlantic Charter" was framed by President Roosevelt and Prime Minister Churchill, Indians at once asked if the third paragraph applied to India. This paragraph read: "They [Roosevelt and Churchill] respect the right of all people to choose the form of government under which they will live; and they wish to see sovereign rights and self-government restored to those who have been forcibly deprived of them." Churchill replied in September that the paragraph referred only to those nations conquered by the Axis and excluded India and Burma. The country burned with anger and disappointment.

On December 4, 1941, the Government of India, apparently foreseeing that Japan was on the verge of entering the war, and desiring to conciliate India, announced that it was releasing all those political prisoners who, like Nehru, were guilty of only "symbolic" offenses. Shortly afterwards (December 15), the Viceroy issued a special plea for unity in support of the war. During Christmas week, the Working Committee of the Congress agreed to coöperate to the extent of blocking the aggressors, but not to the extent of aiding Britain. This endorsement of violence as a method of resistance again alienated Gandhi, who a second time withdrew his support from Congress.

In February 1942, Generalissimo Chiang Kai-shek went to India and encouraged the Indians to rally to the war effort; at the same time he urged the British to give India real freedom.

With the political forces of India and Britain thus jammed and the Japanese, who had taken Malaya and Singapore, rapidly overrunning Burma, Churchill on March 11, 1942 announced that the British War Cabinet had decided upon a plan to settle the constitutional problem in India and was sending out Sir Stafford Cripps, long considered sympathetic to Indian nationalism, to secure the acquiescence of leaders of the various parties.

The British War Cabinet's proposals provided for Dominion Status after the war for an Indian Union to be composed of those provinces and princely States which wished to accede to it, and separate Dominion Status for provinces not acceding to the Union. A constituent assembly was to be called after the war to draw up the terms of a new constitution. Treaties with the Indian States would be revised, and minority rights would be guaranteed by safeguards. During the war the British would retain defense but the Viceroy's Council would be Indianized at once.

After negotiations and conferences in India during several weeks, Cripps returned to England on April 12, his plan rejected by all the important Indian parties. The failure was partly due to the fact that nothing was being offered to India for the immediate present— Gandhi described the proposals as "a post-dated check"—and partly because of specific conditions, which were considered inacceptable. First, the scheme opened the way for partition of the country into at least two and possibly many more separate political entities, and Congress viewed such a partition as potentially disastrous. Second, it continued to reserve for the British all control over the army. To Congress no offer could be satisfactory that left the army under complete control of the British instead of a minister responsible to the elected representatives of the Indian people. Congress wanted some kind of civilian minister or secretary of war, even though the actual command in the field during the war would remain with Wavell, then Commander-in-Chief in India, under the British War Council. In the negotiations Congress found that it could hope for only a very limited kind of control through a ministry which Nehru characterized as one for "Canteens and Stationery." Third, the proposed Indianization of the Executive Council did not in itself provide an Indian government responsible to the legislature. The Council would still have been appointed by the Governor General. The nationalist demand, however, was for a Cabinet of the British model, and it was by no means clear that a Cabinet of the British model could be established except on the basis of a Parliament also of the British model. Fourth, there was no provision that in the proposed Constituent Assembly the autocratic princely Indian States would be represented by elected representatives of the people. The representatives were instead to be nominated by the Princes. This arrangement was in contradiction to the demand which Congress had been making for democratization of the Indian States.

The War Cabinet's proposals, if they had been meant to confuse the Indian political situation, could hardly have been more skill-fully framed. They offered independence on terms liable to shatter India into many parts. Congress considered the offer illusory and re-fused it. The proffer of something which Churchill, who was well-informed on the Indian situation and at the same time a most astute politician, must have known was unrealistic and would be rejected, led to frustration of the nationalists. The proposals suddenly trans-formed the Muslim League program of Pakistan from a bargaining weapon meant to wring concessions from the Congress into a realiz-able goal, and must be considered the most important single step toward the 1947 partition. The princes were at once warned that they would have to look forward to a change in their position, yet were permitted the hope that they could hold their states as separate dominions within the British Empire. The minorities, such as the Depressed Classes, were provided guarantees in a scheme which Congress had to take the odium of declining. The Communists were encouraged, since they had come to support the war after Germany had attacked Russia. Congress itself was divided three ways between those who in their bitterness would have supported nothing British and were willing to sabotage the war effort, those who like Gandhi would have resisted the Japanese with Satyagraha, and those who like Nehru wanted to organize scorched earth and guerrilla resistance. The proposal roused contention and magnified the existing internal dissension at the time when Japan was still pressing forward in the eastern hemisphere and the Germans were still victorious in the western. It seemed to indicate that Churchill believed India had no important contribution to make toward the defeat of Japan.

In the months following, Gandhi urged Britain to "quit India," and his slogan was supported by many for widely varying reasons. On August 8, 1942, Congress passed a resolution on the basis of this slogan, again urging Britain to grant India a government of her own to resist the Japanese, and to recognize India's right to self-rule, otherwise to face "a mass struggle on non-violent lines," under the direction of Gandhi. Gandhi declared that his first step would be to open negotiations with the Viceroy, but the Churchill government had made preparations well in advance of the Congress meeting, and within a few hours after the "Quit India" resolution was passed, the Government of India arrested Gandhi and other leaders. Congress was outlawed, and in rapid steps its chief members were imprisoned to the number of 60,000 and held for periods of varying lengths.

Numerous disorders then occurred, such as burning railroad stations, tearing up tracks, and others, some of which were harmful to military operations. Congress remained helpless and ineffective until just before the end of the war with Japan. Political activity was restricted to the Communist Party, the Muslim League, and the communal Hindu Mahasabha. Both of the latter rapidly grew in membership; the League continuously promoted its campaign for Pakistan, the Mahasabha preached violence against Muslims. Some negotiations were conducted between Congress leaders in jail and Jinnah, but these came to no successful issue. In May 1944, Gandhi was released for reasons of health, and in the following September he conducted futile conversations with Jinnah. Other Congress leaders were released in the first part of 1945 in anticipation of the victory over Japan.

In spite of all the frustration for nationalism it was evident that independence could not be delayed long after the war. Lord Wavell, the Governor General (1943–1947), took various conciliatory steps in advance of a resolution of the problem, especially by convening a conference in Simla in June 1945, attended by leaders of all parties, to devise an interim plan of national government, but this, too, could not bridge the Hindu-Muslim rift. The fate of the Conference was prejudiced in advance, when it was stated that it would proceed on the principle of Hindu-Muslim parity. Congress was willing to talk in terms of Congress-League parity, but it refused to call itself a "Hindu" organization.

Shortly afterwards (July 1, 1945) the British Labour Party swept the Churchill government out of office and in its turn attacked the problem of India. Churchill had been universally regarded in India as hostile to the country's political aspirations and general best interests, but members of the Labour Party had taken an attitude which Indians considered friendly. Most British spokesmen at that time seemed to accept the fact that India must quickly receive independence. One basic reason was Britain's sheer lack of choice. The British power had weakened conspicuously during the war, and it was doubtful if Britain could have afforded the effort to hold India by force. Another was a great public lack of interest in retaining India against her will. Britain was no longer going to receive as much economic profit from India as it had in the nineteenth century and the first decades of the twentieth. Instead India had become a great trouble, if not expense, through its continuous unrest, and in the British public there were many who thought the only answer was to relinquish responsibility at the first possible moment and let India go it alone.

This sentiment was confirmed by events in India during 1945–1946. These included anti-British riots in Calcutta, refusal of the Royal Air Force in India to obey orders in January 1946, and in February of the same year a mutiny of the Royal Indian Navy. Many members of Congress prepared themselves for an armed uprising, which, however, Sardar Vallabhbhai Patel succeeded in restraining. When in that same winter, the government brought to trial for treason the leaders of the Indian National Army, which the Japanese had organized from prisoners of war and used in Burma, popular feeling in their favor was so intense that the action had to be abandoned. In the circumstances, it was clear in Britain that her problem respecting India was merely to save for herself what she could as she withdrew and in the act of withdrawal to keep to a minimum the dislocation and damage bound to result because of the confused and bitter relations which had developed among Indian groups.

In the winter of 1945–1946 new elections were held for the provincial legislatures and in these the Muslim League showed clearly and for the first time in its existence that it had the overwhelming support of the Muslim community. The Mahasabha, however, was repudiated by the electorate and the contesting parties after the elections had been decided were the Congress and the League.

In February 1946, the Labour Government announced that it would send a three-man Cabinet Mission to India to draw up a scheme for giving the country self-government. This went out in March, and on May 16, 1946, the Government published a white paper offering the plan to Parliament. Its provisions respecting the communal issue and the consequent failure of its proposals will be reported in Chapter 8. It proposed in other respects that the newly elected provincial legislature should set up a Constituent Assembly to draft the new constitution, and it indicated that the princely Indian States could not expect Britain to retain paramountcy over them but that they would have to make their own arrangements with the new self-ruling India. Congress and the League quarreled all summer over the plan. No solution seemed yet in sight for the Indian problem and Lord Wavell, who had labored hard to find one, was relieved of his position early in 1947.

The Labour Government now sent out Earl Mountbatten of Burma

as new Governor General. In unexpectedly hurried moves it accepted partition and passed the Indian Independence Act in July
1947, by which independence and partition were to be made effective
a little more than a month later on August 15, 1947.

Thus ended the British Indian Empire. And thus did nationalism
win its victory, though only at the great cost of nearly one-fourth
of India's area and nearly one-fifth of its population.

The history of nationalism in India inspires two reflections, one
concerning the British, the other concerning Indian nationalism. The
first is that, with a moderate degree of political tact, Britain might
have prevented the many serious disturbances that accompanied the
march of India to independence, and might have succeeded in retaining it undivided as a Dominion. If in 1905 Bengal had from the
first been divided according to linguistic boundaries rather than on
the basis of greatest bureaucratic administrative efficiency; if in
1909 the enactment of the Morley-Minto reforms had not been almost
immediately followed by secret planning which led to the surprise
removal of the capital from Calcutta to Delhi; if the reforms of 1919
had not had to fight their way through the brutality of the Amritsar
massacre and military rule in the Punjab; if in 1927 the Simon
Commission had been appointed with at least one Indian member;
if in 1931 the repressive ordinances had not been issued at all, and
especially if they had not come in close conjunction with the (to the
nationalists) disappointing issue of the Second Round Table Conference; if in 1935 the new Constitution had not been framed with
its uncompromising "safeguards" of British power and commerce—
if at any of these junctures there had been more of conciliation and
less of inflexibility, India might well have developed new political
institutions through which unity with Britain could have been preserved.

The other reflection concerns the fact that Indian nationalism rose,
grew, and expressed itself in the religio-social group of Hindus. It
was not possible for this nationalism to win to itself the Muslims, adherents to another religio-centric manner of life, which in its way
was just as intent upon survival as ever was Hinduism. It is true that
the Indian National Congress, the organ of nationalism, never conceded itself to be the voice of Hindu India alone as distinguished
from India as a whole. It adopted a secular program meant to produce a secular state; many of its most prominent leaders sincerely
and consistently upheld secular aims in politics and eschewed re-

ligious and narrow communal aims. Among them were certain Muslims. But the stubborn fact remained that nationalism was a phenomenon of the Hindu community, and this community provided the strength and the direction of Congress, which, when it held power in 1937–1939 was not wise enough to win Muslim confidence. The rivalries already implicit in the situation were exacerbated by the communal activities of the Hindu Mahasabha, which frankly advocated violence against Muslims and goaded Congress as far as it could to communal action. The masses of each community, and more narrowly, the middle classes, which were those fostering political activity, never forgot the contrasts and antipathies of Hinduism and Islam. Hence they could not cross the barrier of communalism and press ahead in common effort to solve the problems posed before their country by the conditions of the mid-twentieth-century world.

7. Hindu-Muslim Communalism

When on August 15, 1947 India was simultaneously given self-government and partitioned into two nations, the western world viewed the gain of independence as the more dramatic of the two changes and the more newsworthy. For it ended the epoch of British political rule, thereby diminishing Britain's world power, and at the same time raised India from her unflattering status as the world's greatest colony. But whatever any distant nations in the West thought of developments, the attainment of full self-rule was neither the more sudden nor the more significant for the subcontinent. Rather, those qualities lay with partition. Self-rule had been in sight for years. But partition was a recent thing. It had not been advocated by a political party until 1940, and then it had appeared unrealistic, a mirage, promoted for propaganda and bargaining purposes but never likely to be realized. Very quickly, however, in 1942 when the Cripps offer was made, it acquired a semblance of reality, yet still no certainty. As late as May 1946, at the time of the Cabinet Mission, partition seemed near to death. Not until June 3, 1947, just over ten weeks before the fateful day itself, did it become a certainty, and when it was effected, it was done with such celerity that there was no time to devise adequate plans for a smooth division, to say nothing of creating the necessary machinery for accomplishing it.

Yet the importance of partition was fundamental. It struck the subcontinent where it lived. It disrupted its new economy, its communications, its administration. It weakened its defense. It divided it into mutually antipathetic and suspicious nations, with a clashing cultural discord inherited from a long past, that only briefly and temporarily had been muted during the eighteenth century and had been steadily rising during the nineteenth and twentieth.

Partition was a direct result of communalism. This is the term given in India and Pakistan to the sense of insecurity which any community feels and the accompanying action it takes to protect itself and further its own interests. It is applied in different localities to groups differentiated by religion, language, region, historical origin, occupation. That is, it has in different areas marked off Hindus, Muslims, Sikhs, Parsis, Christians; speakers of Hindi, Bengali, Marathi, Telugu, and other languages; Mundas, Dravidians, Aryans, Anglo-Indians; agriculturists, jute factory owners, industrial workers. Because a number of these various communities were recognized in British India by separate political constituencies, communalism has had a peculiarly aggravated form in the subcontinent. It is above all applied to the ill-feeling existing in Hindu-Muslim relationships. The Muslims dislike the beliefs and ways of the Hindus, distrust them, and as a minority have feared for their treatment if they should have to live in a state where the Hindu majority had acceded to power. The Hindus in their turn dislike the ways of the Muslims, and, though a majority, have feared the rise to power of the Muslims under whom they experienced centuries of oppression. Before partition the Hindu-Muslim communal hostility was an internal problem of the single undivided India; after partition it became a source of international issues between the two new nations and has helped materially to produce a danger of war. It is the subcontinent's most corrosive inheritance from the past.

The basis of Hindu-Muslim communalism lies in cultural differences. Before partition these appeared to political leaders of the two communities in contrasting ways. The late Mohammad Ali Jinnah, head of the Muslim League, during the latter part of his career consistently said that the differences were not merely those of theology. Hinduism and Islam, he affirmed, were more than two different religions; rather, they were two different civilizations—so numerous and so profound did he consider the antitheses—and, therefore, the two communities were more than a majority and a minority within a single India; they were two different nations which were incongruously associated under a single government. That had long been a Muslim position; it became the fundamental dogma in his political philosophy. But non-Muslim political leaders took a different view. Jawaharlal Nehru, speaking for the Indian National Congress, himself a Hindu, in viewing the communal problem, said in his *Discovery of India* (1946), that the native Hinduism and the intrusive Islam had become so well assimilated to each other that they had

become only modifications of a common civilization. And the late Sir
Tej Bahadur Sapru (1875–1950), a distinguished elder statesman of
India, and a Non-Party Conference committee which he headed,
called the Conciliation Committee, in its report on Constitutional
Proposals (published in December 1945), took the same position.

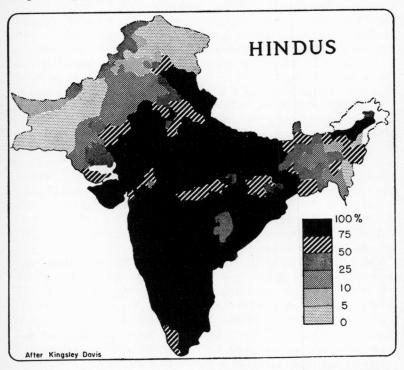

HINDUS

100 %
75
50
25
10
5
0

After Kingsley Davis

Jinnah emphasized the contradictions between the two communities;
Nehru and Sir Tej Bahadur, the correspondences.

In these opposing views is illustrated the most fundamental of
Hindu-Muslim divergences. Islamic civilization is centered around
the religion of Islam, and one of the most characteristic features of
that religion is the demand for doctrinal and cult uniformity. Only
one view of God is acceptable, namely, as Allah; only one series of
revelations concerning Him exists, namely, that of the prophets, of
whom Muhammad is the last and the "seal"; only one book contains

the divine message, the Koran; only one standard of duty lies open
to man, submission to this revelation as a Muslim. But the religion
of Hinduism, which is the core of native Hindu civilization, does not
demand such uniformity, even as an ideal; rather, it is latitudinarian
and tolerant. With orthodox sanction and practice, Hinduism permits

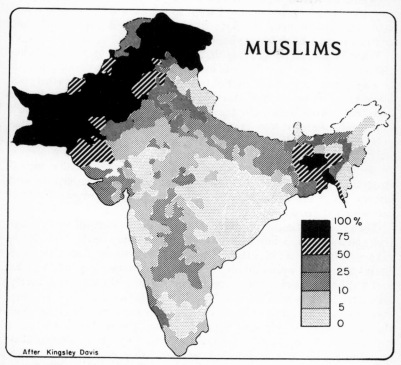

MUSLIMS

100 %
75
50
25
10
5
0

After Kingsley Davis

an unlimited variation in belief concerning the nature of God and a
corresponding diversity in cult and standards of behavior.

Hinduism believes that mankind is incapable of achieving uniformity because human beings are inescapably affected by all their
actions (*karma*) in previous existences, which give them at the in-
stant of birth unequal endowments of intellect and spirit as well
as unequal economic and social position, and therefore impose upon
them different duties. Thus it sanctions the institution of caste, with
its undemocratic implications. But orthodox Islam democratically

views all mankind as born equal; it considers, in fact, that all infants are born Muslims; it is their misguided parents who turn them into Christians, Jews, Hindus, Buddhists, Sikhs, or others. Hinduism, therefore, logically recognizes different capabilities and prescribes different duties for the different castes. It is, from the Hindu point of view, unrealistic to expect human beings, so unequal in their capacities, to hold the same dogmas. Except in the case of the very few rare souls who comprehend absolute truth, everyone is partly right and partly wrong, though in varying degrees.

What Hinduism demands is that, since difference of position, function, and duty exists as a fundamental feature of the cosmos, people of one persuasion should not interfere with people of another but leave them alone in their relative ignorance or wisdom and in the activities corresponding to their limitations. Proselytism is useless and troublesome; it may even be harmful. If an individual performs adequately the duties of his present state, he may in some future existence repair his present spiritual inadequacy and win nearer to supreme knowledge and truth. But Islam, with equally logical deductions from its premises, believes in missionary enterprise and conversion of the infidel and the erring to the single revealed standard which it recognizes.

These contrasting attitudes are not without exceptions in their own communities. Many Muslims, especially today in the Near East, take a wider view of civilization and even of religion than strict and literal orthodoxy would admit; and there are some such too in India and Pakistan. So also there are in India many illiberal and overly dogmatic Hindus who are intolerant of sectarian belief other than their own and scornful of those outside their own narrow group. Yet the basic contrast remains generally true. Hence Islam makes a bifurcation of civilizations into the Islamic, which fundamentalist Muslims regard as God-inspired, and all other civilizations, which are by nature heterodox and false. But orthodox liberal Hinduism may easily admit all civilizations to be reconcilable as merely variations within a single great civilization. It is a corollary of the Muslim view to regard cultural multiplicity as a temporary evil to be replaced by the solitary existence of the one true culture and extinction of its rivals. Cultural amalgamation is equally a corollary of Hindu theory.

Related to this difference in basic outlook upon life is a difference in the social cohesiveness of Muslims and Hindus. With the high

importance which Muslims attach to dogma and their generally
democratic social order, they have developed a strong sense of community. This expresses itself to the eye in congregational worship in
the mosque. There a great courtyard may be filled with a thousand
faithful worshipers, whose voices and bodies rise and fall as one in
the unison of prayer. Any similar phenomenon is unknown in Hinduism. When a Hindu goes to a temple, he worships alone and in under-
tones. Many temples have only recently been thrown open to all
castes. Caste has, indeed, split the Hindu's society and intellectual
freedom has individualized his religion. His human Utopia is a state
of philosophic anarchy; the Muslim's is the well-drilled regiment.
The sense of membership in a community, despite sectarian differences, gave Islam the drive that carried it, within 110 years after
the Hegira (A.D. 622), across North Africa and into Spain and
France in the west and as far as the river Indus in the east. The
Muslim consciousness of community has been strong in India, where
the Muslims were a minority. There, in spite of sectarian theological
and political differences, it gave them a power of aggressive action
out of proportion to their numerical strength.

Again, closely related to the fundamental contrast between Islam,
with its unitary and dogmatic conception of life, and Hinduism, with
its multiple and relative conception, is a difference concerning the
relationship of the state and religion. It is a general Islamic dogma
that Muslims should be governed only by Muslims; Hinduism has
no such religious criterion of rulership. The Muslim theory, in its
orthodox and extreme form, leads to a view of the state as a theoc-
racy (a term decried by Muslims in Pakistan because Islam has no
priesthood), which makes Islam less a state religion than a religious
state. Muhammad regarded himself as the "warner" of his people,
calling them to "submission" (*islam*); their duty was to become "submissive" (*muslim*) to Allah's will. The function of warner was considered a function of the state, to make conversions to the faith the
state's highest purpose. That is why the Islamic religion has been
promoted by military and political means as has no other.

The early Muslims viewed the world as composed of two hostile
military camps. One was the "abode of Islam" where the true faith
was established; the other was the "abode of war" where Islam
was not established and false doctrine prevailed. The ruler of the
faithful was under obligation to convert the abode of war into the
abode of Islam. This he might endeavor to do by making a demand

of conversion upon the unbeliever state. If this were accepted, all was well; but if not, then he must wage a holy war (*jihad*) of compulsory conversion. The conquered were to be treated in two ways according to their previous religious condition. "People of the Book" —Jews, Christians, Magians, Sabaeans—whose scriptures precede the Koran and are considered by Muslims to be in the correct though incomplete line of revelation, had the choice of becoming Muslims or of accepting "protection" and paying a capitation tax. If they refused conversion, their lives were spared but they could not enjoy citizenship. People who were not of the Book had either to become Muslims or be put to death. Obviously, the harsh and extreme application of Muslim theory was impracticable where the conquered folk was stubborn yet necessary to supply labor for the true believing conquerors. For this reason conquered people, including many Hindus, were often allowed to keep their religion and their life, though it might be with impoverishment, humiliation, slavery.

Traditional Hindus have no such theory of the state. They do not regard it as divine will that all people should be Hindus under a single rule. To the traditionally educated Hindu the Muslim theory that state and religion are identical is illogical and untenable. When the Muslims overran India and made forcible conversions, as they often did, the Brahman regarded the conquerors as, in this respect, irrational and mentally immature.

Other important cultural differences separate Hindus and Muslims. The Hindu prestige system, the institution of caste, wherein all men are born to graded places in society, with the Brahman on top as "a god on earth" and the Untouchable at the bottom deeply offends Muslims, since it relegates them, as it does all non-Hindus, to a low status. Islam is socially democratic. It teaches that all men, at least all Muslims, are equal. Again, Hindus decorate their temples profusely with images of gods, human beings, and animals, and use idols in worship as symbols to call a deity to mind. But the Koran strictly forbids the representation of any animate objects, and Muslims destroy the Hindus' temples and images, thus in Hindu eyes committing sacrilege. The Hindu attaches a peculiar sanctity to the cow and considers cow-killing only less heinous a sin than Brahmankilling; the Muslim regards the cow as legitimate food or sacrificial victim and when he can do so with impunity will not hesitate to slaughter the sacred animal. Hinduism uses the native Indian Sanskrit as its classical and sacred language and writes its books in

Hindu-Muslim Communalism

native Indian scripts; Islam uses the imported Arabic and Persian languages and writes in the Perso-Arabic script. Hence the two, with only rare exceptions, have not read and cannot read each other's books. Muslims have generally felt it useless to understand the beliefs and social practices of the Hindus, and the Hindus have been prevented by traditional caste rules from marrying outside their endogamous groups or even interdining and so have been denied much social intercourse which would have helped to bring understanding and toleration.

Bitter and historic enmity divides the two faiths. The Hindus cannot forget the thousand years from the Arab invasion in 711 to the end of the emperor Aurangzeb's reign in 1707, when Muslims periodically plundered their homes, looted their cities, burnt their books, demolished their temples, slew their priests, abducted their women; and they fear a recurrence of these horrors if they should have to live again under Muslim power. With the Muslims it rankles that, under the pax Britannica, they came to take second place to the Hindus whom they had once vanquished and ruled.

Before the agitation that led to partition, in trade unions and peasant groups members of the two communities had often learned to work in coöperation. Among the ruling princes, the antipathy might be suppressed or ignored. It was the middle classes, economically ambitious, that were the chief field in which it appeared. They attached the most value to strict religious dogma; at the same time the system of communal legislative representation and political appointment produced in them heated rivalry and permanent tension, which they communicated on opportunity to the masses. Thereupon on some minor provocation, Muslim mullahs, Hindu priests, or fanatic laymen of either community might by raising the Muslim cry of Din ("The Religion") or the Hindu charge of sacrilege, precipitate a riot.

Several aspects of Hindu-Muslim relations, which showed some degree of cultural assimilation, used to give proponents of the one-nation theory some ground for hope that at a future time, however remote, the hostility might disappear. The one which leaders of the Indian National Congress most often used to stress is the fact that Hindus and Muslims in each locality of India and Pakistan belong to the same racial and ethnic stock. Islam spread in India by conversion rather than by immigration. And conversions were made not so much by force, though force was often used and the memory is bitter in Hindus, as by missionary enterprise among the lowest in the Hindu social and economic scale, who found relief from many disabilities in accepting Islam. In every part of India and Pakistan Hindus and Muslims are alike physically; they can be distinguished only by externals, such as dress, treatment of facial and head hair, sectarian markings, customs of eating, drinking, or other. Moreover, in every locality both parts of the population use a common speech.

Socially, too, there has been occasional assimilation of the two groups, for example, in using similar wedding ceremonies and in sharing each other's religious festivals. Muslim dress has affected, though seldom completely supplanted, native Hindu middle-class costume. The Muslim habit of secluding women became a local practice of those Hindus who could afford it. Caste, though contrary to Muslim doctrine, nevertheless exists in a number of Muslim groups, which could not entirely rid themselves of caste practices when accepting conversion.

On the intellectual level there exists a body of common material, as in the traditional mathematics, astrology, medicine. For several centuries, particularly during the sixteenth and seventeenth, Muslims translated Sanskrit works into Persian, which probably were not read much, yet showed a tendency toward community interrelationship. During that same period both communities had a certain amount of common vernacular literature. In architecture native Indian and imported Persian have blended to produce forms frequently employed in both Hindu and Muslim secular buildings, while in temple and mosque construction there has been exchange of many individual structural and decorative elements. Painting as practiced by both communities during the past three centuries has also been a fusion, in varying degrees in different localities, of native Indian and imported Persian.

Even in religion there have been approaches to each other. Muslim mysticism, that is, Sufiism, though unpalatable to Islamic orthodoxy, renders its adherents and Hindu mystics mutually intelligible. Compromise religions have been preached by persuasive teachers who drew ideas from both Hinduism and Islam. Kabir (1440–1538) was one, there are still sects bearing his name; another was Nanak (1469–1538), the founder of Sikhism. The great Mughal emperor Akbar, who ruled from 1556 to 1605, tried unsuccessfully to bring Hindus and Muslims to a common type of worship but probably doomed it by naming himself God's vice-regent; it perished with him. Generally the reconcilers of the two faiths have done less in bringing them together than in creating new sects to complicate still further the varied array of India's religions.

Finally, the two communities have much of common history. Rulers of one faith have frequently made alliances with rulers of the other against rulers of their own faith. Muslim rulers have often used Hindus as civil administrators and generals, and Hindus have done the same with Muslims. During the British period in India the hereditary rulers of each group were deprived of their political power by the intruding Europeans, and the masses of both suffered economically as their agrarian system was revolutionized and their handicrafts put in competition with western machine industry. The two communities, on high and low levels alike, had a measure of joint interest in gaining self-rule.

The various religious and other cultural differences defined the two communities and produced their primary misunderstandings. But these might have been overlaid and become negligible in their effect upon national life if they had not been supplemented by economic disparities and political rivalries. It happened that in several large areas there was a religious dichotomy of landlords or moneylenders and peasantry. The one would be Muslim, the other Hindu. Thus, in the United Provinces (now Uttar Pradesh), where the peasantry was Hindu, there was a large class of Muslim landholders, called taluqdars. The reverse situation existed in parts of Bengal and the Punjab, where the Muslim peasantry paid rent to Hindu landlords or interest to Hindu moneylenders. In such situations the clash between economic classes was sure to become identified with religious difference.

There was also rivalry between the Hindu and Muslim middle classes created in part by an accident of geography. Because the Muslims had entered India from the northwest and were chiefly concentrated in the north and away from the seaports where the British entered and conducted most of their activities, it was the Hindus, living in and near those parts, who first profited economically from British commerce and first took advantage of the new western education. They became the agents to spread this education, and this fact, too, operated to the Muslim disadvantage and discontent. In Bengal Muslims avoided the learning which was brought by Western unbelievers and propagated by Hindu idolators. Further, when the British reorganized the system of land tenure, the new landlords under the British were Hindus, who had previously been only tax farmers under the Muslim regime. The old Muslim upper classes remained as landowners in their own areas, but the newly appointed Hindus became their upstart rivals as a prestige group and partly displaced them and reduced their numbers.

It was also the Hindus who developed the new bourgeoisie. By the time of the Indian Mutiny in 1857 the Muslim community had only a small middle class against the relatively large Hindu professional, clerical, and commercial groups. This condition persisted down to the time of partition. It was said that in East Bengal, now part of Pakistan, 80 per cent of trade and commerce was in Hindu hands. Moneylenders were almost all Hindus, and the jute business, which is the major industry of East Bengal, was also Hindu. Similarly, about 90 per cent of the professional classes were Hindu. This situation has altered under Pakistan. It was also the Hindus (and Parsis) who became the new industrialists, not the Muslims, most of whose leaders continued to be of the old landholder class.

There was another situation in the nineteenth century operating to Muslim disadvantage. When the Indian Mutiny occurred it was considered by the British to be a responsibility of the Muslims. Most of the Indian Princes involved were Muslim, and the head of a freed India, as the Mutiny would have made it, was to be the titular Mughal emperor in Delhi, around whose shadowy figure the mutineers had asembled their forces. Because of this fact, the British, after quelling the Mutiny, laid the heavier part of the penalty upon the Muslims. It was approximately a decade later before they lifted this discrimination.

During the second half of the nineteenth century the Muslim community contained the larger part of India's dispossessed and unhappy great. It no longer had the political supremacy under the Mughals, whose might had been destroyed by the Hindu Marathas and the Christian British, both of them infidels. The greater number of government posts open to Indians fell to Hindus, and the profits of business were theirs as well. By the time the century was three-quarters past, the old Muslim landlords, who held their position under government title, were still in possession of large sections of Bengal, Bihar, Orissa, and the United Provinces, but in other respects Hindus had the better status. It was inevitable that this situation should produce intercommunity middle-class jealousy.

The Muslim reaction in the nineteenth century to the community's inferior position was twofold. On the one hand it was religious, puritanical, revivalist, fundamentalist; on the other, it was secular and modernist.

The religious and fundamentalist reaction was the older, and consisted of Wahhabiism. This movement originated in Arabia in the late eighteenth century, and its ideas, though not its name, came to India early in the nineteenth century. They gave rise to such organizations as the Ahl-i-Hadith ("People of the Traditions") and Ahl-i-Qur'an ("People of the Koran"), which the Indian Census returned as sectarian groups. Wahhabiism had as its essence the slogan "Back to the Koran!" It strove to eliminate from Islam everything which it considered an innovation since the time of the Prophet, such as paintings, musical instruments, domes and cupolas on mosques. It tried to restore the holy war. In India during the first half of the nineteenth century the movement was widespread. It attacked all elements which Indian Islam had adopted from Hinduism and all the features of modern life which Muslims were inclining to accept. Western learning and culture were, of course, included. The result was to retard progress of the Muslim community and foster strife between it and the Hindus. But, since the Wahhabis were mostly poor, the movement assumed also something of the aspect of proletarian unrest, and as early as the 1830's was alarming the Muslim middle classes, among whom arose later the secular and modernist effort to restore Muslim prestige.

The chief prophet of this second movement was Sir Syed Ahmad Khan (1817–1898). He was one of the most influential Indian Muslims during the nineteenth century. His philosophy was aligned with that of Islamic modernists in the Near East, as in Egypt, who passed beyond the old dogmatism and felt that the holy Koran applied to all peoples at all times. The two camps of Islam and War, they taught, were not so much political conditions as states of the human heart. Muslims should spread Islam by precept and example rather than by violence; the true teaching of Islam was love for all fellow human beings. The political consequence of this teaching was that Islam was not to be an international state under the Muslim banner of religion, but a state of mind and soul among the faithful, who might be rendering temporal fealty to many national governments, including those that were non-Muslim.

Sir Syed was faithful to the British rule in India and did not favor political nationalism. He had been loyal during the Mutiny; he did not share the Muslim resentment of the British discrimination in repressing it. He wished that rule perpetuated, since under it both Hindus and Muslims had the privilege of living according to their own religious law. He pleaded publicly for freedom and independence of thought, and the application of historical criticism to Muslim tradition. He preached a liberal philosophy to the Muslim community, and he had a keen intelligence and a persuasive personality to enhance the effect of his message.

As a part of his program he tried to separate Muslim education from the traditional religious instruction so as to give it a secular character, utilizing modern scientific methods and historical data. In 1875 he founded an institution known as the Muhammadan Anglo-Oriental College at Aligarh, which was immediately successful and in 1920 was chartered as the Aligarh University. It was until partition the leading force in shaping Indian Muslim opinion. Sir Syed had early diagnosed Indian nationalism as predominantly Hindu and therefore potentially prejudicial to the interests of the Muslim community, and he stood apart from the Congress. When the latter organization was founded in 1885, he urged his fellow-religionists to avoid it. As liberalization of India's political system gave Indians increased opportunity in public life, intercommunity rivalry increased. At the Aligarh University anti-Hinduism was expressed in modern terms and applied to modern issues; though religion was not emphasized, sectarianism was promoted in the economic, social, and political spheres. Both the religious and leading secular cultural reactions of the Muslim community in the nineteenth and twentieth centuries, therefore, tended to promote communalism.

Muslim communalism was also in part a reaction against Hindu communal political activity. Particularly irritating to Muslims was the activity of the Arya Samaj, which, differing from usual Hindu practice, promoted reconversion of Muslim groups to Hinduism under the guise of "purification." This practice led in the 1920's and 1930's to considerable intercommunal violence and bloodshed. The Indian National Congress was for long periods under the control of religiously motivated leaders, such as Tilak, who, by means of his aggressive propaganda for "cow protection," alienated Muslims. Gandhi, though deploring communalism and preaching Hindu-Muslim unity, preached unity on what always seemed to Muslims to be

Hindu terms, that is, acceptance of non-violence, Ahinsa, which meant that the cow was to be inviolable; he put it, "The central fact of Hinduism is cow protection." The rank and file of Congress membership was indifferent, if not actually hostile, to Muslim interests. The worst offender of all was the ultra-Hindu political party called the Hindu Mahasabha.

Communal tension between Hindus and Muslims in the latter half of the nineteenth century produced numerous riots in British India. The precipitating cause might be a quarrel over ownership of a parcel of land and the right to erect a religious building on it, or the playing of music by a Hindu wedding procession as it passed a mosque where such a noise constituted sacrilege, or exaction of exorbitant rent or interest by a landlord or moneylender of one religious persuasion from a tenant or debtor of the other, or sacrifice of a cow by Muslims, or the clash of crowds when a Hindu and a Muslim festival coincided. Urban riots were especially common in areas where the disparity of population between the two groups was not great; where one group had a clear numerical or political superiority they were rare.

The growth of Indian nationalism during the twentieth century brought an accompanying increase in the number and intensity of intercommunal riots and took the clash between Muslims and Hindus out of religion and economics into politics. Intercommunity relations grew critical in 1905 over the partition of Bengal, which became a polemical issue of Hindu versus Muslim. The Muslims correctly foresaw that the Hindus might get the partition reversed—as it was in 1911—and to prevent the reversal as well as generally to advance Muslim interests, some of their leaders in 1906, with the blessing of the Viceroy Lord Minto, organized the Muslim League (often called "the League"). Among its specific aims one was to secure for Muslims a due share of government posts. Another was to give the Muslim community a political organization; for it was apparent that India would soon be granted the right to elect some of the members of the provincial councils—the right was later defined in the Indian Councils Act ("Morley-Minto Reforms") of 1909.

It was the Morley-Minto Reforms that inaugurated modern Indian political communalism. In giving the country a limited form of representation in provincial Legislative Councils these reforms introduced the principle of "communal representation" through separate electorates and weightage of representation for minorities. By that system legislative seats and political appointments were apportioned among the general constituency and a number of special constituencies, most of which were defined along communal lines. One of these consisted of Muslims, who had their own representatives, for whom only Muslims voted. The general constituency was the non-Muslim population and corresponded closely with the Hindu community.

When the system of separate representation and separate electorates was introduced, its sponsors stated that it was meant to solve the communal problem; instead it only intensified it. From time to time every minority increased its demands for weightage in representation and appointments. The general constituency, speaking through Congress, resisted these demands, but was compelled to concede more and more. The chief dispute was always with the Muslims. In the two successive constitutions granted India after the Morley-Minto Reforms, namely those of 1919 and 1935, the principle of communal representation was extended instead of curtailed, and it thus became the most poisonous single feature of Indian politics in this century.

During the 1920's the tension between the two communities increased. In part this was due to the prominence of Gandhi in Congress, which made Muslims as a group fear that in a self-governing India the Hindu majority would control Parliament and use the strongly centralized government to discriminate against them. Their alarm seemed to them all too well justified in 1928 at the time of the Simon Commission's activities, when the distinguished lawyer Motilal Nehru and a Congress Committee under his chairmanship drafted a Constitution for India as a Dominion. This frightened the Muslims because it provided for a strong central, non-federal, government, and at the same time took no account of special Muslim claims. The Muslims replied by calling a conference in 1929, presided over by the Agha Khan, head of a small but wealthy Muslim sect, which drew up demands for a separate Muslim electorate, a loose federation of provinces so that Muslim provinces would be practically self-governing, Muslim membership in all Cabinets, central and provincial, and provisions that communal issues brought before legislatures should be decided on terms that would preclude discrimination against Muslims. The Muslim demands and the Nehru draft constitution illustrate the contrast that from then on existed in the political philosophy of the League and Congress.

During the 1930's most of the numerous minor political parties were crowded out of the field and their adherents joined Congress or the League. Congress gained most. Temporarily it received the moral support of several non-League Muslim organizations. The League was reorganized when Congress led by Jawaharlal Nehru in the late 1930's instituted a program of agrarian reform, which alarmed Muslim landowners, intellectuals, and other community leaders.

The political issues between the League and Congress became intensely critical in 1937–1939 during the years of the Congress ministries under the 1935 Constitution. When the ministries resigned, the League celebrated December 22 as a "Day of Deliverance" and continued to commemorate the day each year thereafter until partition. It thanked God in the name of Muslims for "freeing them from the oppression of the Congress ministries" and recited a list of "atrocities" committed by the ministries under the direction of the Congress high command. The chief charge was that the ministries excluded Muslims except those belonging to Congress, whom the League considered renegade and unrepresentative. Other atrocities included the use as a national language of the "Hindi" literary variety of Hindustani rather than the "Urdu," employment of the Congress flag as the Indian national emblem, and adoption as the national anthem of the Hindu Sanskrit hymn *Bande Mataram,* which had an anti-Muslim origin. The League opposed the Wardha Scheme of Education, fostered by Gandhi and supported by Congress, as parochial, communally Hindu, and neglectful of Muslim interests. It also alleged discrimination against Muslims in public office and deplored the promotion of Congress propaganda among the Muslim masses.

In Bengal during the time of the Congress ministries, the Muslims, who controlled the legislature, endeavored to reverse the advantages enjoyed there by the Hindu community by enacting economic legislation to favor Muslims. In the Punjab, where a similar imbalance existed, they made a similar attempt.

During this period Hindu-Muslim communal riots became increasingly frequent and bloody. Riots between Muslims and Sikhs were also frequent. The tension was enhanced by the activities of the Hindu Mahasabha, which attacked the Congress for being too conciliatory of the Muslims.

The Muslims had a genuine alarm that their community might not be able to maintain itself against the Hindu, which during the millennia of history has quietly absorbed other rivals. They feared that their faith might perish in the land, and they and their descendants be reduced economically and socially. Their attention was kept focused on the communal quarrel; their leaders were slow in evolving a social or economic program for the community; they offered little more hope than vague benefits to be derived from establishing a religiously motivated state. This was the meaning Muslims gave to nationalism, and generally they preferred an India under Britain to a free India which might be dominated by the Hindus. Political activity they saw as their rivals' most potent weapon for their oppression; they made it, therefore, their own chief weapon for community protection.

8. The Creation of Pakistan

In the 1940's the Indian Muslim community acquired the goal of a national Muslim state to be created by the partition of India into two separate nations, one Muslim, the other Hindu. The proposed Muslim state was popularly called Pakistan. The Muslim League at a meeting in Lahore, on March 23, 1940, formally adopted the goal but did not then give the proposed state a name.

"Pakistan" was not originally a political term; it was coined to describe a spiritual or religious ideal, which the poet Muhammad Iqbal advanced in 1930 though he soon came to feel that this could be realized only in a separate Muslim state. The name was urged as a political slogan by C. Rahmat Ali and some associates at Cambridge, England, in 1933. The word is derived from Persian *pak*, "the Pure or Sacred," and *stan*, "land, country," and in the religious sense means "Land of the Pure." When it acquired a political sense it was given a second, alternative interpretation as an acrostic referring to the component areas which the proposed nation was to include: *P* for the Punjab; *A* for the Afghan (North-West Frontier) province; *K* for Kashmir; *S* for Sind; (*S*)*TAN* for the last syllable of Baluchistan; the acrostic rather unflatteringly makes no reference to Eastern Pakistan. The other part of India, in contrast to *Pakistan*, "Land of the Pure," was referred to by Pakistan advocates as *Hindustan*, "Land of the Hindus." Though the name Pakistan was not employed in the League's Lahore resolution (1940), it soon afterwards won wide currency.

What part of India was at first claimed for Pakistan? For a long time the League did not define it. In its 1940 resolution it merely stated that "the North Western and Eastern Zones of India" should constitute "independent states in which the constituent elements shall be autonomous and sovereign." Various specific delimitations were offered unofficially by supporters of Pakistan. Many went outside

the boundaries of India to include Afghanistan. Hindus frequently
suspected that the real motive behind Pakistan was to establish
Muslim rule over all India by force, and Muslims often made statements which give some basis for that fear. For example, in April of
1947 H. S. Suhrawardy, of the Muslim League, then premier desig-
nate of the Bengal province, was reported in the *New York Times*
to have said to the convention of Muslim legislators of Bengal,
"The Muslims want to be the ruling race in this subcontinent."

Less sweeping claims were made officially by the League and its
president, M. A. Jinnah. They demanded six provinces of British
India. Four of these were in northwest India, namely, the three
"governor's provinces" of the Punjab, the North-West Frontier Province, and Sind, and the "commissioner's province" of Baluchistan,
all of which were predominantly Muslim in population. The other
two were governor's provinces in northeastern India: Bengal, which
was about 54 per cent Muslim, and Assam, which was only about
one-third Muslim, but was included on the ground that it would be
too weak to stand alone if separated from Hindustan by Bengal.
These six provinces contained about 62 or 63 per cent of India's
Muslims and about 16 per cent of the non-Muslims. Indian States,
such as Kashmir, which were predominantly Muslim and by reason
of geographical position seemed to Muslims designated for Pakistan
were not officially claimed, since constitutionally the States would
have the right to dispose of their own future.

There were from the beginning certain obvious and weighty objections to dividing India into two nations. First, the Hindu-Muslim
communal problem, which the creation of Pakistan was to solve,
clearly would still exist. In Hindustan there would be a Muslim
minority and in Pakistan there would be non-Muslim minorities,
which were already protesting. The Sikhs, for example, who lived
chiefly in the eastern Punjab, were uncompromisingly opposed to
Pakistan or anything that looked like it. Again, western Bengal,
containing India's premier city Calcutta, was predominantly Hindu.
Jinnah indicated at various times that provincial boundary lines
might be redrawn, but he and the League were never reconciled to
any redrawing that would entail, as was nevertheless inevitable,
the loss of Calcutta.

Second, there were certain administrative and economic disadvantages sure to result from Pakistan. Operation of the rail-
roads, postal and telegraph services, and probably some other de-

partments of national life, which were organized on an all-India basis, would be inefficient in a divided subcontinent. Economically, the proposed Pakistan would contain some weak members: Baluchistan and the North-West Frontier regularly required financial assistance from the rest of India. Division could not fail to hinder seriously the exchange of agricultural products and impair industrial development. It was sure, at the minimum, to produce tariffs and customs barriers.

Third, the two parts of the proposed Pakistan would be separated from each other by a gap of 700 miles, across which they could communicate only by courtesy of the proposed "Hindustan." When partition was effected, the area of Pakistan was lessened and the gap became a thousand miles. Finally, the princely Indian States would have to adjust themselves to two independent nations, instead of one. These disadvantages were so certain, so clearly pointed out, so much calculated to affect Muslims as well as Hindus, that they seemed to most foreign observers to forbid creation of Pakistan.

More ominous yet was another consideration. Partition now would reproduce an ancient, recurring, and sinister incompatibility between the Northwest and the rest of the subcontinent, which, but for a few brief periods of uneasy cohabitation, had kept them politically apart or hostile and had rendered the subcontinent defensively weak. When an intrusive people came through the passes and established itself there, it was at first spiritually closer to the relatives it had left behind than to any group already in India. Not until it had been separated from those relatives for a fairly long period and had succeeded in pushing eastward would it loosen the external ties. In period after period this seems to have been true. In the third millennium B.C. the Harappa culture in the Indus Valley was partly similar to contemporary western Asian civilizations and partly to later historic Indian culture of the Ganges valley. In the latter part of the next millennium the earliest Aryans, living in the Punjab and composing the hymns of the Rig Veda, were apparently more like their linguistic and religious kinsmen, the Iranians, than like their eastern Indian contemporaries. In the middle of the next millennium the Persian Achaemenians for two centuries held the Northwest as satrapies. After Alexander had invaded India (327/6–325 B.C.) and Hellenism had arisen, the Northwest too was Hellenized, and once more was partly Indian and partly western. And after Islam entered India, the Northwest again was associated with Persia, Bo-

khara, Central Asia, rather than with India, and considered itself
Islamic first and Indian second.

The periods during which the Punjab has been culturally assimilated to the rest of northern India are few if any at all. Periods of
political assimilation are almost as few; perhaps a part of the
fourth and third centuries B.C. under the Mauryas; possibly a brief
period under the Indo-Greek king Menander in the second century
B.C.; another brief period under the Kushanas in the first and second century A.D.; an even briefer period under the Muslim kingdom
of Delhi in the last quarter of the twelfth century A.D.; a long one
under the great Mughals in the sixteenth and seventeenth centuries
A.D.; a century under the British, 1849–1947.

This ambivalence has made the Northwest a menace to the rest
of the subcontinent. It has always had a typical frontier character,
being turbulent, full of adventurers, proud to call itself "the sword
arm of India," dissatisfied with its skimpy economy, constantly
tempted to use that arm to move eastward and better itself. The
Pakistan proposal, in advocating separation of the Northwest from
India was a twentieth-century illustration of the ancient uncon-
geniality and contained an implied threat of renewed aggression. The
rest of India could not fail to be uneasy about its security.

There was yet another ground for apprehension in having the
Northwest separated; that was its frequently demonstrated inability
to resist a strong invading force from beyond the passes. Its own
resources are small; its political subdivisions (the Punjab, the Frontier areas, Sind, Baluchistan) have little coherence; it needs the
full support of what is now India to make a defense. The British
understood that fact and shaped their military policy in India in
the nineteenth century accordingly. They feared a Russian advance
through Central Asia into Afghanistan and thence by the classic
route through the passes into India. To defend the frontier they
took Sind (1842–1844), destroyed the Sikh kingdom and annexed
the Punjab (1845–1849), and fought two wars with Afghanistan
(1838–1842, 1878–1880). They considered that only a united India
could be defended.

The advocates of Pakistan might also have had some uneasiness
about the defense of Eastern Pakistan. It was to contain the subcontinent's vulnerable eastern frontier with Burma, though this was
less likely to be penetrated than the even more vulnerable northwest
frontier. Eastern Pakistan, however, would be practically at the

mercy of India. It had no natural defenses; it was remote from the dynamic western part of the proposed Pakistan; its people were not warlike. It was less vigorous in promoting the Pakistan proposal. Pakistan would need Eastern Bengal's jute crop as its principal asset in foreign trade, but the area was a strategic liability.

But all the disadvantages inherent in the Pakistan proposal were still insufficient to deter the Muslims. The sense of Islamic community need was more important than all other considerations. Muslims were willing to accept all the disadvantages and risks involved in order to set up their new state.

Much of the strength behind the Pakistan movement came from the personality of the late Muhammad (or Mahomed) Ali Jinnah (1876–1948). He was born in Karachi on December 25, 1876, in a small and unorthodox Muslim sect, and during the first forty-five years of his life had no reputation for Muslim piety or special interest in his community. He chose the law as his career, where he was brilliantly successful, and entered politics early in this century. In 1906 he was secretary to Dadabhai Naoroji (1825–1917), a Parsi, who is known as "the grand old man of Indian politics" and at that time was serving his third term as president of the Congress. In 1910 Jinnah, then prominent in the Congress, became a member of the Imperial Legislative Council, and was already on record as a progressive anti-communal Muslim. He condemned the principle of communal representation, which had been accepted in the Morley-Minto Reforms of 1909, urged general Indian unity, and was considered by Muslim religious fundamentalists to be anti-Muslim. He remained faithful to the Congress until 1920, when Gandhi, with his strong religious motivation, won an overwhelming ascendancy over that body. At that time the liberalizing reforms of the 1919 constitution offered greater political opportunities to Indians than before and consequently brought the ever potent communal rivalry of Hindus and Muslims into heightened activity. During the years 1920–1922, Jinnah and many other prominent Muslims, who had held membership in both the League and the Congress, resigned from the latter body, because they thought that its policies were jeopardizing Muslim interests, and that therefore the Muslim community must organize an effective defense.

In 1934 Jinnah was elected permanent president of the Muslim League. The enlarged political opportunities given Indians by the 1935 constitution further increased the friction between the Hindu and Muslim communities. Under the conditions so created Jinnah converted his position as president into a dictatorship. His followers gave him the title of *Qa'id-i A'zam,* which means "Great Leader," and regularly used it in addressing him or speaking of him. His domination was indicated by numerous items, of which we may cite as typical a resolution adopted March 23, 1942, at a Pakistan celebration in Calcutta, stating, "This meeting emphatically declares the Qaid-i-Azam Muhammad Ali Jinnah, President of the All-India Muslim League, alone represents and is entitled to speak on behalf of the Muslim nation." Jinnah exercised this function without equivocation; anyone opposing him, as even the premier of Bengal in 1941, was forced out of the League. Jinnah was a man of quick and biting repartee, egotistic and sensitive to insult. He had the keenest sort of legal mind, and conducted his arguments with intricate and baffling reasoning. He was noted for his personal honesty, which he carried into his public life, having shown himself unsusceptible to political bribery; on several occasions he refused government offers of high office. In his devotion to Pakistan he attacked ferociously and without prejudice anyone—Hindu, British, or Muslim—who opposed the demand. With his leadership the Indian Muslim community acquired some of that quality of a well-drilled regiment which the Islamic religion had inculcated in the seventh-century Arabs.

During the first three or four years after the Muslim League formally adopted Pakistan as its goal (1940), the vogue of the idea in the Muslim community as a whole was restricted. A number of Muslim parties were relatively indifferent to it; some others were directly opposed. The latter were not only the anti-communalist Muslim members of the Indian National Congress, who were organized as a subparty called the Nationalist Muslim Party, but also other Muslim groups. Among these were the All-India Momin Conference, a rather loosely organized party drawn from the economically depressed Muslim classes; the Majlis-i-Ahrar, a belligerently left-wing and religiously fundamentalist group which originated in the Punjab to relieve the Muslim majority of Kashmir from the discrimination it suffered under the rule of the Hindu maharaja; the Azad party of Sind; the Jam'iat-al-'Ulama, a convocation of Muslim divines; many Shiah, or sectarian, Muslim groups (the Shiahs comprise about 8 per cent of India's Muslim community); the Ahmadiyas, a small sect motivated by a Messiah theory. Most of these bodies either never were effective in politics or by 1946 had lost the effectiveness they once had. The Nationalist Muslims, for example, won only 11 seats against the League's total of 426 in the 1946 provincial elections; the Jamiat-al-Ulama won only 5; the Momins 5, the Ahrars 1.

One group which was always opposed to Pakistan and was the only really strong Muslim organization combating it, was that of the Khuda-i-Khidmatgar ("Servants of God"), the so-called "Red Shirts" of the North-West Frontier Province. This was a group closely affiliated to the Congress; its leader, Abdul Ghaffar Khan, was deeply influenced by Gandhi's teaching and practice of non-violence and introduced similar doctrine and methods among his Pathan followers in resisting the Government of India. In the 1946 elections this group won 19 of the 34 seats reserved for Muslims in the North-West Frontier Province; the League won the other 15. The Red Shirts' seats together with the nine general seats and two of the three Sikh seats gave them control of the province, and Abdul Ghaffar Khan's brother, Doctor Khan Sahib, became premier of the province.

For several years after the League adopted Pakistan, the chief support for it came, not from the Muslim provinces which were expected to constitute the Muslim state, but from Muslims in provinces that were not to be included. It was opposed in Assam as well as in the North-West Frontier Province. In the Punjab, Bengal, and Sind the support was lukewarm and the opposition too strong for the League and Jinnah to overcome until after the Churchill government in 1942–1945 had confined the leaders of Congress and so crippled it. The premiers of those three provinces were at first all outside the League. It was the United Provinces (now Uttar Pradesh) and other regions where the Muslims were numerically inferior to the Hindus and therefore apprehensive that gave Pakistan its early strength.

After the Churchill government in 1942 sent Sir Stafford Cripps to India with constitutional proposals that would have made Pakistan possible, the impression got around among Muslims that the British, who after all had the power, felt that the proposal for Pakistan was reasonable and should be granted—or, at least, that the Churchill government was supporting it. The Cripps offer went a long way toward making the League inflexible on Pakistan.

Whenever it was proposed to Jinnah that a general plebiscite on the Pakistan issue should be held in the provinces which would constitute it, he refused. It was clear in 1946, however, that the Muslims as a whole supported it; for the League's brilliant success in the 1946 elections was based on a campaign in which Pakistan was almost the only issue.

The League and Jinnah often tried to attract moral support for Pakistan from Muslim countries outside India, especially those in the Near East. They got little answer except silence. They specifically inveighed against the further admission of Jews into Palestine, thus aligning themselves with the Arabs, but the Near Eastern Muslim states gave no encouraging response. These states had for many decades been fighting a nationalist battle against Britain and France. In India it was the Indian National Congress which they saw conducting a similar struggle; hence their sympathy was with it, rather than the Muslim League, whose program seemed likely, by dividing India, to perpetuate the very imperialism which they were resisting.

Outside the Muslim community the chief popular support of Pakistan came from the Depressed Castes or Classes (Untouchables, Fifths, Harijan, Scheduled Castes). Under the 1935 Constitution these received special representation through reservation of 151 of the 1585 seats in the various provincial legislatures. They nominated their own candidates, but the electing was by the general constituency, not by a separate electorate, as had been proposed by Ramsay MacDonald in 1932 when the Constitution was being drafted but defeated by Gandhi through his "fast unto death." Politically conscious members of the Depressed Castes were dissatisfied with their gains under the Congress Ministries (1937–1939) and developed their own parties. Their chief leader was Dr. B. R. Ambedkar, educated in the United States, who headed the Scheduled Castes Federation. He gave the League a measure of support, though he never let his party become its satellite. From the Depressed Castes' point of view Muslims or British or almost anyone would have been better as rulers than upper-caste Hindus.

Other support of the Pakistan proposal came from the Communist Party of India, which at its first congress (May 1943) adopted a resolution concerning the solution of India's constitutional problem. The party affirmed that by its plan "Every section of the Indian people which has a contiguous territory as its homeland, common historical tradition, common language, culture, psychological make-up and common economic life would be recognized as a distinct nationality with the right to exist as an autonomous state within the free Indian union or federation and will have the right to secede from it if it so desires." The resolution enumerated a number of such potential nationalities: "Pathans, Western Punjabis (dominantly Muslims), Sikhs, Sindhis, Hindustanis, Rajasthanis, Gujeratis, Bengalis, Assamese, Beharis, Oriyas, Andhras, Tamils, Karnatakis, Maharashtrians, Keralas, etc." By these terms, the resolution stated, the Muslims, if they should wish, would be able to form a separate state, and it defended its stand concerning Pakistan by maintaining that it "concedes the just essence of the Pakistan demand and has nothing in common with the separatist theory of dividing India into two nations on the basis of religion." The recommendation was to lead to "a greater and grander unity of India than our country has ever seen."

The Communist Party of India frequently reaffirmed its position respecting Pakistan, and in consequence was bitterly attacked by the Congress Party. At the end of 1945, because of the Pakistan issue and other matters, there was a complete rupture between it and Congress, though some years before they had worked together against British rule. Later, when the Muslim League, during the quarrel over the Cabinet Mission's plan, observed "Direct Action Day" on August 16, 1946, the Communist Party joined in the demonstrations. It and the Muslim League, however, were never more than strange and temporary political bedfellows, and the Pakistan government has been no friend of Communists.

Various compromise solutions of the Pakistan issue were proposed during the years 1940–1946. The common element in all was decentralization of government. Some proposals would have retained the existing general structure of provinces and states united at the center in a common government, exercising limited powers; others would have redrawn provincial boundaries on linguistic or economic lines; still others suggested an even looser arrangement, that is, the granting of Pakistan, but with the condition that Pakistan and Hindustan should form a federation for defense and promotion of common economic interests.

In promoting Pakistan, however, the Muslim League was inflexible and would accept no compromise. From the time of the War Cabinet's offer in 1942, during the remaining war years, the prestige of the Muslim League as promoter of Pakistan steadily increased. At the same time the strength of the Indian National Congress was

declining under the attack of Churchill's government, which outlawed
both the All-India and the provincial Congress organizations, confined its leaders, and seemed bent on destroying the Congress as a
political force. The 1945–1946 elections in India, which the League
fought on the sole issue of Pakistan, showed the growth of its power.
Though in the last previous elections (1937) for the provincial
assemblies, the Muslim League had been able to win but 104 seats out
of the 482 constitutionally reserved for and elected only by the Muslim community, in 1946 it won 412. The League also won 14 other
seats, including 9 of the 10 reserved for Muslim women; in 1937 it
had won only 5 other seats. Again, in the elections to the Central
Legislative Assembly, the League won all the 30 seats reserved for
the Muslim constituency.

Confirmed then by this solid support, the League and Jinnah demanded Pakistan as an unalterable condition precedent to any further
steps leading to solution of the constitutional problem. The Indian
National Congress refused to accept this, though it was willing to
move from its stand in favor of a strong closely knit central government to one with very much limited powers.

The climax was now not far distant. In March 1946 the British
Labour Government sent out a three-man Cabinet Mission (including
Cripps) to try to solve the constitutional problem, and on May 16,
1946, the Mission's plan was read in the House of Commons by
Prime Minister Attlee as a White Paper. The Cabinet Mission,
though rejecting the Pakistan demand in its full and complete form,
made extensive concessions to it. Two of these we may note here.
The first and more basic was a narrow limitation put upon the
powers of the proposed Indian Union's central government. It was to
deal only with foreign affairs, defense, communications, and the
financing of these subjects. All other subjects were to vest in the provincial governments. In this way the Mission thought to reduce to
a minimum, if not entirely eliminate, the danger that Hindu provinces
might practice discrimination against Muslim provinces.

Second, the eleven "governor's provinces" of British India were to
be free to form themselves into "groups." Each group could have its
own executive and legislature functioning over the provinces in it
and determine the provincial subjects of government to be taken in
common. Since the government of a group was not to be limited to
the narrow range of subjects prescribed for the central union government, it was potentially able to become a very compact, highly

centralized, and efficient political body, in contrast to the central Union. Further the Cabinet Mission's plan proposed to put something like grouping into operation at once, in advance of the drafting of a constitution. It divided the eleven provinces into three "sections," which if they wished could later become "groups." Representatives of the three sections were to deliberate separately in the Constituent Assembly which the Cabinet Mission was providing for. Two of the sections were to be predominantly Muslim in population and corresponded closely to current geographical demands for Pakistan (one was to include the Punjab, Sind, the North-West Frontier; the second, Bengal and Assam); the other, non-Muslim. A province might opt out of the section to which it was assigned in the plan when the new constitution should have come into effect, provided the province's legislature should take such a decision after the first general election under the new constitution. The result at the beginning of the plan's operation was to be a kind of Near-Pakistan.

The Mission further laid down as a principle that, whenever in the Executive and the Legislature there should arise a question touching a major communal issue, decision should require the assent not merely of the majority of representatives present and voting, but also a majority of the representatives of each of the two major communities. This provision seemed to the Cabinet Mission a sufficient safeguard to prevent the Hindu community from forcing its will upon the Muslims.

To carry on government until a Constituent Assembly could be elected, the Mission's plan provided for the appointment of an Interim Cabinet, which was to be a coalition and have "the support of the major political parties."

The whole plan in the end failed and as it was failing the tense relations between the two communities snapped strand by strand. The League demanded parity with Congress in the Interim Government (five portfolios each out of a total of twelve) and the sole right to nominate any Muslim. Congress would allow only five portfolios to the League against six to itself, feeling that in view of its greater strength parity would be unfair—it held 56 seats in the Central Legislative Assembly against the League's 30, and in the provincial legislatures held more than twice as many. Nor would it relinquish the right to nominate a Muslim, since it was not a communal body, as was the League, and was not going to be jockeyed into appearing as one. The League at first boycotted the Interim

Government, but afterwards, when such a government took office (September 2) with its membership nominated by Congress, it agreed to enter (October 12), not having won its points. This Government, however, operated without teamwork, the members apparently never meeting in full session but transacting most of their Cabinet business by correspondence.

In respect to the Constituent Assembly which was to frame India's new Constitution, the League refused to coöperate. Jawaharlal Nehru, President of the Congress, had made an indiscreet statement on July 10, 1946, "The big probability is that there will be no grouping." He had indicated that the arrangement of provinces in sections for the Constituent Assembly, as provided in the Cabinet Mission's plan, was unacceptable to two provinces (Assam and the North-West Frontier Province), then controlled by Congress but included in the Muslim sections, and would therefore be abrogated by them as soon as the sections should meet, instead of at the later time indicated in the plan. The League said that such statements showed that Congress had been insincere in accepting the plan.

When the announcement was made that a government would be formed even without the League's coöperation, the League endeavored to arouse the Muslim community. Jinnah said, "Goodbye to constitutional methods and constitutionalism," and the League adopted a resolution directing "the Working Committee to prepare forthwith a programme of direct action . . . and to organize the Muslims for the coming struggle to be launched as and when necessary." It named August 16 as "Direct Action Day," calling for demonstrations, which it said should be non-violent. But Bengal and Bihar had had almost continuous riots throughout 1946, and that day and several following were marked by the bloodiest communal rioting in Calcutta which India had yet known. Bengal had a Muslim government and the premier, H. S. Suhrawardy, was afterwards accused of complicity. In the weeks following there were communal riots in Bombay and many other cities, and the disturbances in Bihar against Muslims and in eastern Bengal against Hindus broke out again in the most extreme form. The district of Noakhali in Bengal, where Muslims outnumbered Hindus four or five to one, was pacified only when Gandhi made a tour through it. These various disturbances seemed like possible opening moves in the civil war which Jinnah had prophesied would be inevitable if India were given self-government without the accompanying award of Pakistan.

The dispute between Congress and the League over the grouping of provinces in the Constituent Assembly continued uninterruptedly and inconclusively through the summer and autumn. The British Government, evidently trying to stimulate agreement, reaffirmed its position on December 7, just before the Assembly was to meet, and, in reply, the All-India Congress Committee on January 6, 1947, adopted a resolution in which it said that there must be no "compulsion of a province." Matters were not advanced by these two statements.

Hindu-Muslim violence meanwhile remained continuous in Bengal, Bihar, the United Provinces, the Punjab, Assam, and elsewhere. In the Punjab it brought about the downfall of the government which had been set up by the Unionist party, a coalition of Hindus, Sikhs, and non-League Muslims led by Sir Khizr Hyat Khan Tiwana and working closely with Congress. His government, already shaky from Muslim League attacks, had tried at the end of January to curb the disorders. It had arrested a number of Muslim leaders, including sixteen members of the Punjab legislature, some former high officials of the Government of India, and the president of the Punjab Muslim League; had outlawed the Muslim National guard, which since being organized in 1937 had acquired a semi-military character; and had declared illegal the Rashtriya Swayamsevak Sangh, a militant Hindu action body, which later (like the Sikh organization called Seva Dal) at the time of partition was held responsible for organizing and executing much of the violence against Muslims in Delhi. The Punjab disorders, however, did not cease. The Muslim League launched a campaign that drove Khizr Hyat Khan out of office early in March. Riots of extreme violence followed all over the Punjab, so severe as to be like battles, and the Governor, Sir Evans Jenkins, assumed control under Section 93 of the Constitution. Congress power in the Punjab had by this time been destroyed.

In the constantly deteriorating situation the Labour Government now made a desperate—but not yet its most desperate—effort to stop the bloody dispute. Mr. Attlee announced on February 20, 1947 that by June 1948 at the latest the British Government would grant full self-government to British India in one of three ways: either to British India as a unit, or to existing provincial governments, or in some other way that would be "in the best interests of the Indian people." At the same time Earl Mountbatten of Burma was appointed Viceroy in place of Lord Wavell.

When Lord Mountbatten got to India, he made a quick examination of the situation, noted statements of Congress leaders (Nehru, Rajendra Prasad) showing them receptive to partition as a means of ending the bloodshed, found Jinnah aware that he would have to accept a smaller Pakistan than he had been demanding, and discovered the Sikhs ready to concede division of the Punjab. He then returned to London, where he recommended a drastic course of action which was promptly accepted. On June 3, the British Government outlined a plan for partitioning India and the next day announced that the appointed day for independence and partition would be August 15. In July, Parliament passed the Indian Independence Act by which India was divided into two independent nations, each with full Dominion Status, while the Indian States were left free to accede to whichever they wished.

Provision had been made in the case of questionable areas to ascertain preference in joining India or Pakistan by reference to the electorate or its representatives. Two Commissions were appointed to demarcate the division in Bengal and the Punjab respectively, headed by a British lawyer Sir Cyril Radcliffe. When both Commissions became deadlocked, he made a decision (Radcliffe Award), odious now in each nation. In respect of national assets the general basis was 82.5 per cent to India, 17.5 per cent to Pakistan; but in some matters the percentages were altered by Partition Committees. Everything had to be done with the greatest haste. As Lord Mountbatten put it: it had taken three years to separate Burma from India, two years to separate Sind from Bombay, and two years to separate Orissa from Bihar, but only two and a half months were taken to divide all India in two. The result was action without adequate preparation.

The two new nations started off badly. In the capitals great crowds celebrated the independence—in Karachi with the slogan "Long live Pakistan" (*pakistan zindabad*); in Delhi with "Victory to India" (*jay hind*). But this was only a minute fraction of the total response, which was violent, savage, and appalling. For the strife that now occurred was colossal, beyond all that Indian, Pakistani, or British officials had feared. It had begun before August 15. In West Punjab and the North-West Frontier, Muslims murdered Sikhs and Hindus; in East Punjab and the Sikh states, Sikhs and Hindus murdered Muslims. In parts of the United Provinces Hindus and Muslims murdered each other. In the border regions of Jammu and Kashmir Sikhs crossed as refugees from West Pakistan to spread violence.

Peaceful villages suddenly became two hostile camps, one portion of the population trying to exterminate the other. In the cities, especially in Lahore and Delhi, terrorism was in control. Houses were fired, looting went unchallenged, women were kidnapped, massacre took place on the main highways. The leaders of neither side could control the situation. Pakistanis charged that the Sikhs and the armed and drilled Rashtriya Swayamsevak Sangh operated by plan in well-directed organization, as apparently they did; the further charges that high Indian officials abetted them have not been substantiated. Indians charged that Pakistani troops detailed to guard Sikhs and Hindus instead took part in the slaughter. The number of deaths by direct violence is unknown; claims run up to a million. Various Americans and British working at relief in the affected areas at the time have guessed—and they have claimed to do no more than guess—that it was over 100,000, possibly at the outside 200,000. Besides the deaths by violence there were others from disease, hunger, exposure, for floods came at this time, too. The total may have come close to half a million. For weeks there were wide areas where the situation was little short of anarchic. In Bengal, killings were fewer, partly because Gandhi exercised a check there.

A corollary of the violence was mass migration. Fearful Hindus and Sikhs left Western Punjab, and Muslims left East Punjab and nearby regions of the United Provinces. There is probably not a Sikh (except for members of some quietistic sects in Sind) left today in Western Pakistan, and few Hindus. Many Muslims left India. The migration extended over months. In Bengal migrations have continued down to the present. The total number of migrants both ways in all parts of the subcontinent is set at 12,000,000; if the two government's claims are added it comes to a couple of million more. This is the greatest movement of population known to history.

The immediate responsibility for the tragedies occurring at the time of partition must be laid to Hindu-Muslim communal antipathy, fomented by the Muslim League, the Hindu Mahasabha, and many individuals not belonging to either organization but animated by the communal spirit. But Indian National Congress shortsightedness and Muslim League intransigence had set the stage, while the British, by their political policies for fifty years, had augmented the communal mistrust. At the last moment the British were also unequal to the double demand of abrogating power and at the same time protecting those who had been subject to it.

9. Sequel to Partition

When independence and partition were jointly proclaimed, the less sophisticated Hindu nationalists thought that India had at last started on the road to prosperity and the less sophisticated Muslim communalists expected something like the millennium in the new nation they had acquired. Both were quickly disillusioned. The violence accompanying partition produced internal problems for each nation, and at the same time, quarrels between the two developed, many of which are still unsettled.

The first problem was that of caring for incoming refugees. Pakistan had been the scene of the more violence, and its difficulties were the greater. It had a less well organized administration to preserve law and order and protect evacuees leaving its territory and fewer available resources to meet the emergency and help arriving refugees. In each country evacuee railroad trains proceeded slowly to the border, almost invariably suffering long halts with little or no food, often attacked and plundered, frequently violated by murder. Peasants loaded their movable possessions on their carts, yoked up their draft bullocks, took any additional stock on lead, and set out in convoy on a laborious trek to the other nation. They might lose animals on the way, perhaps from starvation, perhaps from hostile raids. The economically less fortunate, the poorest landholders or tenants and landless laborers, who owned no carts, would travel by foot, old people, children, and ailing, as well as the able-bodied. Protection was often inadequate; food was scarce for human beings and might be entirely lacking for animals; medical attention hardly existed.

The refugees would reach their new homeland in desperate straits, and there too might find food and medical services meager. When, for example, a convoy from India came to the Pakistan end of the bridge across the Sutlej at Sulaimanki, it was not enough, even for Muslims who could read, to see the signboard at the camp entrance congratulating them on reaching an Islamic land. The new arrivals needed a more substantial welcome. They wanted more food for themselves than the new state could make available; they required grain or grass for their bullocks and there was none. They wanted medicine, hospitals, mere resting places, which Pakistan was furnishing as well as it could but yet inadequately. Most of all they demanded new land holdings on which to settle and reëstablish their lives, and of these too there were not enough to go around.

For similar refugees coming to India, there were several camps, of which the largest, located at Kurukshetra, about 100 miles north of Delhi, was a model, in organization, sanitation, feeding, and provision for occupation. But most of the others were desperately inadequate. In these unhealthy, poorly organized, demoralizing quarters refugees were held for relocation.

Besides peasantry there were large numbers of the less prosperous villagers and urbanites—artisans, coolies, and others of the lower economic levels—who were generally attracted to cities. Camps were established in the suburbs to accommodate them, but these could not hold all. Three years after partition, in the summer of 1950, many streets in the capitals Delhi and Karachi were lined with flimsy shelters, where families were living, totaling hundreds of thousands of persons, some under only a piece of matting or gunny sack supported on bamboo poles, others, better off, with walls of the same material or of cut and flattened oil cans, while inside were a few cooking utensils and a blanket or two. In front might be some trifling objects displayed for sale. Still other refugees, without families and no shelter at all, slept in the open on the sidewalks. Over all swarmed countless flies. Such people had little or no employment and obtained relief on a bare subsistence basis. They provided critical health and police problems, were a constant drain on public morale, took an important slice of the national resources for their support, and by their very presence inflamed the public of each country against the other.

Promptly, too, there arose a dispute between the two nations concerning possessions abandoned by evacuees, whose rural or urban immovable property was liable to forfeiture, while there were severe restrictions concerning the export of jewelry, other valuables, bank deposits, and securities. These people, some of whom were prominent and influential, indignantly demanded that the nation to which they had fled should recoup their losses from property left behind by evacuees who had emigrated to the other nation. Some managed to effect property exchanges across the borders with refugees of the other persuasion. Some others through the press, friends, or any other available means agitated for the government of their new nation to employ economic sanctions or military force in recovering their claims—that would have meant war.

In each country restrictions of sale and ownership were quickly placed upon evacuees' rural or urban holdings, which often acted as practical confiscation. There were many persons who at some personal risk remained behind to care for their property, hoping when they had disposed of it to migrate to the other country for permanent residence. It became a lawyer's problem to determine who was an evacuee. Was the so far unmigrated relative of someone who had migrated an "intending evacuee" and if so how was the law to deal with him? The legal definition of an evacuee came to be extended, and more and more persons were included in the category. Title to an evacuee's property came by ordinance to vest in the government of the nation he had left. The question inevitably had to be handled at the governmental level and has chronically inflamed the articulate public.

Another dispute which promptly arose concerned Pakistan assets. The successor government of India had been left in physical possession of the cash balances of undivided India, and by agreement was to transfer 55 crores of rupees (Rs. 550,000,000 then about $170,000-000) to Pakistan. After the Kashmir quarrel developed, many Indians, including some high officials, opposed paying the sum on the ground that Pakistan would use the money for war against India. This was one of the issues said to have been espoused by Gandhi in January 1948, when he fasted to obtain generally better treatment of Muslims in India. The payment was arranged at that time. Pakistan maintains that India has unjustly withheld other sums due her. India has, on its side, made certain counterclaims. Negotiations had not led to a settlement by the spring of 1952.

A third subject of caustic dispute has been the distribution of the Punjab Canal waters, a matter of long-term national economic importance to both nations. The situation is briefly as follows. In Western Pakistan, where rainfall is scanty, agriculture depends largely upon irrigation from the river Indus and its five tributaries, the Jhelum, Chenab, Ravi, Beas, and Sutlej. During the British period the old system of irrigation was enlarged by the building of huge dams or barrages, and the Punjab became one of the most prosperous provinces of British India.

The problem that has developed under partition rises from the fact that Pakistan makes the more use of the water, while India controls the upper courses of rivers supplying much of that water. The Ravi, Beas, and Sutlej, which are used to irrigate 11 million acres in West Punjab, 5 million in Sind, and 3 million in the Bahawalpur and Khairpur States, flow through Indian territory before reaching Pakistan. India, therefore, could divert their water from Pakistan's canals, and so seriously injure its basic economy. If India should retain Kashmir, whose ownership is disputed, she could exercise some of the same sort of control over the Indus, Jhelum, and Chenab, which flow from it into Pakistan. The entire Indus system would then be involved, and the total situation would give India a mortal grip on West Pakistan's agriculture.

In 1947 the Punjab Boundary Commission and the Partition Committee dealing with canals took the position that the distribution of water would remain the same as in the undivided Punjab, and that it would not be very difficult to execute such an arrangement. But there was no time to devise a permanent scheme for administering those works which serve both parts of the Punjab. The Arbitral Tribunal, a temporary body created under the Indian Independence Act, set up a temporary scheme, which expired at the end of March 1948, when the Tribunal came to an end. A dispute thereupon started, in which neither side has been willing to make any concessions, though a working arrangement exists.

Connected with the Punjab canal waters problem is a dispute about the construction of a large dam by the Government of India at Bhakra on the upper Sutlej, to provide additional water for Punjab (India) irrigation and a weir eight miles lower downstream at Nangal to furnish power. Pakistan affirms that this scheme will divert from her territory some of the water which she is now receiving, and will also fail to give her the share of power to which she is entitled by international precedent. India points out that the Bhakra scheme is not something she has thought up since partition but that it "has been under consideration or preparation for the last thirty years." Pakistan also claims that India is building a headworks below the junction of the Sutlej and Beas to divert water from those streams out of the Indus Valley area and convey them across the divide to the

Jumna basin to irrigate land there. This would injure agriculture in large parts of Punjab (Pakistan) and the states of Bahawalpur.

In correspondence between the Prime Ministers Liaquat Ali Khan and Jawaharlal Nehru, as well as in other documents, Pakistan asked that the canal waters dispute be referred for adjudication to the International Court of Justice. India replied, however, that negotiation should be continued between the two countries or that a judicial tribunal should be appointed representing both India and Pakistan to deal with the problem. This has left matters in a deadlock, with no resulting injury to India, but with Pakistan's situation urgent. In May 1952, the matter came to the attention of the International Bank for Reconstruction and Development which was trying to devise a plan for comprehensive utilization of the Indus basin waters.

An economic war between the two nations began shortly after partition. In undivided India the areas of the two new nations had had a complementary economic relationship which was vital to both. What is now Western Pakistan produced more wheat than it consumed and sent the surplus to deficit areas in what is now India. Again, the areas in Sind and the Punjab (Pakistan) grew cotton, but lacked enough mills to manufacture it, and so used to ship about a million bales yearly to regions now in India, whence the present Pakistan areas received back most of the 500 million yards or more of cloth required for their needs above their own production. In what is now Eastern Pakistan three-fourths or more of the world's jute crop is raised, including almost all of the best quality. But the raw jute was manufactured in and near Calcutta (now in India), where are located about 57 per cent of the world's jute looms. On the other hand, coal in the subcontinent is almost exclusively an Indian product and Pakistan needs to import about three million tons of it annually. Pakistan has an annual deficit of about 370 million pounds of sugar, which would normally be supplied from India's surplus. Iron is mined in Bihar and made into steel in Bihar and Bengal in India. This and other miscellaneous products needed in Pakistan, which is virtually without factories, were most readily supplied from the products of industry situated in the present India. Foreign trade of the subcontinent flowed chiefly through four main ports—Calcutta, Bombay, Karachi, Madras—on which the railway systems converge. Karachi served Western Pakistan, but Eastern Pakistan had no good port, and has been struggling to make one of Chittagong. A decade before partition the economic interdependence of India's parts seemed natural, advantageous, and bound to continue. But with partition the system was rudely shattered.

Just before partition, India and Pakistan made a Standstill Agreement to run until the end of February 1948 (six and a half months), which provided for free trade and precluded any interruption as by customs barriers. Existing import and export policies were to be continued, and there was to be free movement of goods, persons, capital, and money remittances, without transit duties. The arrangements quickly broke down. In November 1947, Pakistan imposed an export levy of Rs. 15 on each bale (400 lbs.) of jute. This was a blow to the jute mills of Calcutta, which could not keep busy on the meager and inferior Indian-grown jute. To meet the increased cost of raw jute, India increased the price of the manufactured product, and the Government imposed an export duty on it which was far in excess of Pakistan's export duty on raw jute. Later, Pakistan levied an export duty of Rs. 60 a bale on raw cotton, again striking at Indian industry, and a 10 per cent ad valorem export duty on raw hides, skins, and cottonseeds. The ostensible purpose of these duties was to produce revenue, but in the existing atmosphere of animosity, they were regarded by the public in both countries as acts of hostility. India retaliated with export duties on machine-made cloth and cotton yarns, oilseeds, vegetable oils, and manganese, and also raised the price of coal. Pakistan spokesmen accused India of trying to break Pakistan economically, and especially to destroy the economy of Eastern Bengal, where the burden of the jute war fell. This region was already dissatisfied with its unfavorable tax position in relation to Western Pakistan, and Pakistanis claimed that India hoped to produce discontent and in consequence a movement for reunion.

The crisis came in September 1949, when most sterling bloc countries including India devalued their currency but Pakistan did not. The refusal to devalue again was regarded in India as hostile. India had an adverse trade balance with Pakistan estimated at Rs. 350,000,-000 (about $73,500,000 at the present rate) and non-devaluation would make her pay 44 per cent more than before for imports of raw materials from Pakistan. Pakistan also was considered by India on the basis of "a very rough guess" to owe her a debt of 3 billion rupees, payable in Indian rupees, now worth only two-thirds as many Pakistan rupees. India immediately severed trade relations, thus depriving her mills of needed supplies and causing shutdown, but also denying Pakistan her necessary coal imports and the profit from disposing of her exportable products.

The advantage seemed at first to lie with India, which had a basically stronger economy, but Pakistan's position was saved by the Korean War and the western nations' rush to stockpile cotton, jute, and wool. Meanwhile, India's diminution of industry further weakened her economy, which was already crippled by the urgent need to use all available resources for the purchase of food. India, therefore, came to see that she had to end the trade war, and on February 25, 1951, the two nations signed an agreement to run until the end of June 1952, and in so doing India accepted Pakistan's rupee valuation. A new agreement was concluded in August 1952, to run until the end of June 1953, but it was less comprehensive than the earlier agreement. It excluded jute, cotton, rice, and coal, which have been the main commodities in India-Pakistan trade.

A long running quarrel developed over the treatment of the Hindu minority in Pakistan and the Muslim minority in India. The critical area was the two Bengals (Indian and Pakistani); to a much less extent Kashmir, Hyderabad, the Punjab, and Uttar Pradesh (United Provinces) were involved. The intercommunal violence accompanying partition never completely subsided and there was a constant movement of population each way between India and Pakistan. In the process Pakistan was assuming a more homogeneous character; non-Muslims were all but purged out of Western Pakistan; and the Hindus of Eastern Pakistan, who were estimated at about 12 million at the time of partition, were steadily being reduced. The Muslim portion of the population of Pakistan, which was 76.7 per cent for those regions in 1941, was estimated to be 83.3 per cent in 1949; it was still higher in 1951. The state was rapidly moving toward Muslim control of not only its government, but also of its economic life. Hindus were dropping out of business, factory work, and agriculture. In India, however, where the Muslims were a minority, the shift in their percentage was slight—from 11.9 per cent of the population in 1941 in the areas later included in the Indian Union to 11.1 per cent in 1949. There was no appreciable change toward establishing a religious structure of the administration except for a diminution of Muslim elements in the police and military, nor was there evidence of religious reconstitution of the national economy.

By the latter part of 1949 the tempo of violence between Hindus and Muslims in Bengal in consequence of the economic war had accelerated rapidly. Hindus forced out of business in cities of Eastern Bengal and migrating to Calcutta were bitter against the Pakistan government which they charged had encouraged the dispossession and had withheld their property as they left. Hindu peasants fearful of attack, on arriving in India found no place to go and were equally bitter. Retaliation was inevitable, and many imperiled Muslim peasants of Western Bengal and inhabitants of Calcutta emigrated to Eastern Bengal, where they too found themselves destitute.

The press in each of the two Bengals published inflammatory, exaggerated, and poorly authenticated accounts of atrocities, often based upon events long since passed but freshly printed as though current news. Presently communal organizations in Western Bengal (India)—the Hindu Mahasabha, the Rashtriya Svayamsevak Sangh, and the Council for Protection of the Rights of the Minorities—demanded that partition be repudiated and Eastern Bengal be forcibly made a part of India, or that it be constrained by economic pressure. Anti-Muslim riots broke out in Calcutta in January 1950, and in February anti-Hindu riots followed in Dacca, capital of Eastern Bengal (Pakistan), and then in other parts of the state. The Prime Ministers of the two nations each charged that the other nation was carrying on hostile propaganda and arousing the public against the minority within its borders. Hindus again fled from Eastern Bengal in great numbers, bringing their suffering and anger to Calcutta. When the Holi festival of the Hindus came in the first week of March 1950, tension was high not only in Bengal but in other parts of India and disturbances were numerous.

By this time Hindus were speaking of a "deep-laid plot" in Eastern Pakistan to expel all Hindus, and the execution of it was ascribed to the Ansars ("helpers," originally of the Prophet), a kind of militia said to be 40,000 strong. In Pakistan responsible officials—the Prime Minister of the country and the Prime Minister of East Bengal—spoke of a "master plan" directed by India's Deputy Prime Minister Patel to spread hatred of Muslims. Suspicion grew on each side, and it was reported that India was mobilizing troops for war. Both Jawaharlal Nehru and Liaquat Ali Khan, the two Premiers, however, had no desire for war, and each by endeavors in his country's part of Bengal calmed the population until they could meet and effect negotiations. On April 8 they signed the Delhi Pact affirming the rights of minorities in their respective states in explicit terms.

The agreement assured minorities of "complete equality of citizenship irrespective of religion, a full sense of security in respect of life, culture, property, and personal honour, freedom of movement within each country, and freedom of occupation, speech, and worship, subject to law and morality." Minorities were to have equal right to participate in the public life of the country, and their allegiance and loyalty were stated to be due to the State of which they were citizens —"it is to the Government of their own State that they must look for redress of their grievances," not to the government of the other state. Other provisions dealt with property rights of migrants and the right to return to their homes, and were to affect the 1,500,000 who had left East Bengal and the many Muslims who had fled from Bihar and West Bengal. Antagonistic propaganda was to be curbed. The Pact allayed public fear, and the war scare was dissipated.

Communal antipathy, however, was not dispelled. Eleven days after the Pact was signed (that is, on April 19,1950), two members of the Indian Cabinet, Shyama Prasad Mookerjee and K. C. Neogy, resigned. Mookerjee, a prominent member of the Hindu Mahasabha, made a long statement in which he condemned the agreement as a product of "drift and indecision," offering no solution of the basic ill, which he described as "Pakistan's concept of an Islamic state and the ultra-communal administration based on it." He complained that blame had not been fixed squarely on Pakistan as the aggressor, nor were Hindu refugees receiving compensation. He asserted that the agreement would not stop the exodus of Hindus from Pakistan.

In the other nation six months after the Pact was signed, on October 8, 1950, Jogendra Nath Mandal, Minister for Law and Labour and the only Hindu in the Pakistan Cabinet, himself a Panchama (Untouchable) from Bengal, resigned his position as a mark of protest against the treatment of Hindus in Pakistan, especially in Bengal. He accused Pakistan of "squeezing out Hindus from Pakistan," a process which he said "has succeeded completely in West Pakistan and is nearing completion in East Bengal." He regretted his own former collaboration with Pakistan, which had seemed to him a way of safeguarding the interests of the depressed classes in Pakistan. The resignation was a sharp denial of Pakistan's claim to be treating Hindus fairly, and the Pakistan Prime Minister denounced him as a warmonger, who had been traitorously intriguing with communal Hindu elements in Calcutta against Pakistan.

Minority commissions were set up in the two Bengals, and government officials in both India and Pakistan and prominent nonofficial citizens have from time to time issued reassuring statements. But from each side have come continued tales of mistreatment of minorities, and as the refugees come with their stories they keep the public agitated. In the spring of 1952 Pakistan and then India decided to impose passport and visa regulations upon travel between the two nations. The first result was an alarmed increase in migration between the two Bengals and an accompanying increase of ill feeling between the two nations.

Very quickly after partition political issues arose between India and Pakistan concerning the accession of certain princely states. Strictly speaking, the Indian Independence Act, 1947, applied directly only to former British India and not to the Indian States, which were, in theory, independent. But it had a provision opening the way for the Indian States to accede to one or the other of the two Dominions. It was evident that the States could not exist except as parts of the new Dominions, while it would also be dangerous to the Dominions for the States to remain independent political entities. Lord Mountbatten, as Governor General, used his good offices before partition to induce them to accede and in so doing to recognize in one of the new Dominions the paramountcy previously recognized in Britain.

Three States, however, held out, not wishing to accede to the Dominion to which by reason of geographical contiguity and their system of communications they would naturally have allied themselves. These were the two largest, namely, Kashmir in the extreme northwest and Hyderabad in the south, and the small state of Junagadh in the west (and a petty holding called Manavadar). Junagadh (and Manavadar) endeavored to accede to Pakistan; Kashmir formally acceded to India; and Hyderabad strove to maintain its independence, with implications that, if accession could not be avoided, its ruler would have preferred to accede to Pakistan rather than India. All three cases became subjects of controversy between India and Pakistan. The status of Junagadh and Hyderabad seems now to be settled; that of Kashmir remains in hot dispute.

Junagadh, named after its capital city, was a small coastal state of 3337 square miles and a population of 671,000 in 1941, situated in the peninsula of Kathiawar, connected by all land routes with India, or with states that had acceded to India, and therefore contiguous to it. Its population was about four-fifths non-Muslim (543,000), but the ruler was Muslim. He entered into a Standstill agreement with Pakistan on August 15, 1947, and signed an instrument of accession on September 15, 1947. India promptly objected in August and proposed that the matter be referred to a plebiscite, but Pakistan ignored the suggestion for many weeks. Early in September India sent troops to points nearby. Many of the state's subjects had protested the accession and organized resistance had developed. As disorder broke out, a provisional government was formed, and the Government of India took over the city of Junagadh on November 9, 1947, to save it from "administrative breakdown." Later a plebiscite was held, the result was overwhelmingly in favor of accession to India, and Junagadh has now been integrated in Saurashtra (the United States of Kathiawar). It can scarcely be doubted that the Junagadh question is dead, as Nehru has often said, and Pakistan cannot realistically hope ever to receive its accession. But the Pakistan government tries to keep the issue alive, perhaps only to use it as an argument in the Kashmir dispute, and as recently as the summer of 1950 issued a wall map of its territories showing Junagadh among them.

The case of Hyderabad was much more complicated than that of Junagadh. Though it became an issue between India and Pakistan, Pakistan has never made the kind of claims about Hyderabad that it has about Junagadh.

The Hyderabad State, named after its capital city, was the second largest among the Indian States in pre-partition India, covering 82,313 square miles and having an area about that of Kansas. It had the largest population, which in 1941 was a little under 16.5 millions. It lies completely landlocked in southern India, where it occupies most of the plateau known as the Deccan. The people and their rulers were communally opposed to each other. The inhabitants were 87 per cent non-Muslim, of whom most (81 per cent of the total) were Hindu. In their hands lay most of the trade. The ruling dynasty, however, was Muslim and the ruling class was drawn mostly from the élite top stratum of the Muslim community. The head of the state was the Nizam, very wealthy, hard-working for an Indian prince, but inelastic in his official attitudes. The public economy was exploited generally in favor of him, some 1100 feudal landholders, and a few commercial and industrial middlemen, chiefly Muslim.

Economically and educationally the masses were below the general Indian average. The system of forced labor for the state was declared abolished only in 1947. The great body of Muslims aside from the landholders were urbanites, among whom were many sunk in the bleakest poverty and hence predisposed to profit, if opportunity offered, at the expense of non-Muslims. The state was, in broad terms, retarded politically, economically, socially, culturally, in character conservative, if not actually mediaeval, its institutions outmoded, while such modern developments as it owned were directed toward the satisfaction of narrowly communal Muslim interests.

Hyderabad was regarded by Indian nationalists during the struggle for independence as a natural opponent of liberal political institutions and an ally of imperialism. In 1938 a Hyderabad State Congress was formed and became a member of the Indian States People's Conference, through which it had a spiritual association with the Indian National Congress. Its purpose was to establish responsible government in the state, and it quickly inaugurated a campaign of Satyagraha, which the Nizam's government repressed.

If the Nizam had been willing to negotiate with this group in 1938 and 1939, he might have avoided the humiliation he suffered in 1948. For by banning the State Congress until 1946 and keeping its leaders in jail, he left the field open to communal organizations, both Hindu and Muslim, and to the communists. On the Hindu side the active bodies were the aggressive Arya Samaj and the Hindu Mahasabha. The latter was particularly strong in the northwestern part of the state where the population was Maratha and cherished an anti-Muslim tradition inherited from its great leader Sivaji (1630–1680), an ardent Hindu. On the Muslim side the active group was the Majlis-i-Ittihad-ul-Muslimin ("Assembly of the Association of Muslims") commonly called the "Ittihad," which was founded in 1927 as a cultural body, but through the years had become increasingly political. In 1947, under a president named Qasim Razavi, the Ittihad developed a fighting corps known as Razakar volunteers, who pledged themselves to "fight to the last to maintain the supremacy of Muslim power in the Deccan." As independence for India drew near, this body practiced ever greater violence against Hindus.

The communists, working through an organization known as the Andhra Mahasabha or Andhra Sangham (both of which mean "Andhra Association"), were active in the eastern part of the state. This and the adjacent part of the Madras province constitute the region known as Andhra, where there exists a regional nationalism of Telugu-speakers. The communists had led a peasant revolt there which in 1943–1944 refused to pay taxes or to supply forced labor and successfully resisted police action. Its success in the Hyderabad state led to its spread in neighboring Andhra territory in British India.

A further element to confuse the total picture was the state's official claim that it had substantially equal status with the Paramount Power (Britain). The theory, however, was never more than a fiction. Hyderabad had been subordinated to Britain in fact since 1798, but from time to time circumstances had developed which had prompted the current reigning Nizam to claim equality. The present Nizam had been rebuked for this in 1919 and again, in the plainest of terms, in 1926, when the Viceroy Lord Reading in an official document told him that the British Crown was supreme in India and "no Ruler of an Indian State can justifiably claim to negotiate with the British Government on an equal footing."

As self-rule drew near for British India, the Nizam asserted his intention of remaining independent. In February 1947, when independence was assured though partition was still in issue, his government released a note to the press in which it indicated that Hyderabad would not join the proposed Indian Union. The Hyderabad State Congress responded three weeks later that the people of the state would tolerate no attempt to keep Hyderabad out of the Union, and initiated a Satyagraha campaign. Later the chief promoter, Ramanand Tirth, and other leaders, were arrested. When the Indian Independence Act formally provided for partition, the Nizam announced that he would join neither dominion until he could see developments. Just after partition, on August 21, 1947, in a public decree he proclaimed the "resumption" of independence. To this India at once objected in a statement which declared that "an issue like this involving the defense of India, the integrity of her territory, the peace and security of the country, and above all the common interests of the State of Hyderabad could not be allowed to be solved by mere legalistic claims of doubtful validity."

It was obvious that the Nizam, if he should feel it necessary to relinquish his hope of sovereign status for Hyderabad, would only with the greatest reluctance accede to India. Accession to Pakistan would have been preferable but was impracticable; further, many sympathizers with the Ittihad were opposed to any status except full sovereignty. He therefore wished, as the next best solution, to conclude a treaty with India as between equal sovereign states. India, however, pressed for accession, and, failing that immediately, a Standstill Agreement. One was signed at the end of November 1947, after serious Muslim demonstrations in the state against it, and negotiations for a final settlement continued, but with each party promoting its original objective.

Shortly afterwards sharp quarrels broke out between India and Hyderabad. India in January 1948 charged Hyderabad with violating the agreement by lending 20 crores of rupees (at that time worth about $62 million) to Pakistan—Hyderabad replied that the loan had been arranged before the agreement was negotiated. The Razakars, whom the Government of India estimated, probably with exaggeration, at 100,000, were now engaging in serious mob violence against Hindu villages in Hyderabad and others across the border in India, and India demanded that they be suppressed. Hyderabad replied that the Razakars were needed to supplement the police force, and maintained that raids on Hyderabad were being organized in Indian territory. India insisted that the Nizam liberalize his government, and, as he temporized, India applied an economic blockade.

During these developments the communists are accused of having helped first the Hyderabad State Congress, then the Razakars. Their own power increased until they had "liberated" over 2000 villages (according to their own claims) and had acquired actual control of the government in a large part of the state. In May, when it looked as though India might employ force, the Nizam's government removed its ban on the Communist Party, which then instructed the "liberated" villages to resist Indian troops if they should attempt to pass through.

In these disturbed circumstances negotiators produced an agreement on June 15, 1948, but the Nizam would not sign it. India then began to prepare for invasion, and Hyderabad appealed to the Security Council. But before the appeal was considered, India, on September 13, entered Hyderabad from five different points in a "police action" to restore law and order, and in a "hundred-hour war" had taken it over. Hyderabad was kept as a state, and the Nizam left as ruler, but an Indian military administrator was put in charge. The Razakars were disbanded, the communist revolt quelled, and steps were taken to institute liberalized government. In the aftermath large numbers of Muslims appear to have been killed, some in private revenge, while others, according to claims made in Pakistan, were slaughtered by troops. The Nizam, when a new government was formed, withdrew his complaint at the United Nations.

In British and American newspapers there was considerable criticism of India's conduct. This was resented in India, on the ground that the case was imperfectly understood. Whatever the legal rights and wrongs of specific acts in the Hyderabad controversy, India could not have tolerated the state's existence as a sovereign political entity. To do so would have jeopardized the economy, political structure, and security of India itself.

Pakistan had no legal claim at issue in the Hyderabad dispute, but its sympathies were strongly involved and it gave the Nizam support before the Security Council, while its press and public reaction were unanimously anti-Indian on the subject. The dispute, like that concerning Junagadh, had features which Pakistan has claimed are analogous to features of the Kashmir dispute, though with India's position reversed. Pakistan has, therefore, used both cases repeatedly in arguments to support its side of that greater controversy.

10. The Quarrel over Kashmir

The quarrel over Kashmir is the most critical of all between India and Pakistan. It has led to an undeclared war, which three times (December 1947, May 1948, August 1951) has threatened to become overt. The stakes are of major economic, political, and strategic significance to Pakistan, while to India Kashmir has become a symbol of national prestige and international justice. The seriousness of the dispute brought it before the Security Council on the last day of the year 1947, where it still lies unsettled in spite of the efforts of a United Nations Commission for India and Pakistan and three distinguished mediators.

Kashmir, properly referred to as the Jammu and Kashmir State, was the largest of the Indian States before August 15, 1947. It had an area of 84,471 square miles, being about the size of Minnesota, and in 1941 had a population of about 4,022,000, of whom 3,101,000, or about 77.11 per cent were Muslims. The rest were Hindus (20.12 per cent), Sikhs (1.64 per cent), Buddhists (about 1.0 per cent), and a few Christians. The ruling family was Hindu. Almost all the state is mountainous or high plateau country, but it has two small cultivable plains, one of which is the renowned Vale of Kashmir, about 85 miles long and 20 to 25 miles wide, and the other the Jammu flatlands at the foothills of the Himalayas, a part of the Punjab plain. It contains Mount Godwin Austen in the Karakoram range, the world's second highest peak, and has throughout a spread of scenic splendor possibly unequaled anywhere else in the world. The beauty, too, of the women in the Vale of Kashmir has long been proverbial in both Asia and Europe.

The state consists of a number of separate parts, which possess no geographic, linguistic, cultural, or historic unity, but were first united politically in the second quarter of the nineteenth century. It has been administered in three divisions. The first of these is Jammu, situated in the south. Its capital, the city of Jammu, is the state's winter capital and the seat of the ruling dynasty. This is a family of so-called Dogra Rajputs, which rose from obscurity in the 1830's under an adventurer named Gulab Singh (1792–1858). By associating himself with the Sikhs he built a kingdom piece by piece through conquest, intrigue, and finally the blessing of the British. In 1846, because he had been friendly to them in their dark hours of the First Afghan War and had abstained from helping the Sikhs, his masters, in the Sikh War, the British gratefully let him pay them £750,000 and then confirmed him and the heirs male of his body to hold "forever in independent possession" a territory approximately that of the present state. Jammu Province contains one-seventh of the state's total area and nearly one-half (1,981,400) of its population.

North of Jammu Province beyond the first Himalayan range known as the Pir Panjal is the division of Kashmir, accessible from Jammu City by a single road that was regularly snowbound in winter until snowplows were introduced in 1948. This contains the renowned Vale of Kashmir, through which flows the river Jhelum. In this land of mountains and lakes, glaciers, rivers, and canals, rice fields and flower-covered alps, plane trees and deodars, ancient civilization and modern crafts, live most of the rest of the state's population. Here is situated the city of Srinagar, the summer capital. The Muslims entered the Vale of Kashmir only in the fourteenth century, but once in they rapidly converted the population. In 1941, of its 1,729,-000 inhabitants all but about 113,000 were Muslims. The minority consists mostly of the élite Kashmiri Brahmans or Pandits. The Muslim peasantry there is notoriously poor and timid in its dealings with authority.

The third division of the state is called the Frontier Districts. It is a miscellaneous group of diverse areas lying east, north, and northwest of the Vale of Kashmir, covering three-fourths of the state's area but having a population of only 311,500.

The state has considerable strategic significance. It marches with Tibet and Sinkiang on the east and north and Afghanistan also on the north. The long narrow Wakhan strip of Afghanistan separates it from the Soviet Union. Communications, however, are difficult with all these regions. The state commands the northern flank of Western Pakistan; the upper reaches of four of the rivers (Indus, Jhelum, Chenab, Ravi) on which the agriculture of the latter area depends are in or border it. All the state's communications by road, rail, and river led into what is now Western Pakistan until in 1947–1948 India built a road from Pathankot in Eastern Punjab to Jammu.

Though the British gave Gulab Singh the state to hold "in independent possession," they did not mean in sovereignty. Alarmed by Russian advance in Central Asia, in 1885 they compelled the Maharaja Partab (or Partap or Pratap) Singh to accept a Resident. This he did with such bad grace that he was temporarily deprived of the throne. Neither before nor after Partab Singh's time did the ruler relish having a Resident. Hari Singh, Maharaja at the time of partition, had an additional grievance against the British, who had let him figure as "Mr. A" in a notorious divorce suit in England in 1925 shortly before he became ruler. As Maharaja, Hari Singh was a playboy, extravagant, devoted to polo and horse-racing, uninterested in his subjects' economic improvement, incompetent in politics.

The uncongenial elements composing the state never acquired a common national consciousness. The two élite Hindu groups, the Dogras in Jammu and the Brahmans in Kashmir, were favored in state affairs and held almost all the political posts; the Muslim majority got only a small fraction of them. The state army was recruited almost wholly from the Dogras. The rule was backward, oppressive, and unpopular among the masses. Dogmatic Hindu law, such as that concerning cow-killing, was sternly enforced upon all subjects, including Muslims and Buddhists who had none of the Hindu feeling for the cow. Forced labor for the state existed until the 1920's, when it was legally abolished as one of several reforms instituted after a minor popular revolt. During the next decade uncorrected economic, administrative, and social ills produced an accelerating popular discontent, which led to another set of political reforms including creation of a puppet legislative assembly in 1932.

The principal reform organization was the Jammu and Kashmir National Conference, formed in 1938, when it took over the "Muslim Conference," which had been organized in 1932. The new Conference (like the Hyderabad State Conference) was affiliated with the States People's Conference in India, and had an ideological association with the Indian National Congress, especially the latter's left wing. The chief mover in the States People's Conference was Jawaharlal Nehru (himself member of a Kashmiri pandit family which emigrated to India about 1716), and the founder and president of the Jammu and Kashmir National Conference (as of the previous Muslim Conference) was Sheikh Mohammad Abdullah, a former schoolteacher, a Muslim but not a communalist. In 1943 the National Conference had prepared a program of far-reaching social, economic, administrative, and political reforms in a draft constitution and an economic plan, which were entirely secular in motivation and provisions. In 1946 it demanded "absolute freedom" from Dogra rule and called upon the Maharaja to "Quit Kashmir!" The leaders, particularly Sheikh Abdullah, were frequently arrested, and at the time of partition Abdullah was serving a three-year sentence imposed in September 1946.

If on partition the Indian States had been assigned to the two Dominions on the principles which applied to the provinces of British India, that is, religious predominance and geographical contiguity, the State of Jammu and Kashmir would presumably have gone to Pakistan, though it might have been divided, and the eastern parts of Jammu province, which were predominantly Hindu, or possibly the whole province given to India. But since choice lay with each separate state, the Maharaja Hari Singh, as autocratic ruler, had the right and duty of making the decision. This he was not equal to. He disliked the idea of becoming a part of India, which was being democratized, or of Pakistan, which was Muslim. He did not yield to Mountbatten's urging to make a decision, not having much trust in the British. For some time he seemed to think he could remain independent, but the realities of the situation made such a status absolutely impossible.

Apparently with the motive of avoiding any final decision he inquired of both Dominions about making a Standstill Agreement. India held back, but Pakistan accepted the proffer. On August 15, after a telegraphic request from Hari Singh's government on August 12, it made such an agreement, involving the continuation of railway, post and telegraph, and commercial communications. Pakistan also understood the agreement to imply control over defense and foreign affairs, in short to convey to it all the rights which the Government of undivided India had had respecting Kashmir, and to lead to eventual accession. It seems doubtful that this had been Hari Singh's intention since he had approached both governments at once. When later in the general confusion that prevailed in the Punjab after August 15, the state failed to get the supplies of petrol, sugar, cloth, and other items due it and badly needed, its government was apprehensive. And when the state failed to follow the Standstill Agreement with accession, the Pakistan government, too, became apprehensive and suspected that the Maharaja was secretly planning not to accede to it.

During the communal strife in the Punjab Sikh and Hindu refugees crossed the border into Jammu province and in their anger clashed with the Muslims they met in Jammu. From Jammu there were raids into Western Punjab and from the latter there were raids into Jammu. The situation got out of hand for the local police.

At the end of September, the Maharaja released Sheikh Abdullah, who promptly made an address to a large public gathering in which he seemed to favor independence for the state. Possibly the Maharaja hoped to make use of Abdullah's support. He continued to hold in detention the leader of the Kashmir Muslim Conference, which Jinnah had endorsed and which openly favored accession to Pakistan.

At about this same time India started to build the road from Pathankot to Jammu. Pakistan took this to indicate that India was preparing to receive the state's accession. Also in September a Muslim revolt against the state government broke out in the area of Poonch, the western part of the Jammu province.

Everything was now prepared for the dramatic catastrophe which came in the latter part of October. It consisted of an invasion of Kashmir by armed Muslim tribesmen, some from nearby Hazara, others from around Peshawar, over a hundred miles distant. Their route was through Pakistan, and they came with the knowledge and assistance of Pakistan officials. They were permitted to have their base of operations in Pakistan, and Pakistan allowed additional tribesmen to go to the fighting front and often helped with motor trucks.

On October 20 tribesmen crossed the state's border at Muzaffarabad, apparently then only about 2000 strong, and moved up the Valley of Kashmir toward Srinagar. On the fourth day a provisional Azad ("Free") Kashmir was proclaimed with its own government. The Maharaja fled across the mountains to Jammu. On the sixth day, when the invaders were not far from Srinagar, looting industriously and murdering Muslims as well as Hindus and a few Europeans, and the state forces were completely unable to halt them, the Maharaja executed an instrument of accession to India, with the advice of V. P. Menon, Secretary to the States Ministry of India, and the support of Sheikh Abdullah. The next day (October 27) Lord Mountbatten, as Governor General of India, accepted the accession provisionally. Legally this seemed to satisfy the procedure prescribed in the Indian Independence Act, and India was free to dispatch troops, and did so. Immediately they began to arrive in Srinagar by air, barely saving it from the undisciplined tribesmen who were loitering on the way to loot. These troops pushed the tribesmen back by stages and gradually cleared the Valley.

Pakistan refused to recognize the accession, calling it a violation of the Standstill Agreement, and instead assisted the Azad Kashmir government. In the Maharaja's part of the state, control now lay with the Jammu and Kashmir National Conference and on October 31, at the "request" of the Maharaja, Sheikh Mohammad Abdullah was sworn in as Head of the Emergency Administration. Later under a governmental reorganization he became Prime Minister. From then on the Maharaja was the forgotten man of Kashmir, and in due time he was virtually retired from his position and his son Karan Singh performed the royal functions.

Pakistan now openly gave the Azad Kashmir government weapons, vehicles, and regular troops who went to Kashmir as "volunteers," commanded by General Akbar Khan under the pseudonym "General Tariq," and permitted and assisted ordinary volunteers recruited in its territory to go to the front. Pakistan had an open road into Kashmir from the headquarters at Rawalpindi in the Punjab just across the border; India could at first enter only by air to Jammu, and from there could reach Kashmir either by further air flight or by the mountain road through the 9300-foot-high Banihal Pass over the Pir Panjal. The Azad Kashmir and Pakistan forces had a clear advantage in communications; the Indian and Kashmir state forces held the large centers, especially Srinagar and Jammu.

Lord Mountbatten in accepting Kashmir's accession had said that when the invaders had been expelled and law and order reëstablished, "the question of accession should be settled by a reference to the people." A few days later (November 8) Nehru confirmed the principle of decision by the people in a telegram to Liaquat Ali Khan, Pakistan's premier, but reiterated that the invaders must be driven from Kashmir and peace restored before a reference would be possible.

Liaquat Ali at once announced his agreement with the idea of a plebiscite, but stipulated certain conditions on which his government would urge the Azad Kashmiris to cease fire and disband. These were withdrawal of Indian troops and immobilization of the State forces, substitution for Sheikh Abdullah's government of a coalition government (including the Azad Kashmir elements), and following these two steps the holding of a plebiscite under international auspices. These accessory conditions Nehru declared unacceptable. Here was born an issue which ever since has been debated continuously.

Several small states in the far northwest which were feudatory to Kashmir, namely, Gilgit, Hunza, and Nagir (Nagar), at about this time repudiated their connection and acceded to Pakistan. Meanwhile the warfare continued indecisively, though India regained some of the territory held by the Azad Kashmir forces. Pakistan was not yet formally in the fighting.

In Western Pakistan enthusiasm for the Kashmir action was intense. It was a symbol of secession from Hindu India, which Muslims viewed as a sinister intriguer against their rights. In the gunfire of war they could convert their resentment and hatred from words to deeds. In India the feeling against Pakistan was strong, but tempered by consideration of other problems. In certain regions, such as South India, the Kashmir fighting seemed rather distant in comparison with current local matters. Some persons there spoke of it as a relatively unimportant issue which was being contested by North Indians at a cost far beyond its worth to India as a whole—better to withdraw and let Pakistan have Kashmir; such surrender, though morally questionable, would be politically sound.

Each nation confidently professed to believe that it would win in a plebiscite, if one were conducted fairly. Pakistanis relied on the communal issue, that is, the bond of Islam, and the Kashmir Muslim majority's dislike for the Hindu rule of the past hundred years. Indians and members of the Jammu and Kashmir National Conference, often conceding that on the date of partition the popular will might have favored Pakistan, argued that revulsion against the atrocities committed by the invading tribesmen and the increasing popularity of Sheikh Abdullah's liberal reform movement now outweighed Muslim unity.

Now began the stage of official public debate. On December 31, 1947, when discussions between the two nations had produced no solution and the military operations were proving indecisive as well as costly, India laid the matter before the Security Council, charging Pakistan under Article 35 of the United Nations charter with "an act of aggression against India," and giving specifications. Pakistan met the charge with vigor, dispatching one of its ablest public servants, Chaudhry (also Sir) Mohammed Zafrullah Khan, to Lake Success to conduct its side of the case. India appointed as chief of its delegation, N. Gopalaswami Ayyangar, an elderly and distinguished member of the Indian Civil Service and Prime Minister of Kashmir, 1937–1943, who later in 1951 became India's Cabinet Minister for States and in 1952 Minister of Defense.

At Lake Success Pakistan obtained the first advantage. India's case was that the invasion of Kashmir by tribesmen and the support given them by Pakistan was illegal. But Sir Zafrullah, instead of merely defending the charge, took the offensive and attacked India. He described the deaths of Muslims during the post-partition violence in East Punjab (Indian territory) as genocide; he characterized the enforced accession to India of the state of Junagadh, after its Muslim ruler had tried to accede to Pakistan, as aggression and an act of hostility against Pakistan; and he branded India's reluctance to give Pakistan its agreed portion of pre-partition India's assets in money, military munitions, and other items, as non-implementation of an international obligation. Along with all these allegations, he charged India with "fraudulent procurement of the accession of Jammu and Kashmir State," and in a larger sense yet of being insincere in its attitude toward partition and the accompanying creation of the new state of Pakistan, which it hoped to strangle. In the Security Council the debate came to concern not so much India's complaint against Pakistan as Pakistan's demand that the future of the Jammu and Kashmir State be considered.

After more than three months' consideration, the Security Council on April 21, 1948 adopted a resolution advising that both Indian troops and the tribesmen should be withdrawn, and that a United Nations Commission on India and Pakistan (UNCIP) should go to Kashmir to exercise its good offices in helping the two nations restore peace, and arrange a fair plebiscite.

This resolution pleased neither India nor Pakistan. In regard to troop withdrawal and the conduct of the plebiscite it agreed essentially with Pakistan's terms of November 1947, which India had already rejected. Pakistan did not like the resolution either, for, though it provided for widening the Kashmir government by adding to it representatives of the Azad Kashmir government, it still left Sheikh Abdullah at the head. In such circumstances, Pakistan contended, an impartial plebiscite would be impossible. Both nations, therefore, rejected certain terms of the resolution.

When the Commission got to Pakistan, July 7, 1948, it at once got a frank acknowledgement from Zafrullah Khan that Pakistan troops were fighting in Kashmir. This fact was widely known but had not previously been admitted by the Pakistan government. In the eyes of the Commission it constituted "a material change in the situation," and it stated so in correspondence with the Pakistan government. Pakistan, has since named May 8, 1948 as the day when it first sent regular troops into Kashmir. Pakistan also admitted in August 1948 that the Azad Kashmir forces were under the operational control of the Pakistan army.

After a month's inquiry, the Commission on August 13 presented to the two governments a resolution which provided for a cease-fire and the subsequent negotiation of a truce agreement. The Government of Pakistan was to use its best endeavor to secure the withdrawal of the tribesmen and Pakistani nationals ("volunteers") not normally resident in the state who had entered for the purpose of fighting. After these had left, and as the Pakistan regular forces were being withdrawn, the bulk of Indian troops too were to be withdrawn in stages agreed upon with the Commission. Only those would be left which were needed to maintain law and order.

This proposal India found acceptable and assented to on August 20, with certain "clarifications"; Pakistan, on September 6 also agreed to accept the proposal, but only on condition that India would also accept the Security Council's proposals of April 21, which at the time had not been agreeable to either nation. Since those earlier proposals of the Security Council partly contradicted the Commission's own later proposals, the Commission in a reply (September 6, 1948) released to the public observed that Pakistan's "Government have found themselves unable to accept without reservation the proposals of the Commission," and treated Pakistan's reply as a refusal. A truce did not seem possible at that time, and the blame was placed at Pakistan's door. Pakistan then continued the discussions.

During this period Sheikh Abdullah's government ruled in Indian-occupied Kashmir, endeavoring to initiate the type of reform to which the Jammu and Kashmir National Conference had long been committed. In the part of the state controlled by Pakistan the Azad government was at least nominally in charge. India resumed her military offensive in September, and Pakistan then complained to the Security Council, which instructed the Commission to continue its efforts.

After further negotiations the Commission, on December 11, 1948, enlarging a suggestion it had made in the August 13 resolution, offered a program for a free and impartial plebiscite, to be inaugurated after the cease-fire and truce arrangements had been fulfilled and peace had been restored to the state. This program departed from the Security Council's plebiscite proposals of April 21 by making concessions on some of the points to which India had objected. The government of the state, headed by Abdullah as Prime Minister, was to be left unaltered. The plebiscite administrator, who was to be named by the Secretary General of the United Nations in agreement with the Commission, was to be appointed to office by the Government of the State of Jammu and Kashmir, and was to derive from the state the powers he should consider necessary for organizing and conducting the plebiscite and ensuring its freedom and impartiality. Final disposal of Indian and state armed forces was to be determined by the Commission and Plebiscite Administrator in consultation with the Government of India, after the cease-fire and truce proposals of the August 13 resolution were implemented. In the part of the state held by Pakistan, Azad Kashmir, and other pro-Pakistan forces, it said, "final disposition of the armed forces in that territory will be determined by the Commission and the Plebiscite Administrator in consultation with the local authorities."

India agreed to the proposals on December 23 and Pakistan on December 25, and a resolution embodying them was formally adopted by the Commission on January 5, 1949. The cease-fire line, essentially along the then stabilized military front, was made effective as of January 1, 1949 (later, on July 27, 1949, the line was agreed upon and in due time was demarcated).

Unfortunately difficulties arose almost at once. India understood that the "local authorities" who were to administer the territory in Azad Kashmir hands meant the State Government headed by Sheikh Abdullah, and that the Azad Kashmir government was finished. Pakistan, on the contrary, held that in that area "local authorities" meant just the Azad Kashmir government, which was therefore not eliminated. Disagreement also arose about the method by which the withdrawal of the Pakistani and Indian troops would be synchronized.

At this point the situation became deadlocked, and has remained so. The Commission recommended that the two nations submit their disagreements over the implementation of the resolutions of August 13, 1948, and January 5, 1949, to Fleet Admiral Chester W. Nimitz, who had been accepted by them as Plebiscite Administrator. Pakistan was willing, but India refused, and the whole question again came back to the Security Council in December 1949. The then President of the Security Council, General A. G. L. McNaughton of Canada, on instructions of the Council, endeavored to mediate, but unsuccessfully. The Security Council, on March 14, 1950, asked the governments of the two nations to prepare and execute within five months a program of demilitarization precedent to the making of arrangements for the plebiscite, and provided for appointing a mediator to help in framing and implementing this program. The two nations accepted the resolution.

The mediator was Sir Owen Dixon, a distinguished Australian jurist. He reached Delhi May 27, 1950, and worked in India, Pakistan, and Kashmir until August 22, when he issued a public statement of failure. In the negotiations the first breakdown had concerned the terms of demilitarization, the next the terms of a plebiscite. The differences concerning demilitarization were the old ones. In respect to the plebiscite, Sir Owen brought before the two governments the question of a limited or partial plebiscite. But Pakistan would agree to nothing less than one that was over-all and would settle the fate of the entire state, while India would not accept partial plebiscite in the Valley of Kashmir if the local government were to be superseded by a United Nations administrative body and troops were to be introduced drawn from Pakistan sources as well as Indian. These features, Nehru said afterwards, were contrary to the Commission's previous resolutions. Sir Owen in closing his report made a strong plea for partition as a solution with a plebiscite in a limited area.

A spark to touch off the explosive situation appeared in the autumn, a couple of months after Sir Owen Dixon had reported. On October 27, 1950, the General Council of the Jammu and Kashmir National Conference adopted a resolution recommending that the state government convene a Constituent Assembly, under the provisions of the Constitution of India, to determine the "future shape and affiliations of the State of Jammu and Kashmir." The Conference, as we saw above, had been working towards a liberal constitution for the state since at least 1943, and after attaining power had gone ahead with its economic program. The proposed Assembly, to be elected by the people, would on the one hand build a new order in the state, and on the other would attempt to settle the question of the state's accession. It was clear that the elections for it could be held only in the part of the state held by India, which, however, contained by far the greater part of the population. It was also clear that the elections would be arranged and supervised by Sheikh Abdullah's government. Pakistan felt that in such circumstances the issue was prejudiced: the Assembly was bound to be just a creature of the Conference; it would do the will of Sheikh Abdullah, which was also the will of Nehru and India. Though the legality of its deliberations and actions might be doubtful, it would nevertheless present the world with an accomplished action, which would make Pakistan's position even more difficult than it already was. Pakistan, therefore, protested at once and strongly.

In the Security Council, on February 21, 1951, the United Kingdom and the United States introduced a joint resolution, which disapproved the plan for convening a Constituent Assembly as contrary to the Council's resolutions previously accepted by both India and Pakistan and endorsed Sir Owen Dixon's proposals for demilitarization.

The resolution contained various other provisions which the two nations had previously found offensive and both promptly objected. Thereupon the United Kingdom and the United States lowered their sights and submitted a new resolution, still condemning the Constituent Assembly and providing for a new mediator but assigning him no duty except that of expediting demilitarization. The Security Council adopted the revised resolution on March 30; Pakistan accepted it; India rejected it. The Security Council appointed Dr. Frank P. Graham as the new mediator. He went out in early June. India refused to help him implement the resolution, though it treated him with full courtesy. In the inauspicious circumstances it was not surprising that his preliminary report in October was inconclusive, scarcely even encouraging.

The circumstances had been, in fact, worse than inauspicious; they had become warlike and menacing. In July India had charged Pakistan before the Security Council with violations of the cease-fire line and complained of anti-Indian and pro-jihad (holy war) propaganda. Pakistan's premier in rebuttal declared that 90 per cent of India's army was at Pakistan's border. Communalists on both sides urged action. Both nations massed troops, but the crisis passed. When Dr. Graham made his third report on April 22, 1952, he felt that progress had been made toward an agreement on demilitarization though several vital points were still unsettled. In May the United Kingdom and the United States suggested that Dr. Graham return to India and Pakistan to try again to settle the dispute.

The Constituent Assembly was elected while Dr. Graham was conducting his negotiations. In some districts no candidates offered themselves against those of the Conference; in others a few candidates offered and later withdrew. Abdullah's party won an overwhelming, all but unanimous, victory. Pakistan claimed intimidation. The Assembly convened on October 31. On November 6 Sheikh Abdullah called upon it to decide "the state's future political affiliation."

The position of the two nations respecting the accession of the state has been fairly clear. Pakistan believes that an over-all plebiscite, if conducted on unprejudiced terms, would result in a decision in its favor. Certain districts in Jammu might vote in favor of India, but the total would cancel these out. Therefore Pakistan wants a simple, universal, and prompt plebiscite, with no provision for partition, and wants it under the best terms obtainable, which means, viewed practically, under United Nations auspices. It vigorously opposes any consideration of the legality of its own presence in Kashmir, and, whenever that issue rises, counters by questioning the legality of Hari Singh's accession, and charges conspiracy.

India, on the other hand, stresses the illegality of Pakistan's support of the raiders and its presence and actions in the state, and wants that question settled before any other is considered, being convinced that a juridical decision would affirm the charge. Such a decision would lead to an order for Pakistan to evacuate the portion of the state it holds. Out of this development would flow abolition of the Azad Kashmir government and confirmation of the Abdullah government's right to control the entire state and to be the source of the Plebiscite Administrator's powers, as provided in the Security Council's resolution of January 5, 1949. In any plebiscite India wants to preserve every advantage to which it can get legal title.

Meanwhile India does not need to press for a decision. It is in possession of the larger and better part of the state, and time operates to its advantage. But Pakistan cannot afford to wait. It gets no profit from the part of the state it holds, only expense, and in being kept on the edges and away from the best parts loses prestige, while Sheikh Abdullah with his reform program that has been abolishing landlordism has an opportunity to increase his support. If a plebiscite were delayed long enough, Pakistan seems to fear, he might have a chance even in a fair election. Pakistan spokesmen have, therefore, accused India of practicing delay and obstruction for this reason. The question of Kashmir is Pakistan's most important foreign problem; failure to reach solution of it is becoming a national depressant.

Partition with limited plebiscite, as proposed by Sir Owen Dixon, seemed to offer better possibilities of solving the problem than anything previously proposed. Certain areas could be assigned to India and Pakistan respectively on the basis of known preference. The northwestern frontier districts now occupied by Azad Kashmir and Pakistan forces would go to Pakistan; the eastern districts of Jammu would go to India. The people of the western part of Jammu would probably prefer to go to Pakistan; this might be decided by a plebiscite. In Kashmir Province, containing the Valley of Kashmir, a plebiscite could be conducted after complete demilitarization and under United Nations auspices according to the resolutions of August 13, 1948 and January 5, 1949. The eastern and northern frontier districts of Ladakh and Astor (Baltistan) might vote with the Kashmir Province, since all their communications are with it, and go with it as a unit.

Sheikh Abdullah never appeared very warm toward merging the state closely with India. He maintained that by the instrument of accession "Kashmir is completely free and autonomous in all but three subjects—communications, defense, and external affairs." It was no surprise, therefore, that the Constituent Assembly took a similar view, and in July 1952 was able to negotiate a pact with India giving it special status. Its citizens are to have special rights while in their state; it can pursue its social and economic reforms in spite of certain sections of the Constitution of India; it is to elect its own Chief of State, unlike former Indian States now integrated in India, where a former prince holds that position. The Assembly abolished hereditary rule in the State; Hari Singh, the Maharaja, agreed to abdicate; and the Assembly then elected his son, the heir-apparent Karan Singh, now a commoner, as the first Chief of State for a period of five years. This pact and the other developments were, of course, bitterly criticized in Pakistan.

Late in November 1949, when the disputes between India and Pakistan and the communal violence in Bengal and elsewhere had raised public feeling in them both to a point where the likelihood of open hostilities had become a real fear, Prime Minister Nehru tentatively proposed that the two nations should issue a joint declaration to abstain from war with each other. On December 22, 1949, he submitted a draft of his proposal to the Prime Minister Liaquat Ali Khan. The latter expressed agreement with the basic motive of Nehru's proposal, but evidently also felt that acceptance of the simple declaration as proposed by Nehru would tie Pakistan's hands in cases where India had a present advantage and would not proceed to a final solution. Nehru had not included in the draft any procedure which would compel a settlement in case first negotiations failed.

Liaquat Ali, therefore, presented a counterdraft, which corresponded fairly well in its first part with Nehru's draft, but then added specific provisions concerning procedure and the subjects then under dispute to be so settled. The steps were to be, first, negotiation, which, if it failed, was to be followed by mediation, which, if it failed, was to be followed by arbitration. A time schedule was to be set for the successive stages. From then until the end of November 1950 the two Prime Ministers engaged in a long and repetitious and fruitless correspondence, since published, on the subject of the No-War Declaration, in which they reviewed the various disputes and went over the old ground but in neither case budged an inch from an original position. India would not agree to Liaquat Ali's proposed procedure; Pakistan affirmed that without an agreed procedure settlement of disputes could be blocked indefinitely. During the period of the correspondence the crisis of March and April 1950 over the minorities came and went and the Delhi Pact was signed. Though the two nations could not agree upon a formula for settling their disputes, they were able in that moment of extreme tension to avoid war.

11. Progress of the Nations

Since independence the two nations have achieved a number of positive ends. The most conspicuous for India are integration of the former princely Indian States into the structure of the republic and the framing of a Constitution. In Pakistan they are construction of an operating national administration, and development of a working economy.

Pre-independence India was administered at the center by a Governor General (Viceroy), who was appointed by the British Crown on the advice of the British Cabinet. It contained two kinds of political entities. The first was British India, consisting of (a) eleven Governor's Provinces, whose Governors were appointed by the British Crown and functioned under the Governor General; in these provinces were elective legislative bodies and ministries responsible to them; the provinces were Assam, Bengal, Bihar, Bombay, Central Provinces and Berar, Madras, the North-West Frontier Province, Orissa, the Punjab, Sind, the United Provinces; and (b) six Chief Commissioner's Provinces, administered directly under the Governor General and possessing no legislatures; they were Ajmer-Merwara, British Baluchistan, Coorg, Delhi, Panth Piploda, and the Andaman and Nicobar Islands.

The second was princely India, known as the Indian (formerly Native) States, 562 in number, autocratically ruled. Some of them had acquired legislatures, usually of very much limited powers, whose members were partly elected by a small electorate, partly appointed by the ruler. The Constitution of 1935 had provided for federation of British India and the Indian States, but this had never been effected and the Central Government was still operating under the 1919 Constitution. At the center and in the provinces of British India legislatures had been freshly elected during the winter of 1945–1946, and in 1946 the provincial Legislative Assemblies so composed had acted under the provisions of the British Cabinet Mission's Plan of that year to elect a Constituent Assembly which was to frame a new constitution. The Indian States, being unfederated, were not in a legal position to participate in the Constituent Assembly.

On becoming dominions India and Pakistan acquired status like that of the other dominions in the Commonwealth. In each there was a Governor General appointed by the British Crown on the advice of the Dominion Cabinet, to be a ceremonial head of state. The Indian Cabinet had asked that Earl Mountbatten, the last Governor General and Viceroy under the old order, should be Governor General under the new, and he was so appointed. He remained in this position until June 1948, when Chakravarti Rajagopalachari, who was then Governor of West Bengal, succeeded him, to continue until the new constitution went into effect, whereupon, as India became a sovereign republic, the position lapsed. At that time Babu Rajendra Prasad, a Congress party stalwart of long standing, became head of state as President of the Republic.

Pakistan would not have Lord Mountbatten as Governor General, and Jinnah took the position, holding it until his death in September 1948. His successor was al-Haj Khwaja Nazimuddin, who had been premier of East Bengal. He was succeeded in October 1951 by Ghulam Mohammed, who had been Finance Minister in the Pakistan Cabinet.

In each dominion its portion of the Constituent Assembly that had been created in undivided India after the 1946 elections acted as an interim parliament. In the provinces the legislative assemblies which had been elected in 1945–1946 continued to function; in the case of the divided provinces of Bengal and the Punjab, the legislature was split also.

The new India's Cabinet has been headed since the beginning by Pandit Jawaharlal Nehru, who had headed the Interim Government (1946–1947) up to partition. In Pakistan the premiership fell to Liaquat Ali Khan, the Muslim League's second-in-command, who had been Finance Member of the Interim Government 1946–1947. When he was assassinated October 16, 1951, he was succeeded by Khwaja Nazimuddin, then the Governor General.

One of the first tasks which the Government of the new India set itself was to eliminate the contradiction in form and spirit between the autocratic rule of the Indian States and the liberalizing rule of the provinces. This had been an avowed Congress policy since 1938. Until it was done the country could not have a constitution uniformly applicable throughout all its parts. The procedure was first to get the accession of the Indian States and secondly to assimilate them to the new national political structure. The means lay at hand in the authority which the new dominions had received under the Indian Independence Act to call into effect by an Order in Council the unused provision of the 1935 Constitution for federation. The task of bringing the states into line fell to the late Sardar Vallabhbhai Patel, Deputy Prime Minister and Minister for States and Home Affairs. He was another party stalwart, noted for his mental brilliance, sharp repartee, inflexible will, "the iron man" of the Congress. He had an able assistant in V. P. Menon, Secretary of States Affairs.

The Indian Government knew what it wanted, and the princes were in a defenseless position. Most rulers hastened to conform to the obvious necessities when the Government told them its will. The first step was to have the states sign Standstill Agreements at the time of independence or shortly thereafter. Lord Mountbatten took a large part in urging them to do so. Then came the process of accession and "integration" (Patel's term) of the approximately 550 states that were in India's orbit. There were three kinds of integration. A number of small states, not separately viable, were merged with those former Governor's provinces that had fallen to India and are now known under the First Schedule of the Constitution of 1950 as Part A States.

Of the medium-sized and the other small states 275 were integrated into five large political unions, in each of which a Council of the rulers in the union elected one of their number Rajpramukh ("chief of state"). Such a union had to develop an elected legislature and government by a cabinet responsible to it. Three of the largest states —Kashmir, Hyderabad, Mysore—were allowed to retain separate existence, and the rulers of Hyderabad and Mysore automatically became Rajpramukhs. Kashmir elects its Rajpramukh. These unions and separate states have identical status under the Constitution of 1950, which calls them Part B States.

Finally 61 medium-sized states were made into seven units and these and three of the former Chief Commissioner's Provinces (Ajmer, Coorg, Delhi) were placed under the direct administration of the Central Government and are classified by the Constitution of 1950 as Part C States. A Bill has been passed to bring these states democratic institutions.

In this way India ended the princes' autocratic rule, and the princes were reduced in income and prerogatives until most of them are now a kind of landed gentry. The transition has proved far simpler and more successful than many observers, even some who were favorable to Indian nationalism, had foreseen. In the 1951–52 elections a number of former princes ran for legislative office and won.

Pakistan has also effected the accession of those former Indian States that lie within its orbit—always remembering that the status of the Jammu and Kashmir State is in dispute. It has not yet required integration and assimilation. In the case of Kalat in Baluchistan it had to suppress a revolt.

Work on the new Constitution of India was begun before partition by the Constituent Assembly, which, however, was being boycotted by the Muslim League. The Assembly convened in New Delhi on December 9, 1946, and on January 22, 1947 adopted a resolution that India should become an "independent sovereign republic," thus to fulfill the Congress aim of "full self-rule." Late in 1948 after partition, the drafting Committee presented a draft, on which debate began in November. The revised document was finally approved by the Assembly about a year later, on November 26, 1949, and the Constitution was made effective on January 26, 1950, the official Indian Independence Day, celebrated annually in commemoration of the day in 1930 when Congress first formally celebrated the adoption of full self-rule as its goal.

The Indian Constitution as printed is a book of 251 pages, comprising 395 sections and eight schedules, one of the largest, perhaps the largest, such document known. It was drafted by a committee of distinguished Indians, under the chairmanship of Dr. B. R. Ambedkar, an Untouchable, who was Law Minister of the Indian Cabinet. It embodies many principles for which the Indian National Congress had been an advocate before independence. For one, it is secular, meaning to discriminate neither for nor against any religious group. For another it denies, by simply ignoring, the "two-nation" theory, on which the Muslim League succeeded in getting India split into two nations. It makes no provision for separate electorates or administrative appointments to Muslims, Sikhs, or any other community, with the exception of some temporary ten-year concessions to Anglo-Indians, the Scheduled Castes (Untouchables), and the backward Scheduled Tribes. Thus it repudiates political communalism.

The positive purposes of the Constitution are indicated in its Preamble, which declares that India is to be "a Sovereign Democratic Republic," which has as its purpose ". . . to secure to all its citizens: Justice, social, economic, political; Liberty of thought, expression, belief, faith and worship; Equality of status and opportunity; and to promote among them all Fraternity assuring the dignity of the individual and the unity of the Nation."

A Bill of Rights is contained in Part III, which specifically declares invalid any laws of the State (meaning the Union, the separate States, and local authorities) infringing them. It provides for equality before the law and forbids titles. It prescribes that "no citizen shall, on grounds only of religion, race, caste, sex, place of birth, or any of them, be subject to any disability, liability, restriction, or conditions with regard to—(a) access to shops, public restaurants, hotels and places of public entertainment; or (b) the use of wells, tanks, bathing ghats, roads and places of public resort maintained wholly or partly out of State funds or dedicated to the use of the general public." It says specifically " 'Untouchability' is abolished and its practice in any form is forbidden."

Citizens are to receive equality of opportunity for public employment through a clause providing that "No citizen may, on grounds only of religion, race, caste, sex, descent, place of birth, residence, or any of them, be ineligible for, or discriminated against in respect of, any employment or office under the State."

With respect to the rights to freedom of speech, assembly, and others, there is a modifying provision for "reasonable restrictions." Freedom of conscience and the right to profess, practice, and propagate religion are guaranteed subject to public order, morality, and health. But the State reserves the right to regulate or restrict economic, financial, political, or other secular activity, to provide for social welfare and reform, and to throw open Hindu (including Sikh, Jain, and Buddhist) religious institutions of a public character, meaning chiefly temples, to all classes and sections of Hindus.

In institutions supported wholly by state funds no religious instruction may be offered, and in no institution recognized by the state or receiving any financial assistance from the state may any student be required to attend religous instruction or religious worship except with his own or his guardian's consent.

The Constitution contains a list of directive principles of state policy, which are "fundamental in the governance of the country and it shall be the duty of the State to apply these principles in making laws," though they "shall not be enforceable by any court." They include the fostering of an "economic system which does not result in the concentration of wealth and means of production to the common detriment; development of decent working conditions for workers; equal pay for equal work of men and women; old-age, unemployment, and disability benefits; protection of children; the fostering of village panchayats (councils)." The state is required by the Constitution, within ten years after the date of its enforcement, to provide free compulsory education for all children under fourteen. The Government is also to bring about prohibition and to prevent "slaughter of cows and calves, and other milch and draught cattle"—two provisions that echo Hindu religious dogma. In its foreign affairs India is to promote international peace and security, maintain just and honorable relations between nations, foster respect for international law and treaty obligations, and encourage the settlement of international disputes by arbitration. Many of the various foregoing provisions, prohibitions, and principles, such as the abolition of untouchability, are still to be implemented by effective legislation. Those concerning international relations Pakistan spokesmen repeatedly declare India ignores in their various relations.

The governmental structure is federal, but its prevailing tone is centralization of power. The head of state is a President, who is also Supreme Commander of the Defense Forces. He is elected for a five-year term by an electoral college consisting of the elected members of both legislative chambers of the Central Government and the elected members of the legislatures of the states, whose separate votes are weighted to correspond to the population of their constituencies. The President is "aided and advised" by a Council of Ministers headed by a Prime Minister whom he chooses and with whose advice he chooses the other ministers. The President is intended to function as a ceremonial head of state, acting on the advice of the Prime Minister; his position, therefore, is analogous to that of a constitutional monarch. There is a Vice-President, elected in a joint session of both houses of the central legislature, who presides over the upper house.

The central legislature is bicameral. The upper chamber is called the "Council of States" and consists of 250 members, of whom 12 are appointed by the President for distinction in literature, art, science, or other fields. The rest are elected by the elected members of the lower houses of the state legislatures. The members of the Council of States serve for six years; one-third of the total number complete their terms each biennium.

The lower chamber is called the "House of the People." It consists of 500 members, elected for a term of five years, by universal adult (21 years or over) suffrage so that each member represents not more than 750,000 persons or less than 500,000. The Council of Ministers is responsible as a whole to this body as the British Cabinet is to the House of Commons, and must command its confidence to function. No one not a members of the House of the People may remain a minister longer than six months.

To become a law a bill other than a "Money Bill" must be passed by both chambers. As with the British Parliament, the upper Chamber cannot initiate a Money Bill and cannot prevent passage of one passed by the lower Chamber, but may, if it acts within fourteen days, make recommendations concerning it. The President may "assent" to a bill, withhold his assent, or refer it back with recommendations, which, however, the Parliament need not accept, whereupon the President may no longer withhold assent.

The judiciary belongs to the central government, which appoints it, and has ample safeguards; there are no separate state judiciaries. At the top is a Supreme Court, which decides constitutional issues.

The administrative machinery of the states is modeled in many respects on that of the central government. Part A states have Governors appointed by the President (that is, the national Cabinet) to hold office during his pleasure, normally for a term of five years. Part B states are headed by their Rajpramukhs. Each Governor or Rajpramukh, like the President, is aided and advised by a Council of Ministers, which is responsible to the state's legislature—if the legislature is bicameral, to the lower house. The Governor or Rajpramukh is closely dependent upon the central government and is more than a ceremonial head; there are certain functions which he exercises "in his discretion" and not on the advice of his ministers. Part C states are administered by the President through a Chief Commissioner, a Lieutenant-Governor, or the Governor or Rajpramukh of a neighboring state.

Six Part A states have bicameral legislatures—Bihar, Bombay, Madras, the Punjab (East), Uttar Pradesh, West Bengal. In the other three the legislature is unicameral—Assam, Madhya Pradesh, Orissa. Of Part B states Mysore alone has a bicameral legislature. An upper house is called Legislative Council, the lower house Legislative Assembly. An upper house in any state may be created or abolished by the central Parliament if the lower house of that state passes a resolution for such action. The Legislative Assemblies have a representative for each constituency of approximately 75,000 persons. A Governor or Rajpramukh, besides having the power to assent to a bill, refuse his assent, or refer it for reconsideration, may reserve it for the assent of the President of the Union.

The division of powers between the Union and the states is clearly defined. All powers not specified, that is residual power, vest in the Union. The Constitution gives the Union and the states concurrently broad power over economic and social planning, commercial and industrial monopolies, companies, and trusts, social security and social insurance, employment and unemployment. The way is thus laid open for economic and social development under whatever degree and variety of government control conditions may make advisable.

In the case of an emergency "whereby the security of India or any part of the territory thereof is threatened, whether by war or external aggression or internal disturbance" (actual or potential), the President may issue a Proclamation of Emergency which remains in force for two months and longer if approved by both houses of parliament. During that period the guarantees to individuals under the Bill of Rights may be suspended, the President may issue administrative orders for any state, and the Union parliament may legislate on subjects normally restricted to states' action. There is a similar emergency provision for the government of any state to be assumed by the President.

The first elections to the House of the People and to the state legislatures under the new Constitution took place in the winter of 1951–1952, and the number of eligible voters was estimated at about 176 million. Of these about 106 million (60 per cent) valid votes were polled for the House of the People and about 102.5 million (58 per cent) for the State Legislative Assemblies. There were eight principal parties and over forty other local parties in the various contests. For balloting purposes the boxes were designated by party symbols. Congress was overwhelmingly victor in the central and most state elections. In May Dr. Rajendra Prasad was reëlected President and Professor Sarvepalli Radhakrishnan, the well-known philosopher who had been India's Ambassador to the U.S.S.R., was elected Vice-President. Nehru was renamed Prime Minister and in May re-formed his Cabinet.

Though Pakistan, like India, has a Constituent Assembly, it has not yet adopted a Constitution. It did, however, in March 1949, adopt a Resolution of Aims and Objectives, which states that Pakistan is to be "a sovereign independent State" and a federation, and is to have guarantees of fundamental rights. The resolution puts strong emphasis on the part of Islamic religion in the operation of the new state. It opens with the words, "In the name of Allah, the Beneficent, the Merciful"—translation of a familiar Muslim invocation—and proceeds directly to say, "Whereas sovereignty over the entire universe belongs to God Almighty alone and the authority which He has delegated to the State of Pakistan through its people for being exercised within the limits prescribed by Him is a sacred trust . . ."

The resolution promises safeguards for the legitimate interest of minorities, but shows its major concern to be with Muslims, who "shall be enabled to order their lives in the individual and collective spheres in accord with the teachings and requirements of Islam as set out in the Holy Koran and Sunna (tradition)." This religious purpose flows naturally from the prepartition declarations of the Muslim League that Pakistan was to be a Muslim State. In harmony with it, at conferences on education called by the government and meant to adduce material for use in framing the Constitution, it has been recommended that all schools in Pakistan should be required to offer instruction in the Islamic religion to Muslim students.

Since partition, Pakistan has been preoccupied with setting up its own housekeeping. At the time of partition it had no national capital. It had inherited the capital of the Punjab, Lahore, when that province was divided, but Bengal was ruled in Calcutta, and Pakistan created a provincial capital for East Bengal at Dacca, an ancient center of culture, education, and political distinction, but lacking administrative equipment. For national capital it chose its then second largest city Karachi, a seaport, without a historic tradition, but having an advantage over its first city Lahore, the cultural center of Western Pakistan, which was militarily exposed to India. The national government moved into the buildings in Karachi built for the Sind provincial government, which latter had to find makeshift quarters and is to be relegated to Hyderabad, a hundred miles to the northeast.

The new government was allotted office equipment from the old Indian government, the pertinent portion of the files, and other necessities, but the division had to be made hastily and Pakistan had the disadvantage of being on the receiving end, not the distributing. Further, rail communication was precarious because of the disturbances in the Punjab. Pakistan felt that it received less than its share, whether by intent in New Delhi or by arson or other sabotage on the railway.

Another handicap was that the trained office personnel of the Government of undivided India was Hindu more than Muslim and elected to remain with India rather than transfer to Pakistan. On the higher administrative levels similar situations existed; the Muslims had less than a proportionate amount of trained executives and administrators. This was an effect of the Muslim failure to patronize modern education.

Added to this was the fact that Karachi was quite unprepared to accommodate the administrative machinery of a nation then numbering somewhere around 70 million persons. In the census of 1941 Karachi's population had been only 360,000 (248,000 in 1931); in the 1951 census estimate it was given as 1,118,000.

There were few available houses for officials, quarters for the new workers, shelter for the great number of refugees who poured in. Nor were the materials at hand for building new accommodations. Old residents lucky enough to have good houses but unlucky enough not to be in government service, were firmly dispossessed. Houses of less value, especially those of non-Muslims, located in something less than the best parts of the city, if left vacant for a day or two, or perhaps only a few hours, were liable to be occupied informally without process of law by refugee squatters, whom the Government either could not or would not evict. One result was a steady exodus of non-Muslims, among whom were many Parsis prominent in the city's commercial life. As they left they took their capital, as far as they were able, into flight with them, depriving the city of means that might have helped it adapt to the critical conditions. Conciliatory words from the Government, which recognized the disadvantage in letting these people leave, did not assuage their fear as they heard what was happening in the Punjab or as close as in Hyderabad, only a few hours away by train or motor road.

Another severe handicap lay in the fact that Eastern Pakistan was a thousand miles distant from Western. There was no rail connection;

communication by water, which required a voyage all the way down the Arabian Sea, around Ceylon, and up to the extreme end of the Bay of Bengal, 2700 miles or more, was slow at best. With crowded port conditions at Karachi and only a third- (or fourth-) class port, Chittagong, available to receive ships in Eastern Pakistan, little could be sent by sea. Because of the economic war with India, what facilities Chittagong had were soon preëmpted for shipping raw jute, Pakistan's chief source of foreign exchange. Mail service and personal travel could use air, and Pakistan quickly established its own line, but this needed supplementing by ground and water to be adequate. In the circumstances government was a difficult matter, particularly since the Bengalis and the Western Pakistanis as groups had no very high degree of congeniality.

The chief asset of the state of Pakistan in getting a start lay in the spirit of the personnel in its service. Karachi had in the autumn of 1947 an air of creative enthusiasm and crusading zeal something like that among the hastily assembled staffs of the newly established war agencies in Washington in 1941–1942. Most of the executives in Karachi were filling posts several echelons above any they had held in government service before; many were in government service for the first time, and the average age was low for the degree of responsibility. But they had drive; they were working for God and their new country, which they had struggled to create and at whose birth many of them had lost jobs, property, kin. Just across the border was Hindustan, "Land of the Hindus," whom they called "the enemy," and from whose malignancy they felt they had freed themselves. They were convinced that they could outmatch him again. His mere presence was a stimulus to build their nation. The ramshackle offices in the old secretariat held the amateur's ardor and a democratic camaraderie different from the routine and often jaded calm of the professional bureaucrats in New Delhi. By 1950 some of this first fine freshness had gone, as had the Great Leader, but the Pakistanis still saw the plotting Hindu foe to the eastward, denying them Kashmir, checking the flow of their rivers, fighting an economic war. Though fissures were now appearing in their body politic, when they thought of him and India their anger mounted and they united in action.

Since partition Pakistan has energetically made itself a nation. Its central government firmly controls all parts of the country. It has built up a strong military machine for a nation of its resources, and at a great price, too, for such resources. It has handled a tremendous refugee problem that might have brought anarchy to both the Punjab and East Bengal. It has established diplomatic relations with many nations, and organized a hard-working and competent international propaganda machine. It has pled its own case with great skill in the United Nations.

Its most important achievement has been the winning of relative economic security. Partition brought great economic disadvantage to Pakistan. At the same time Pakistan was supporting the fighting front at the extreme north, some 800 miles by rail from Karachi, which was the only port of ingress for equipment, fuel, and other supplies. When coal supplies from India failed to arrive, Pakistan converted as many locomotives as possible to oil burners, for which oil had to be imported, and curtailed drastically the passenger and normal freight service. In consequence during 1947–1948 the railway stations throughout Sind and the Punjab held large quantities of un-moved wheat and cotton, which being unmarketed, became an economic liability.

The refugee situation that followed partition contained a second economic problem besides that of relief and rehabilitation. The farms vacated in the Punjab by Sikhs were left without care at a critical time. They could not be saved by incoming refugees, who came too late and in confusion and could not be moved in rapidly enough to take over. During the season of 1947–1948, therefore, much was lost. In the spring of 1948, when it was time to sow for the next crop, the canal waters dispute caused further damage. This was the situation in Western Pakistan. In Eastern Pakistan the refugee movement and the economic war involving disposal of jute brought additional serious loss.

Further, during the entire period since partition, Pakistan has been organized on a war footing. In addition to its revenue budget, it has carried every year a second (capital) budget which got its receipts from the floating of loans, issuance of treasury bills, and similar methods. When these two budgets are considered together, it is clear that Pakistan has been going further and further in debt, largely because of military expenditures.

When Pakistan was new and to all appearances economically shaky, it had indifferent credit standing. Foreign suppliers would sometimes demand advance deposits in foreign banks to guarantee payment when due. It gained foreign credit by supplying foreign demands for cotton and jute in other markets than the Indian. By May 1952, however, the market for those commodities seemed threatened by glut, wheat was being sought abroad, and Pakistan's economic prospects were darkening.

The successes achieved by the two nations have not allayed their concern about their present and future. In the years since partition each has had little to rejoice about and much to lament. They have lost great national heroes in Gandhi, Jinnah, Patel, and Liaquat Ali Khan; they have been in a quarrel with each other that for a period could hardly be distinguished from war; living conditions have been poor to desperate, especially in India which has had to meet a continual food shortage. India lost by partition the areas producing exportable commodities (cotton, jute, hides) and in consequence of that and of the need for food purchases has lacked the exchange to procure steel and other metals, capital goods, railway equipment, oil, chemicals, dyes, vehicles, and has had to curtail drastically all luxury imports.

Though India was faced with such a prospect even as it gained independence, the Government did not at first meet it squarely. It started to slide down the easy road in December 1947, by relaxing food controls too soon. At that time, with the public blessing of Gandhi, it completely removed the controls on food grains and sugar, and shortly afterwards began to ease the controls on cloth. This action was contrary to the judgment of Nehru and represented the will of the right wing of Congress, that is, the industrialists, among whom were Birla, Dalmia, and others, whose businesses all profited. The expected result occurred, that is, the result expected by economists, though not by Gandhi. Prices rose, inflation was rapid. By July 1948, the wholesale price index had reached nearly 390 against a base of 100 in 1939, and in 1949 and 1950 it exceeded 400 for many commodities. In July food grains and cloth were returned to control. Inflation then decelerated temporarily, but not permanently. In July 1951 prices had advanced again until they stood at over 4½ times the prewar figures.

At the time of putting food and cloth back under control, the Indian Government liberalized the import policy. To finance the increased amount of imports, it drew against the sums available from the sterling balances due it in London. These were a debt to prepartition India accumulated by Britain during the second World War, when India liquidated all the obligations incurred for railroad building and other forms of British capital investment, and Britain, reversing its role, became India's debtor.

It had not been easy for Britain and India to reach an agreement on what size debt should be acknowledged and how it should be repaid. After a number of conferences, not always free of acrimony, it was agreed just before partition that the sum should be set at £1,160,000,000 (at the exchange rate then this was $4,640,000,000) for India and Pakistan jointly. Against this amount Britain received credits for military installations left in the subcontinent and annuities for British civil and military officers who had served the Government of India. India ended up in August 1948, when these had been deducted, with a share of about £800,000,000. Of this sum a certain amount was made available as credit for immediate use. To this last were added sums that India had earned. For the year 1948–1949 the amount to be available was fixed in July 1948 at £81,000,000; for each of the next two years (1949–1951) it was to be £40,000,000. But India quickly exhausted the first amount, and in August 1949 the sum for the ensuing two years (1949–1951) was increased to £50,000,000, while an additional £50,000,000 was made available to meet outstanding obligations. India was at the same time getting from the Sterling Pool more than twice the amount of dollars agreed upon. In 1949 India had to restrict imports from dollar areas. Devaluation in September 1949 led to an increase of exports and an improvement in the balance of payments situation, which had become alarming and still remains unfavorable.

The country's economic position has been worsened by poor rains and consequently poor crops in South India during the years 1947–1951 and in much more acute form in North India in 1950–1951, when too much rain in some areas and flooded rivers in some others produced what would have been famine but for large imports of grain. India utilized all funds available to meet this emergency and in 1951 received from the United States as loan a credit for the purchase of up to 4,000,000 tons of wheat at $190,000,000. Throughout the period since independence India has had to import more than the usual amount of foodgrains. Further, defense, which means mostly the Kashmir war, has every year taken more than half the central government's revenue, expenditures having each year exceeded the estimates.

While Pakistan had raw materials to export to salvage her economic situation, India, being deprived of some of her most important ones, could not get exchange by means of them to import the raw materials needed to produce exportable manufactures. The situation might have been helped by industrial expansion, for which India has many resources. There is some small capital in the country for investment, but this was frightened by the Congress Plan for economic development issued early in 1948, which proposed nationalization of public utilities, defense, heavy industries, and conversion of private enterprise in these fields within five years' time. Profits in industry were also to be shared between owners and workers.

After industrialists had protested such a program, the Government adopted an industrial policy resolution in April 1948, designating certain government monopolies (armament, atomic energy, railways, any industry vital for defense in an emergency), and fields in which it would initiate all new undertakings (coal, iron and steel, aircraft manufacture, shipbuilding, communication equipment, mineral oils). But in these latter it would not take control for at least ten years, at which time it would review the situation. Many other industries were to be left to private enterprise, provided they advanced satisfactorily, but certain others, since they required government capital, were to be developed under government planning and regulation.

In 1949, the Government introduced the Industries (Development and Control) Bill, embodying its previous plan, but held it in abeyance for two years. In the meantime Patel had died, and the right wing had no leader of equal influence. On September 4, 1951, shortly after Nehru with elections coming up had got his way on Congress policy, Harekrushna Mahtab, Minister for Industries and Commerce, again presented the 1949 Bill to Parliament which enacted it in October, providing wide powers to nationalize industry and applying controls to all private enterprise. Said he, "the old free economy system, irrespective of social planning, has gone." This program, like that of Congress in 1948, seemed drastic, being more thoroughgoing than that of the Labour Party in Great Britain. Industry considered it as undesirable as the earlier one, and therefore capital was still not forthcoming for development.

Neither did foreign capital offer itself for investment in India, as Indians had confidently expected it to do at the close of the war. Private foreign investors thought the climate unfavorable. The Government had prescribed that at least 51 per cent of the stock of any company formed in India would have to be Indian-owned and the management would have to be Indian-controlled. These limitations voiced the Indian fear of western economic imperialism; they were afterward lifted when it was clear that western capital would not enter when so restricted.

During the period since the end of the war and for some years before, economic planning had been an Indian preoccupation. Big business had led off in 1944 with the "Bombay Plan." Following this, the Government, Congress, and the provincial governments all produced plans. India became for a time the economists' Never-Never Land. Few of the plans took a realistic view about the amount of domestic and foreign capital that would be available for economic development; analysis not beclouded by wish-fulfillment generally showed that it was only a fraction of what the plan would need for implementation. Two plans, however, were produced in 1950 and 1951, which were in the realm of financial reality. The first was the Colombo Plan for Co-operative Economic Development in South and South-East Asia, jointly devised by the various Commonwealth Governments. It called for a total expenditure of £1868 million (about $5.23 billion) in six years, of which about two-thirds would be for India, and something more than one-seventh would be for Pakistan. The coöperating Governments were to provide the money by contributing some of it and securing the rest from outside sources.

The other plan was prepared under the auspices of the Government of India by its Planning Commission. This was established in March 1950, to develop means of implementing the aims expressed in the Constitution of giving the population social justice up to the capacity of the country's resources. It had prepared India's proposals for the Colombo Plan. It then coöperated with the central and States Ministries and issued a Draft Outline of *The First Five Year Plan* in July 1951. This called for the expenditure of Rs. 1793 crores (about $3.77 billion), of which the Commission expected India to raise from its own resources and the Colombo Plan Rs. 1493 (about $3.14 billion), while the remaining Rs. 300 crores (about $620 million) would have to come from outside. The latter plan has received some fairly sharp criticism in India, but has nevertheless been generally regarded as offering concrete and feasible means to assist in solving India's development problems.

In Pakistan no general over-all plan has yet been produced but a variety of projects have been devised for both the eastern and western parts of the nation. As Pakistan becomes better organized, it will have more energy to put into national planning.

12. Political Parties

In each country the party structure since independence has been almost monopolistic. In India the Indian National Congress has been dominant from having fought and won the battle of independence and from having constructed while doing so the country's most powerful party machine. In Pakistan the Muslim League has had a corresponding supremacy for having split the old India and so brought the new nation into existence and for possessing the only well-built party apparatus. Other national parties in both countries define their status and objectives in relation to either the Congress or the League.

The Indian National Congress at the elections held in 1946 still campaigned on the issue of nationalism versus imperialism, and the Hindu-Muslim communal issue of partition. By means of the first issue it had for some decades succeeded in transcending the conflicts between mutually antipathetic ideologies, as those of violent revolution and constitutional evolution, or religious conservatism and social modernism, or a controlled economy and *laissez faire,* and so had fairly well kept together the secularly motivated part of the small electorate (about 11 per cent of the population could vote in the provincial elections). Because of the partition issue it had been guaranteed almost the total vote of the Hindus. Both issues became dead letters in August 1947. The subsurface fissures of Congress were already showing before that date; after it they widened. Gandhi's death at the end of January 1948 was a blow to Congress unity, for all elements in Congress respected him, though some disagreed and some were actually opposed. Some of the cracks have now become cleavages, and various new parties have split from Congress.

Yet Congress is still the dominant political party in the new India. In the 1951–1952 elections for the House of the People it got 45 per cent of the total vote cast and won 74 per cent of the total seats elected (362 of 480). Its nearest rival, the Communist Party of India with its allies, won 27 seats and got 5.5 per cent of the vote. For the State Legislative Assemblies Congress got 42.5 per cent of the votes cast and won 68.6 per cent of the total seats, gaining a majority (2248 out of 3283) in all Part A and Part B states except Madras, Orissa, Hyderabad, PEPSU,* and Travancore-Cochin. The nearest rival in number of votes was the Socialist party with 9.7 per cent of the votes but only 3.84 per cent of the seats (126). The Communist Party of India and allies got the second largest number of seats (180 or 5.5 per cent), though only 6.0 per cent of the total votes.

In its 1951 Election Manifesto, Congress led by Nehru declared itself unequivocally for a secular socialist state. It announced as its aim "freedom of the masses from want" and stated that "economic progress must therefore be given first priority." This was to be achieved by "co-operation and the avoidance, as far as possible, of competition and conflict." The Manifesto called for "a planned approach" to development, in which the first and vital step in the effort "to live the good life" was to free the land from the burden of old and out-of-date agrarian systems of tenure. "Increased agricultural production," it said, is "absolutely essential" and the conditions of agricultural labor have to be improved. Improvement of cattle breeding it called another need; so, too, the encouragement of small and cottage industries. "Basic industries," it said, "should be owned or controlled by the State." This would lead to a mixed economy with a "public sector as well as private sector," all fitted into the "National Plan." It advocated controlled distribution of commodities with a well determined price policy. It included the development of scientific research. It proposed to encourage corporate savings for developmental purposes. Economic equality and social justice were strongly supported. The rights of labor were recognized. Railway services were to be rehabilitated and improved. Transport services should be nationalized. The public services should be supported by a training program. Corruption must be ended. Education, public health, the control of epidemic disease, provision of sanitation, were to be furthered. The depressed classes and tribes were to be helped in their self-development. Part B and Part C states should be brought as rapidly as possible to the condition of

* Patiala and East Punjab States Union.

Part A states. Displaced persons from Pakistan should be rehabilitated. Every citizen should have "full freedom to profess and practice his religion." Women must be relieved of "social and other disabilities." Redistribution of provinces on a linguistic basis "ultimately should depend upon the wishes of the people concerned."
Foreign policy was to continue to be "an independent line in her
[India's] own national interest and in the interest of peace." This
was Congress' definition of the good life for India. The voters gave
it their overwhelming approval.

It is significant that the Congress program repudiated all religious
conservatism and communalism. Forces of the latter sort had tried,
however, to assert themselves. In September 1950, at the party's
annual convention, conservatism, headed by Purushottamdas Tandon,
an old-timer who opposes vaccination, modern medicine, and other
innovations, won the contest for the presidency over Nehru's candidate. Nehru, however, under threat of resigning if not supported,
got Congress at the same meeting to endorse his domestic and foreign policies. But he did not then have full control over Congress
and found himself frustrated at a number of points including the
membership of the Central Election Committee, which was to
nominate the candidates for the 1951–1952 general elections. Tandon
had won control over this body in May. In August 1951, therefore,
Nehru submitted his resignation from both the Congress' governing
body (the All-India Congress Committee) and the Central Election
Committee. Since he was Congress' best vote-getter and could
possibly carry the country for any existing party he might join or
any new one he might create, other Congress leaders got Tandon to
step down. Nehru then took the presidency and with it domination
of the Central Election Committee.

Nehru with his liberal economic and social philosophy, therefore,
in the middle of 1952 seemed to have control of the Congress. The
conservative industrialists have uneasily remained with Congress,
having no place else to go. Religious conservatives of a modern
dye have stayed too, presumably not convinced that they should
bolt the Congress for any existing extremist religious organization
like the Hindu Mahasabha.

But there were dissidents who did bolt, some because Congress
was not radical enough, some because it was not conservative
enough. One such group was led by Acharya J. B. Kripalani, a
Gandhian stalwart. His candidates were defeated for the Central

Election Committee in May 1951, and shortly afterwards he left Congress. In June 1951 he took the lead in forming a new party known as the Kisan Mazdoor Praja (Peasants, Workers, and People's) or simply Praja Party. This expressed itself as dissatisfied with Congress' measures for the peasantry and labor, advocated redistribution of land and coöperative farming, but opposed nationalization of industry. In foreign policy it agreed with Nehru's policy of "strict neutrality." It specifically opposed communism. It won 9 seats in the House of the People and 77 in the State Legislative Assemblies.

Another defection from Congress in anticipation of the 1951–1952 election was that of Dr. B. R. Ambedkar, leader of the All India Scheduled Castes Federation, the strongest organization among the Untouchables. He was dissatisfied with Congress' failure to put through Parliament enforcing legislation for the anti-Untouchability provision of the Constitution, and he therefore resigned from the Cabinet in October 1951. "What is the position of the scheduled castes today?" he is reported to have asked. "So far as I see, it is the same as before—the same old tyranny, the same old oppression. The same old discrimination which existed before exists now and perhaps in worse form." He condemned the Nehru government's policy in dealing with Pakistan—he had favored the creation of Pakistan when it was an issue—deploring the military expenditures and urging settlement of the Kashmir question by partition and limited plebiscite. He also criticized the Congress party for its neutrality in the cold war, which he said had left India friendless, and for championing the cause of communist China and so forfeiting "financial and technical aid from America on a large scale." This party won only two seats in the House of the People and twelve in the State Legislative Assemblies.

A defection from Congress of much longer standing is that of the Socialists. The Socialist Party had its origin in 1934 when the Congress Socialist Party was organized by Jaiprakash Narain and other liberals, including Jawaharlal Nehru, to work for agrarian and labor reform. It constituted at that time a left wing of the Congress and, though Jaiprakash had a Marxist philosophy, he and the party were opposed to the Communist Party of India. Instead he became a devoted follower of Gandhi, though often disagreeing with him. By 1947 most of the Congress Socialists were discontented with Congress for its failure to take an aggressive position for social reform. They were also unrelenting opponents of communalism, and when Gandhi was assassinated they all but accused Patel of having been responsible through letting Hindu communalism run loose in the land. Shortly afterwards they entered candidates against Congress in an election in Bombay, and in March 1948 voted to become an independent party known as the Socialist Party of India. Jaiprakash Narain's chief associates are Acharya Narendra Deva, Ashok Mehta, chief promoter of a labor strike in Bombay in 1950, Rammanohar Lohia, former close disciple of Gandhi and associate of Nehru, Kamala Devi Chattopadhyaya, a woman who has long fought hard for advanced socialist principles, and Achyut Patwardhan. The party protested against the Congress-controlled government's failure to provide the masses with food and housing and to check black marketing. In August 1951, when Nehru offered his resignation from the All-India Congress Committee, various commentators thought he might align himself with Jaiprakash Narain, who was an old personal friend, co-worker, and congenial political theorist. This party won 12 seats in the House of the People and 126 in the State Legislative Assemblies.

The Muslim League, which now hardly exists in India, won one seat in the House of the People and five in the Madras State Legislative Assembly. Muslims were expected to give their votes to Congress or the Socialists or the Scheduled Castes Federation or perhaps one of the new parties.

The.leading communal party in India is the Hindu Mahasabha ("Hindu General Association"), whose vague beginnings go back to the first part of the century when the Muslim League was being founded (1906). For many years the Mahasabha was headed by Pandit Madan Mohan Malaviya, long Vice Chancellor of the Benares (Banaras) Hindu University, a traditional orthodox Hindu, who had a ceremony of rejuvenation by rebirth in his eighties but to little effect since he died soon afterwards. The Mahasabha became prominent about 1934–1935 under V. D. Savarkar, who had served a jail sentence for terrorism. Its platform has always been to preserve India for the Hindus. It actively attacked the Muslims in the decade before partition and consistently fought the Congress for trying to reconcile Hindus and Muslims in an India which they would jointly occupy without discrimination. It never had much of a following but during the war years, when the British War Cabinet kept Congress leaders in jail (1942–1945), the Mahasabha became powerful beyond its intrinsic importance, and contributed notably to Hindu-Muslim terrorism. Gandhi's assassin (Vinayak Godse) had earlier been a member of the Mahasabha, and this fact led the public to express intense hostility against the party. Savarkar was tried for complicity but he was acquitted. Another leader of the party was Dr. Shyama Prasad Mookerjee, who was Minister of Industry and Supply in Nehru's Cabinet, but resigned April 19, 1950, in protest against the government's pusillanimous attitude, as he regarded it, toward Pakistan on the treatment of Hindu minorities. The present president is Dr. N. B. Khare, formerly a member of Congress.

Associated with the Mahasabha until 1938 was the R. S. S., that is, the Rashtriya Swayamsevak Sangh ("National Volunteer Association"), also sometimes called the Sangh, a fascist-type action organization, founded in 1925 by Dr. K. B. Hedgewar. In recent years the leader of the R. S. S. has been Madhav Golwalkar. This group was held responsible for a large part of the violence in the Punjab at the time of partition. In 1948 after Gandhi's assassination, when communal feeling was running high, the Indian Government outlawed the Sangh and put its leaders under arrest. At the same time the Mahasabha went into seclusion. Both the Mahasabha and the Sangh emerged in 1949 to engage again in pro-Hindu communal activity directed toward reconstituting Indian unity (*Akhand Hindustan*), that is, abolition of Pakistan, and the establishing of a Hindu *Rashtra* ("realm"), and both feed upon and nourish Hindu hostility toward Pakistan. The two organizations now have no formal connection, and differ in that the Mahasabha claims to be a political party and the R. S. S. a cultural body, but in the words of Asutosh Lahiri (like Savarkar a former terrorist) in 1949, when he was General Secretary of the Mahasabha, "ideologically there . . . is . . . no difference between the Mahasabha and the R. S. S." In the 1952 election the Mahasabha won four seats in the House of the People and twenty in the State Legislative Assemblies.

Dr. Shyam Prasad Mookerjee, dissatisfied with the Mahasabha as well as with Congress, in 1952 led the organization of a new party called the Bharatiya Jan Sangh ("Indian People's Party"), which contested the election on the issue that Congress had failed to take a strong enough line on the plight of the Hindu refugees from East Bengal, the issue on which he resigned from the Congress. It won three seats in the House of the People and 32 in the State Legislative Assemblies.

There are other lesser parties, for example, the aggressive revivalist Sikh party known as Shiromani Akali Dal, which wants a Sikhistan, that is, a separate state or nation composed of the area where the population is predominantly Sikh. It is led by Master Tara Singh, a venerable former schoolmaster, who looks like a benevolent grandfather but has been jailed by the Government of India for defying orders against assembly and is held by Muslims to have incited Sikhs to much of the violence at the time of partition. It won four seats in the House of the People and 33 in the State Legislative Assemblies (Punjab and PEPSU).

Another party is the Akhil Bharat Ram Rajya Parishad, "All-India Society for the Rule of Rama" (i.e., return of the Utopian Age), which won three seats in the House of the People and 32 in State Legislative Assemblies. Still another party is the All-India Forward Bloc, heir to the tradition of Subhas Chandra Bose, centered in Bengal. This party has two subdivisions, both radical and violent, one Marxist and the other "Subhasist," led by R. S. Ruikar. Neither is affiliated with the Communist Party of India. There is a large number of other small local parties. In addition in the elections a number of candidates ran independently, winning 37 seats in the House of the People and 291 in the State Legislative Assemblies.

In Pakistan the Muslim League, after partition, was for a brief time allowed to decline but it became evident by the spring of 1948 that the leaders of the Government were going to revivify it. The feeling in Pakistan was at first that a political party should not be permitted to have a large influence in government.

The government, however, came under considerable criticism from communally minded Muslims for various reasons and the League was an instrument at hand which could be used to maintain its prestige. The provincial League organizations therefore were encouraged and began to regain their importance. By mid-September 1950 the Government of Pakistan was not only strongly supporting the League but was demanding that it have a monopoly of the political situation. At that time on the second anniversary of Jinnah's death, in a speech on government policies, the Prime Minister, the late Liaquat Ali Khan, referred to Jinnah's insistence on the "three golden principles of unity, faith, and discipline." He quoted a speech of Jinnah's made in March 1948, wherein he warned against internal "enemies of Pakistan . . . [who promote] sedition and treachery" and seek to create "new political parties" and affirmed that "the Muslim League is a sacred trust in your hands." Liaquat Ali inveighed, therefore, against political division in a period when Pakistan had great problems to solve such as the quarrels with India and Afghanistan. Though admitting shortcomings in the League, he said, "It is our duty to make the Muslim League a strong organization and a living force." He assailed in the most vigorous terms those who would found other parties, calling them "traitors, liars, and hypocrites," and singled out for specific attack H. S. Suhrawardy and the Awami Muslim League. "Those who are founding different political parties," he said, "are aiming at weakening this national organization (the Muslim League) and thus to cause disruption. It is the duty of us Leaguers to strengthen the League. The existence of Pakistan depends on this."

There are few opposition parties in Pakistan. The Awami ("People's") Muslim League headed by Suhrawardy has undoubtedly been a thorn to the Government. Suhrawardy, member of a wealthy and aristocratic family, was a prominent Bengali politician before partition, and was premier of the province at the time of the Muslim League's "Direct Action Day," August 16, 1946. After partition he seemed undecided where his future career lay. Should he seek a place in Pakistan or should he stay in India and try to lead the Muslims to participate non-communally in the new nation's public life? He seemed inclined at first toward the latter, but evidently was discouraged by the poor prospect for any organized Muslim effort. When he turned toward Pakistan he was met with coolness and suspicion in various high quarters and seemed to have no bright future with the Muslim League dominated government. He then endeavored to build up the Awami Muslim League as his organ, appealing to the masses and the forlorn refugees inhabiting the disheartening camps around Karachi. He criticized the Government for rashness and precipitancy in supporting the United Nations on the Korean Issue while at the same time being dilatory and weak in not demanding that the Security Council adopt and enforce a decision against India on the Kashmir issue—positions in basic contradiction to each other, as Liaquat Ali Khan pointed out with relish.

While Jogendra Nath Mandal was with the Pakistan government the Scheduled Castes Federation seemed to have status in the country, but with his defection that group may not now have the leadership to make it effective. Minor opposition parties include a Socialist Party and an Azad ("Free") Pakistan Party, which seems close to communism in its ideology. Active in the latter is Iftikhar ud-Din, publisher of two newspapers in Lahore which support Communist ideology.

In the North-West Frontier Province there existed before partition the Khuda-i-Khidmatgar ("Servants of God") party, commonly called "Red Shirts," affiliated with the Indian National Congress. They had opposed partition and when it became unavoidable had unsuccessfully campaigned for secession of the province or part of it from Pakistan to become an independent area known as Pakhtunistan or Pashtunistan or Pushtunistan ("Land of the Pakhtus" [or Pashtus or Pushtus], i.e., the Pathans). The party has since been liquidated and its leaders, including the two brothers, Abdul Ghaffar Khan and Dr. Khan Sahib, thrown into jail.

All the political parties in India and Pakistan so far mentioned have their origin within the subcontinent and may be considered indigenous in contrast to the Communist Party, which owes its origin to outside stimulus. Communism came to India from Russia shortly after the first World War. All Asia at that time promptly became a field of the new Russia's activities, and especially India as the most important part of the British Empire, which Lenin and others had openly named as an antagonist. A number of Indians, among whom the most prominent came to be M. N. Roy, a Bengali Brahman, received training in those years in the Russian communist training schools. Because of agitation in India in 1924 a group of four communists (the "Cawnpore Conspirators") were sentenced to imprisonment for conspiracy against the King-Emperor. One of them was S. A. Dange (party leader in 1952). That year the Communist Party of India was organized but it had little strength because the chief communists had been jailed.

In 1926–1927 several British communists, including S. Saklatvala, an Indian who had been elected to the British Parliament, came to India to establish cells of workers' and peasants' parties in Bombay, Bengal, the Punjab, and the United Provinces. The Party held a conference in 1928 in Calcutta and decided to act in accordance with the program of the Comintern and the policy adopted from time to time by the Party with the agreement of the Communist International. It organized a militant left-wing labor movement, which participated in many strikes. In March 1929, the Government of India arrested 31 leaders, all but two of whom were communists, in the well-known Meerut Conspiracy Case. Most of these were released in 1933, but the four most prominent were held longer. When another wave of strikes broke out in 1934, the Government of India banned the Communist Party and it went underground to stay until 1942. It seems to have had a membership in 1934 of 150; by 1942 the number was perhaps between 2500 and 2700 (its own varying claims ran up to 5000), recruited from various outlawed groups or individuals and from Congress socialists who were dissatisfied with the meagerness of gains under Congress. Congress and the communists contended during this period to dominate the labor movement and the peasant organizations, and in 1942–1944 when the Government held Congress leaders in detention but lifted its ban on the communists, the latter gained control of the principal organizations.

Before the Communist Party was banned, the communists in India had opposed Congress and its leaders, including Gandhi, as tools, conscious or unconscious, of imperialism and bourgeois feudalism and capitalism, deceiving the people and betraying the nationalist struggle, a menace to the proletarian revolution. The left wing of Congress, that is, the group including Jawaharlal Nehru, Jaiprakash Narain, and other socialistically inclined leaders, they condemned unequivocally when it emerged in 1931, and later they denounced as a bourgeois blind the Congress Socialist Party which was being formed when the Communist Party of India was coming under government ban. When the ban was imposed and communism in Europe was entering upon its struggle with fascism and nazism and generally promoting a united front, the Communist Party of India too changed its policies. It urged a united front in India against imperialism and gave Congress its support, though recommending some changes in Congress tactics, for example, abandonment of non-violence. It usually supported Congress in the 1936–1937 elections but was not satisfied with the work of the Congress ministries (1937–1939).

When the second World War broke out in 1939, the Communist Party of India, following the general communist line, stigmatized it as an imperialist war and admonished India not to support it, and in March 1940 the Government of India took communist leaders into custody under the Defense of India Rules. When the U.S.S.R. became involved in the war, the Indian communists called the Russian part of the World War a people's war, but still did not support the British part. They did not cease their hindrance to the Indian war effort until the Japanese were advancing in Southeast Asia and threatening India, whereupon they accepted the British war as also a people's war and urged India to support it. By this time the Indian political parties had shown that they were at best only lukewarm about the war, and after the Cripps Mission (March 1942) had failed, the Government of India removed the ban from the Communist Party in July 1942, and released the leaders whom it had confined over two years before. At this time the party published a lively organ called the *People's Age*. During the period from August 1942 to March 1945, when the Government was holding Congress leaders in confinement, the Communist Party strengthened both its position and its membership. By the end of the war it had grown to at least 25,000 (party spokesmen claimed more).

During the war years 1942–1945 the Communist Party, with P. C. Joshi as its General Secretary, maintained a wary coöperation, first, with the Government of India, which, though using its support in prosecuting the war, continued to arrest its leaders; second, with the Indian National Congress, which welcomed its support in advocating release of Congress leaders but deplored its compromise on the Pakistan idea, and regarded its support of the war as traitorous to nationalism; third, with the Muslim League, which being a group dominated by landlords found the communists uncongenial but appreciated the Communist Party's support of the Pakistan proposal; and, finally, with the Untouchables, whose social aims it approved but whose failure to support the war effort it criticized. At the end of 1945 the association of Congress and the Communist Party, as brittle during the war years as that of the United States and the U.S.S.R., was shattered, and has never been repaired. While the final struggle between Congress and the League over Pakistan was in progress (1946–1947), the Communist Party sided with the League rather than the Congress, which latter by that time was operating the Interim Government under Nehru's leadership.

After partition the activities of the Communist Party increased still further. It made capital of the Indian government's removal of economic controls late in 1947, which sent food prices up, and in 1948 it staged a large-scale operation among the peasantry in the eastern Hyderabad state and the adjacent parts of Madras. Various leading figures in the national and state governments, especially Patel, who was Home Minister as well as Deputy Prime Minister, accused the Communist Party of fomenting strikes and sabotage and other types of violence. In February 1948, the communists called an Asian Youth Conference in Calcutta, which is generally considered to have planned a communist campaign for all South and Southeast Asia. Immediately afterwards in the same place the Communist Party of India held its second Congress (February 28–March 6, 1948), where it removed from the Secretary Generalship P. C. Joshi, who had held the position during the days of the united front, and installed B. T. Ranadive, a communist labor leader, and adopted a new and violent program which was published (July 1948, May 1949) and defended at length in a *Political Thesis*.

The basic motives of the Party as stated therein include severance of India from the Commonwealth; no "collaboration with Anglo-American imperialism"; adult suffrage and proportional representation; self-determination of nationalities, with "a voluntary Indian Union; autonomous linguistic provinces"; accession of the former Indian States to either nation, not on the basis of ruler's choice, as had been the procedure adopted, but by reference to the people; extension of full democratic rights to the tribal and backward peoples; coöperation between India and Pakistan; abolition of landlordism, liquidation of rural indebtedness and abolition of usury; confiscation by the State of foreign capital in banks, industrial and transport concerns, plantations, mines, etc., and nationalization of those concerns; nationalization of big industry, banks, insurance companies, and guarantee of workers' control; minimum living wage; eight-hour day; economic planning; repeal of repressive legislation; elimination of bureaucratic administration; arming of the people; right to free education; equal democratic rights for women.

These demands were to be promoted by *Shanti Senas* ("peace armies") and common "Left coöperation" in a "Democratic Front." The fight was to be waged by a united working class with the aid of strikes, support of the All-India Trade Union Congress, warfare against the non-communist labor organizations, the Congress, the Muslim League, the Socialist Party, the rousing of the peasantry under the All-India Kisan Sabha, organization of students, youth, women, Untouchables, organization of mass political action. The movement was to support the U.S.S.R. and Chinese People's government. This program appears to have been the Party's manual and directive at least until early in 1951 and possibly until October.

The Indian Government set out in March 1948 on a policy of repression in Bengal, where the Communist Party was strongest, Bombay, Madras, and other centers, and outlawed it in several states. In February 1949 the Government reported discovery of a plot to wreck railways and bridges, and that same month there were raids on arms depots near Calcutta by groups which the Government said belonged to a Revolutionary Communist Party of India (distinct from the Indian Communist Party). The Government arrested large numbers of persons in an anti-communist drive (for example, a report shows 3000 in one week in February 1949, and there were many others).

At the end of 1949 the Government issued a booklet describing "Communist Violence in India," and citing instructions found in captured documents for armed assaults on authority through guerrilla bands preparatory to a general revolution, methods of silent killing, raiding of police stations, and many other similar activities. Communists have also been held responsible by the Government for much other miscellaneous disturbance, such as inciting the head-hunting Naga tribes in Assam to raid their neighbors (later the Nagas were reported to have yielded to pressure to refrain and adopt a less anti-social attitude. In March 1952, certain Naga tribes were reported to be seeking independence). Over 300 communists were said in October 1950 to have been arrested in Assam, and over 1000 others there in March 1951. In February 1950, at the request of Patel and for the purpose of checking subversive persons, the Indian Parliament passed a repressive act valid for one year giving the Government wide and unusual powers of arrest and detention without trial.

In preparation for the elections of 1951–1952, the Communist Party took several steps to get back on an operating footing in the country. In February 1951, it made a "peace offer" to act as a regular political party in the open if the Government would withdraw its preventive measures. This the Government rejected. In July the communists in the Hyderabad State made a similar offer to the State government. At the end of April, the Communist Party's headquarters in Bombay issued a "fundamental program" of political and economic emancipation for the Indian people, in which it repeated the demand for establishment of a people's democracy under the leadership of the working classes and the Communist Party, confiscation of feudal estates without payment, nationalization of industry and other large enterprise, support of the U.S.S.R. and the Chinese people's republic, withdrawal from the Commonwealth, and alliance and friendship with Pakistan and Ceylon. It called for a united democratic front of all left organizations. At the beginning of August it established its right to enter candidates for the elections in areas where it was not banned; meanwhile the number of areas where it was banned had been notably reduced by court decisions ordering various states to lift their bans. The party aimed at that time to function through local leftist groups.

In late October the party announced that it had failed in its fight to overthrow the government by violence and would cease its hostilities in Hyderabad, and on November 8, one of the party's local officers in Delhi announced that a third national congress of the party had been "held somewhere in India late in October" and that Ranadive had been removed from the position of General Secretary. This was understood to mean that the party was for the time being relinquishing terrorism, evidently meaning to fight the elections wherever it could. Its election manifesto contained many of the usual demands of the Communist Party and also a clause demanding that India withdraw from the British Commonwealth and join "the peace camp led by the Soviet Union and the People's Republic of China." At the end of November 1951, S. A. Dange, a leading communist since the foundation of the party, having come out from underground and acting as its head or chief spokesman, announced that the party would contest 500 seats for the state legislatures but would not enter the contests for the central House of the People, though later it did and won some seats. He outlined plans for a mass peasant revolution but rejected violence as a method to overthrow the government, and stated that under governmental persecution and intraparty purging the party's membership, which had stood at 80,000 in 1946, had declined to 30,000.

The communist movement has been much less active in Pakistan than in India. It has, however, a number of open members and sympathizers, as in India, is vigorously opposed by the Government, and has been supported by various newspapers, among them the *Pakistan Times* (Lahore), one of the nation's two largest English language newspapers, its Urdu counterpart called *Imroz,* and some others. The most prominent members or supporters have been Iftikhar ud-Din, publisher of the *Pakistan Times,* and a member of Parliament; Faiz Ahmed Faiz, editor of the same newspaper, president of the Pakistan Trade Union Congress, member of the World Peace Council; Syed Sajjad Zaheer, general secretary of the Communist Party of Pakistan; Syed Sibtey Hassan, formerly a correspondent in the United States for the *People's Age* (communist organ in India during the war).

The chief of the Government's charges against the communists in Pakistan is that of a conspiracy to assassinate its leading figures and establish a military dictatorship. The Government announced the discovery of this on March 9, 1951, and arrested sixteen prominent military and civilian persons. The leading ones were Major General Akbar Khan, Chief of Staff of the Pakistan army, who in 1947 had borne the pseudonym "General Tariq" as commander of the Pakistan forces operating with the Azad Kashmir forces in Kashmir; Faiz Ahmed Faiz; Syed Sajjad Zaheer. The Constituent Assembly (functioning as the Pakistan Parliament) passed a Special Tribunal Act in April, authorizing abrogation of usual judicial procedure, and in June, fifteen (or fourteen) of those arrested were brought to secret trial. The communists claimed that the conspiracy trial was a blind, and that the real motive for the arrest was that the accused were opposing secret negotiations of the Pakistan government with the United States. The Pakistan government has also considered communists largely responsible for riots in East Bengal in February 1952, which agitated various issues including that of language.

The communists sell large numbers of well-printed books at cheap prices, and speak much in public and in private. They make an important point of showing that communists concern themselves with national cultural aspirations, and support the claim by stimulating small amateur and semiprofessional theatrical groups. In this way they appeal to some of the same sort of sentiment that gave nationalism its strength. They get a great deal of their material into the newspapers in editorials and news items. Their workers industriously circulate among the masses. The communist achievements in Russia and China are exploited to the maximum as examples of what India might expect if it became a communist country. Early in 1952 an exhibition was staged in Bombay, the headquarters of the Communist Party of India, to show the agrarian, industrial, and cultural advance of Russia and China. Many Indian literary, artistic, motion picture, and other sorts of cultural figures are invited for visits by the governments of those countries. The total effect of this program has been large, and has, of course, been pointed to show a contrast with the United States.

Since the elections of 1952 the communists in India have been making alliances with other parties to capture control of state legislative assemblies. The issue has been squarely joined by Congress, whose leaders (for example, Nehru in the House of the People and Chakravarti Rajagopalachari in the Madras State Legislative Assembly) have responded vigorously to communist attacks and charges. The Communist Party General Secretary, Ajoy Kumar Ghosh, said in February that it would now abjure violence, and implied that it would employ parliamentary devices to achieve its objectives. This seemed a natural consequence of gaining second place in the national party structure. The Communist Party of India has, in fact, been pursuing a consistently obstructive policy in the various legislative bodies. But the Government of India is convinced that the communists, and like them the religious communalists, have active programs of armed violence. In August 1952 it was fighting in the House of the People for a bill to prolong for two years the Preventive Detention Act of 1950, by which the Government is empowered to hold suspected subversives for twelve months without trial. The Government had been partially provoked by communist disturbances in the Telingana (Telugu-speaking) area of the Hyderabad State, which Nehru described as "civil war." The bill contains provisions much like some of those of acts and ordinances imposed against the nationalists during the struggle for freedom. The new abrogation of civil rights is a measure of the present Government's exasperation.

13. Education, Language, Press

The most useful modernizing tool which Britain bequeathed to India and Pakistan was a system of public education. It is true that it was below western standards: that by 1941 it had made only 15.1 per cent of the population aged ten and above literate; that many pupils attended for only a year or two and then lapsed into illiteracy; that it presented modern social and physical science incompletely; that it ignored the traditional Indic material in the humanities side of its program and instead presented western British materials; that it gave college instruction a disproportionate place in the system; that it had little of technical and applied science. Nevertheless, it brought new and stimulating ideas to India, introduced the country to a secular view of life, gave it a common language, put it into direct contact with the learning, thought, politics of the outside world. Both nations want to enlarge and improve it as much and as fast as their resources will permit.

At the close of the second World War the subcontinent had eighteen universities, some of which were examining bodies for affiliated colleges, while some others gave "postgraduate" (a term equivalent in India, as in Britain, to the American "graduate") instruction, and the rest gave both postgraduate and undergraduate instruction. There were around 450 colleges, including four-year and intermediate colleges, second grade colleges, and about 115 professional colleges, dealing with law, medicine, teaching, agriculture, commerce, engineering, technology, art. The enrollment in them all was about 160,000. The number of graduates in a year was coming to about 16,000 in arts, 2600 in law, 860 in medicine, 330 in engineering, 1900 in education, 720 in commerce, 260 in agriculture. There were in British India in those years approximately 4200 high schools, with about 1,350,000 students, among whom were 171,000 girls; less than 1000 secondary schools teaching professional subjects; about 10,300 middle schools (equivalent to American "grammar schools"), with 1,420,000 pupils; 187,000 primary and special schools, having about 12,000,000 pupils out of possibly 40,000,000 children of primary school age. In British India about 5.2 per cent of the entire population was receiving instruction—the percentage was probably not much different in the Indian States as a whole, though both the lowest and the highest rates of literacy and school attendance were found in them. All the instruction in British India was costing annually only about Rs. 317 million (equivalent at the rate of exchange then to about $98 million, at today's rate about $66.6 million). Of this 60 per cent came from the government, about 25 per cent from students' fees, and the rest from philanthropic sources of various kinds. The schools were chiefly in the cities; most of the more than 650,000 villages in the subcontinent had nothing at all.

Various important studies of India's educational system were made during the British period, of which the latest was begun in 1938 and published in 1944. This was an elaborate *Report by the Central Advisory Board of Education,* entitled "Post-War Educational Development in India," commonly known from the name of its chairman Sir John Sargent as the "Sargent Scheme." This was aimed to provide both basic mass education, which it was hoped would become universal in a period of forty years, and also secondary, higher, and professional education adapted to the social, economic, and political needs of India as a modern state. The scheme was criticized, on the one hand, as taking too long to achieve, on the other, as being too expensive to be realized and therefore over-optimistic. To many observers who were not involved in Indian politics it seemed to be a realizable combination of restrained idealism and fiscal courage.

Since partition both nations have added many new universities, colleges, professional and technical schools, high schools, lower schools. Pakistan was only three months old and still trying to organize itself amid the confusion and shortages of Karachi when the Minister of Education (as also of the Interior, Information and Broadcasting, and Commerce), Fazlur Rahman, convened an Educational Conference to make recommendations for the guidance of immediate operations and the deliberations of the Pakistan Constituent Assembly. An Advisory Board of Education was established, which has met at various times since. In December 1951 it adopted a six-year plan for educational development to cost Rs. 1,154 million ($358 million). The plan aims to provide free compulsory primary education for the entire nation by the end of twenty years.

In India equal, though differently channeled, interest has been directed to the problem. The most ambitious response appears in clause 45 of the Indian Constitution, which reads: "The State shall endeavour to provide, within a period of ten years from the commencement of this Constitution, for free and compulsory education for all children until they complete the age of fourteen years." This is a bit of optimism that makes Sir John Sargent with his forty-year plan look like a discouraged Jeremiah, and doubtless no informed person in India dealing with education has ever thought it had the remotest chance of achievement. To provide such basic education each of India's roughly 500,000 villages would need at least one primary school, in many cases several, amounting to three or four times the total number of schools now existing. No way has yet been pointed out to find the necessary teachers, buildings, equipment, and financing for this expansion on the most modest terms imaginable, in so short a period.

There is a pressing cry in both countries for amplification in the natural sciences and technological fields. But since these are notoriously expensive because of the cost of laboratory equipment and the training of instructors, India and Pakistan will not be able to expand them rapidly and will have to continue to utilize western institutions. In the humanities, modern college education may be expected to make increased use of the great resources of the Indic and Islamic civilizations in language, literature, art, speculative and analytical thought. A movement to do so became vigorous in Bengal in the 1920's and led to certain innovations at the University of Calcutta, which have since spread elsewhere. Training for specialized government service and for the many developmental projects planned in each country requires a great expansion of the educational system. Research facilities in general are poorly developed, whether for natural, social, or humanistic studies, and many distinguished scholars of the area have publicly and vigorously lamented this fact, including Sir C. V. Raman, winner of the Nobel Prize for Physics in 1920. Libraries, laboratories, investigating institutes, are few and inadequately supported, though several of high standing and distinguished accomplishment can be mentioned (Calcutta School of Tropical Medicine, Haffkine Institute, Poona School of Social and Economic Research, Bhandarkar Oriental Research Institute, Deccan Oriental Research Institute, Indian Statistical Institute, and others).

The current social and political problems arising in India and Pakistan from language center around the question: what should be the language or languages of government and higher education? The conflicts are those of Aryan with Dravidian, Indic with English, Hindi with Urdu, and each of the latter two with other Aryan tongues. We shall consider these in order.

Aryan has now for three thousand years been encroaching upon Dravidian. A century ago Bishop Caldwell spoke of Aryan contempt for Dravidian and the self-assertion of Dravidian in reaction. When the British introduced English in the first half of the nineteenth century, they did so as the preferred alternative to both Sanskrit and Persian (not to the vernaculars, which were then disesteemed). Nationalist promotion of the vernaculars as the medium of instruction in education appeared in the late nineteenth century and the first half of the twentieth. Their literatures began to gain prestige then and a press developed in them. The most striking illustration was the establishment at Ahmedabad under Gandhi's inspiration of the Vidyapith at the time of the First Non-coöperation Movement. There the medium of instruction was Hindi and the cultural material studied was Indian. Rabindranath Tagore, too, in the institution he founded at Shanti Niketan (Bolpur, Bengal), now become the Visva Bharati ("Universal Indian") University, used Indian languages for the medium of instruction and their literature as material for study. The Osmaniya University in Hyderabad employed Urdu.

Nationalism was intent on displacing English both as the official language and as the medium of instruction, but the question was with what. Here Hindu-Muslim communalism affected the question. The Indian National Congress wanted Hindi, or, when it listened to Gandhi, Hindustani. Muslims wanted Urdu. Hindustani, Hindi, and Urdu are varieties of the same language. Hindustani is the current spoken form, providing the phonology, grammatical structure, and basic vocabulary. Hindi and Urdu are literary forms of Hindustani, and are differentiated from each other in the learned or highly cultivated vocabulary and in script. Hindi borrows words freely from Sanskrit, is generally written in an indigenous script known as Devanagari (or Nagari), and as so written is chiefly current among Hindus. Urdu borrows copiously from Persian and Arabic, usually is written in the Perso-Arabic script, and is largely restricted to Muslims. Hindi and Urdu came to be rival symbols of Hindu-Muslim communalism. Gandhi tried to resolve the language quarrel by advocating Basic Hindustani written in both scripts, and continued to do so as late as January 1948, shortly before his assassination. The Congress Ministries during their period of power (1937–1939) were not always thoughtful of Muslim susceptibilities and sometimes promoted Hindi rather than Hindustani, thus leading Muslims to react by affirming claims for Urdu.

The attack which nationalism made upon English, therefore, also induced communal controversy over the substitute as to whether it should be Hindi or Urdu. It also aroused regional linguistic jealousy among the Dravidians, living in South India, proud of their own literary tongues. Further, in various parts of India where Aryan languages were current, there was jealousy of Hindi. The Bengalis, who consider themselves the intellectual leaders of India, thought their language should be second to none; to a less extent speakers of Marathi in western India had a similar feeling; to a still less extent did Gujaratis, also in western India.

These various linguistic rivalries now carry over into India and Pakistan. In each country nationalist sentiment urges that English be demoted from its present dominance. But in India the choice of Hindi as the replacement is unpopular in southern, eastern, and western parts of the country, and in Pakistan the choice of Urdu, though accepted in West Pakistan, is questioned in East Pakistan, where Bengali is the vernacular. In each nation, therefore, the linguistic problem is a double one: first to find a suitable substitute for English; second, to persuade the people of the nation as a whole to accept any single one of its tongues as that substitute.

India has committed itself to Hindi, and the Constitution in Section 351 proposes that the State should positively promote the development of that language (as against Urdu or any other), saying:

It shall be the duty of the Union to promote the spread of the Hindi language, to develop it so that it may serve as a medium of expression for all the elements of the composite culture of India and to secure its enrichment by assimilating without interfering with its genius, the forms, style and expressions used in Hindustani and in the other languages of India specified in the Eighth Schedule, and by drawing, wherever necessary or desirable, for its vocabulary, primarily on Sanskrit and secondarily on other languages.

It is doubtful that the decision for Hindi solves the problem of finding a suitable national language. It is, first of all, not at present a feasible substitute for English. That fact is revealed by the Constitution itself. This says in Section 343(1): "The official language of the Union shall be Hindi in Devanagari script." But after giving this acknowledgment to national cultural aspirations, it goes on to say in Section 343(2): "Notwithstanding anything in clause (1) for a period of fifteen years from the commencement of this Constitution, the English language shall continue to be used for all official purposes of the Union for which it was being used immediately before such commencement." And still further in the same section it states in 343(3): "Notwithstanding anything in this article, Parliament may by law provide for the use, after the said period of fifteen years, of—(a) the English language . . . for such purposes as may be specified in the law." More stringently and specifically the Constitution, dealing with a field where the use of language may be administratively critical, provides in Section 348 that

until Parliament by law otherwise provides—(a) all proceedings in the Supreme Court and in every High Court, (b) the authoritative texts—(i) of all Bills . . . (ii) of all Acts passed by Parliament or the Legislature of a State and of all Ordinances promulgated by the President or the Governor or Rajpramukh of a State, and (iii) of all orders, rules, regulations and bye-laws issued under this Constitution or under any law made by Parliament or the Legislature of a State, shall be in the English language.

(There are certain minor modifications.) In accordance with this provision the official text of the Constitution is in English.

In Pakistan, since a Constitution has not yet been adopted, there is no provision about language, and English is at least by default the current official language. The Pakistan Educational Conference called by the Ministry of Education in 1947, after discussing this touchy subject, adopted a resolution which avoided the phrase "official language" but indicated the majority sentiment: "This conference recommends to the Constituent Assemby that Urdu should be recognised as the lingua franca of Pakistan." The Minister of Education (Fazlur Rahman) in the opening address of the Conference had said, ". . . English . . . must for some considerable time to come retain its pride of place both in the sphere of our University education and as a means of international communication." He spoke in the same vein at an educational conference in December 1951. It has not been possible to gain for Urdu a place as the national language or the medium of instruction in East Pakistan or in Sind, but it is a compulsory subject in the educational curriculum. In April 1952 the Prime Minister of Pakistan, recognizing the seriousness of the dispute over language, asked the Pakistan press to coöperate in keeping the language question out of politics.

Both countries are greatly dependent in government upon English. It is the only medium through which legislative representatives and officials from all parts of the nation can communicate with one another. In education and business the situation is the same. At the Pakistan Educational Conference in 1947, mentioned above, delegates from Bengal (East Pakistan) frequently complained that they could not understand speeches in Urdu. The courts, except on low levels where small cases are handled, could not today proceed in any other language than English. Decisions have been rendered and precedents are established and quoted in English all over the land. The legal vocabulary is that of English law; none of the native languages, not even Sanskrit or Persian, is equipped at present to express the necessary concepts. The same considerations apply in framing legislation. Indian languages can, however, be used for many administrative procedures, and are beginning to get such usage. On November 1, 1952, Uttar Pradesh replaced English with Hindi as the official language. It is evident, however, that Hindi still lacks the vocabulary to supersede English. For international communication neither Hindi nor Urdu is usable.

Though the Constitution of India prescribes Hindi as the goal for national language, it recognizes in Section 345 that separate regions within the nation need to use their local languages internally in public affairs. But (by Section 346) for communication between one State and another and between a State and the Union the language shall be that authorized as the official language of the Union, unless two or more States agree to use Hindi (in place of the present official English). To prevent a majority language from dominating unfairly in a State, the President of the Union may, by Section 347, on demand, if he is satisfied that a substantial portion of the State's population desires the use of a language spoken by them to be recognized by that State, direct that it be recognized in all or part of the State. The end result could well be, in theory, that in the government of a State where Hindi is not a local language, such as Madras, officials might need to use in their interstate and intrastate affairs jointly English, Hindi, Tamil, Telugu, and Kannada. In practice, however, it might equally well be that English would remain the sole official language for any but the lowest levels of governmental usage, and a good many realistically minded citizens say so.

Closely associated with the problem of language as a vehicle for legislative, administrative, and judicial functions and as a means of intellectual and business communication is that of language as the medium of instruction in the educational system. Cultural nationalism in both India and Pakistan urges use of a native language instead of the present prevailing English, but the issue is again which one to employ. In India the Congress has demanded Hindi and in Western Pakistan there is sentiment for Urdu, but again there are local objections, as in the case of the adoption of these two as official languages. The issue arises only on the higher levels of education, that is, in colleges, technical and professional institutions, and graduate schools, possibly to a limited extent in high schools. For education below those levels the local vernaculars are necessary and satisfactory.

On the higher levels, however, vernaculars lack the scientific vocabulary to replace English. But the nationalist sentiment which demands the ouster of English insists that the native literary languages supply a terminology made from their own lexical resources. That is, English terms would be translated into forms made from Hindi or Sanskrit or Urdu or Persian or Arabic elements through derivation or compounding. Such proposals to manufacture a vocabulary, though fair to hear, are liable to be a delusion, because the meaning of scientific terminology depends largely upon usage by scholars, and newly fashioned terms with no scientific history and context have little meaning or chance to acquire it.

For education, therefore, as for government, the provisions of the Constitution of India, unless administered thoughtfully and without political demagoguery, would impose a heavy language burden upon the country, and the implications of the Pakistan Educational Conference, if put into statute form, would do the same there.

The language problem includes a subsidiary problem of script. The various vernaculars of the subcontinent use different local systems of writing, though the different systems, with the exception of the imported Perso-Arabic used for Urdu, are all indigenous and derived from the Brahmi script, which was current by the third century B.C. The most widely used indigenous script is Devanagari, cited in the

Constitution of India, Section 343, which is employed for Hindi and Marathi. All scripts, whether indigenous or imported, are alphabetic but are complicated to write and difficult to learn. The symbols for different sounds may vary in appearance according to position in the word, whether initial, medial, or final, or when combined with other symbols in ligatures, which are numerous. Hence, while our own roman script with its small and capital letters (some of which are duplicates), requires a learner to master only about 40 shapes, an Indian script, though having no capitals, may present literally hundreds of forms.

The central and several state governments of India and Pakistan have been concerned with the problem of simplifying scripts so as to ease the learning process and fit them for typewriting and modern printing. Newspaper publishers and others printers have also been so concerned, and to a less extent so have business interests. Some newspapers in India and Pakistan, publishing in Bengali, Hindi, Tamil, or Urdu, have experimented with script reform so as to adapt them to mechanical type-composing machines (linotype, monotype). Such adaptation requires changes in the appearance of some symbols.

Since independence the Governments of Uttar Pradesh, Bombay, and Madras have had active Script Reform Committees; some other states have had less active committees. The Government of India has also had a committee, which seems to be waiting to see what the states do. The Government of Pakistan now seems prepared to use the Naskh form of the Perso-Arabic, which is common in western Islamic countries and has been adapted to printing, but in printing it is being simplified in Pakistan. The problem in both India and Pakistan is to simplify the scripts in such a way that, though the writing is made easier, the appearance of the symbols is kept near enough to the accepted traditional forms to be neither ambiguous nor offensive to public taste, which is extremely sensitive on the subject.

The easiest and most successful method of script reform would be to use the roman script with modification, as was done in Turkey. With the aid of simple diacritical marks it is possible to adapt it to the phonetic demands of any language used in India. Scholars do so successfully now. Roman would have the advantages of being simple to learn, easy to use on the typewriter and in printing, and widely employed elsewhere. Some of India's leading linguistic scholars proposed this change in the 1920's and 1930's, and Nehru as recently as in February 1949 said "It would be desirable to explore the possibilities of the roman script," but such advice is not welcome at the present time. Nationalism asserts Indian and Pakistani cultural prestige, and script is an item deeply cherished in that connection. No language group in the subcontinent is willing that its language should be written in a European script.

A bothersome problem to the Government of India since independence has been that of linguistic provincialism. This is the desire of linguistic groups to constitute separate states. It is based partly upon the latent desire of a culture group, especially one identified by language, to have political integrity. Partly in India, however, it is also the consequence of propaganda by the Indian National Congress in its campaign for independence. As part of its complaint against British rule, Congress deprecated the provincial structure of India, calling it illogical because the boundaries cut through cultural groups and so frustrated their natural aspirations. Congress, in its Constitution adopted in 1920, organized itself in the area of British India in "Congress Provinces," which were mostly delimited by language boundaries, and demanded reconstitution of India's provinces according to this division. At the time of independence there were twenty of these. After independence, when Congress was responsible for Government, the issue of linguistic provincialism became embarrassing. Some of the language groups had hoped that, when independence was obtained, their political aspirations would be realized. The Government, however, now found reorganization impracticable.

The areas most insistent were the Andhra, that is, the region where Telugu is spoken, lying in Madras and Hyderabad; the Kannada, lying in Mysore, Madras, and Hyderabad; the Kerala, where Malayalam is spoken, lying in Travancore, Cochin, Madras, and Mysore; the Maharashtra, where Marathi is spoken, lying in Bombay, Hyderabad, Berar, and the Central Provinces (now Madhya Pradesh); Gujarati, lying in the northern part of Bombay; and Gurmukhi, consisting of Sikh States in the Punjab. There was a little talk in Bengal, not very serious, of absorbing the few regions outside it where Bengali was the prevailing tongue.

Congress was able to still most of these demands, but that for an Andhra province was for a long time too strong. The first draft of the Constitution conceded the future creation of Andhra; this was, however, omitted from the final version. The Sikh States still agitate for a Sikhistan or Gurmukhi area as a separate State if not an independent nation. In the south the demands are still strong and it is not yet entirely certain that at some future time the region may not be reorganized in part on linguistic lines.

Linguistic provincialism exists in Pakistan among the speakers of Pashtu (Pushto, Pakhtu), who would like their entire area, which lies in Pakistan and Afghanistan, to be a single political unit, preferably independent of both countries. The demand is strong and reflects the Pashtu-speaking tribesmen's contempt for the plainsmen of the Punjab.

A serious problem has arisen in India since independence in connection with freedom of the press. This has periodically been a critical issue since the foundation in 1780 of India's first newspaper, *The Bengal Gazette,* often known after its founder as *Hicky's Gazette* or *Hicky's Journal,* which was suppressed in 1782 by Warren Hastings for various offenses, including attacks upon his wife. Other newspapers in English were established shortly afterwards in Bombay and Madras, and in 1816 a vernacular press was born in Bengal. The leadership has consistently to the present lain with the English language press. It had and has today the best newspapers of India and Pakistan, gets the best and freshest news service, publishes the best editorials and columns, gives the fullest commercial and other specialized coverage. The vernacular press is secondary to the English language press, drawing upon it for news and ideas, containing as a rule inferior editorials, being less responsible and less original, and, with only some few exceptions, being poorly printed. By American standards both English-language and vernacular newspapers have small circulation. The maximum is around 100,000.

For the first forty years of its life the Indian press was subject to rigid control, in the beginning (until 1799) by penalties such as stoppage of circulation or deportation of editors, after 1799 by Regulations promulgated by Lord Mornington, and then by a series of further restrictive rules imposed from 1823 to 1827. In 1853 these were repealed in a Press Act, which was adopted contrary to the presentiment of the far-seeing Sir Thomas Munro, Governor of Madras, that a free press and an autocratic government were incompatible—"What is the first duty of a free press?" he asked, and himself answered, "It is to deliver the country from a foreign yoke." He predicted that the freeing action would come about through the sepoy army, which later did revolt. A part of the press protested Lord Dalhousie's (1848–1856) annexations in Oudh, which led to the

Indian (Sepoy) Mutiny, and during the time of the Mutiny Lord Canning (1856–1862) imposed severe censorship, which afterwards lapsed. In 1867 a Press and Registration of Books Act was passed. At the time of the Second Afghan War, in 1878, Lord Lytton (Governor General 1876–1880) imposed a Vernacular Press Act, which aroused violent protest and was repealed shortly afterwards, in 1882, under Lord Ripon (1880–1884). From then until 1907, the Government dealt with journalistic sedition under sections of the Penal Code.

In 1908 a Newspaper (Incitement to Offences) Act was passed, to curb the anti-British acts accompanying the growth of nationalism, and in 1910 a still more stringent Indian Press Act was adopted. The reaction to this was so strong that in 1922 the Acts of 1908 and 1910 were repealed and instead certain modifications, less harsh than the repealed legislation but nevertheless restrictive, were made to the Act of 1867. But in 1930, when the Second Civil Disobedience Campaign was launched, the Government imposed a strict Press Ordinance, which in 1931 was put on the Statute Book as the Indian Press (Emergency Powers) Act. The various press restrictions were constantly attacked by nationalists, and when the Constitution of India 1950 was adopted, it included a guaranteee in Section 19(1)(a) of "freedom of speech and expression," subject however to the modification that nothing should "affect the operation of any existing law in so far as it relates to, or prevent the State from making any law relating to, libel, slander, defamation, contempt of court or any matter which offends against decency or morality or which undermines the security of, or tends to overthrow, the State."

After independence the Indian press, which had been encouraged by Congress during the nationalist struggle to extreme kinds of utterance, felt free to attack the new rule and to attack foreign countries, the United States being the most frequent object. The most violent were organs of communism and communalism, both of which were at times guilty of sedition and incitement to public violence and murder by almost any definition. National Government security seemed threatened. Action through the courts proved ineffective as a curb, because of the constitutional guarantee mentioned above. The Supreme Court held that in suppressing certain such papers, the Government action was unconstitutional.

The Government, therefore, in the person of Prime Minister Nehru, in May 1951, introduced an amendment to the Constitution to permit severe restraint upon public expression and the freedom of the press.

The country's press opposed it unanimously, or so nearly so as to make any exceptions negligible, and many Congress members of the Indian Parliament privately questioned it too. It was felt that genuine cases of treason, slander, obscenity, incitement to violence, and other crimes could be controlled through existing penal law. After heated public argument, Nehru agreed to modification of the original proposal. At last on June 1, Parliament, acting under party discipline, by a vote of 228 to 19, amended the section mentioned above to read that nothing in the guarantee of freedom of speech and expression should affect the operation of any existing law

in so far as it imposes or prevents the State from making any law or imposing restrictions in the interests of the security of the State, friendly relations with foreign states, public order, decency or morality . . . and in particular nothing . . . as it relates to or prevents the State from making any law relating to contempt of court, defamation or incitement to an offense.

The Government then introduced a bill of enforcement of wide coverage which was enacted October 6, 1951. When President Prasad made his opening speech to the newly elected Indian Parliament on May 16, 1952, he listed a new press bill as part of the Government's legislative program.

The situation has been admittedly a bad one, but it is doubtful if the solution is good either. Certain organs, such as the weekly *Blitz* (Bombay), which follows the communist line, have been unscrupulously irresponsible, and its deputy editor was arrested on March 11, 1952, for attacking the impartiality of the Uttar Pradesh Assembly's speaker. The editors of this same weekly and of another, called *Current,* were indicted in the fall of 1952 for conspiracy of forgery in publishing an alleged letter of United States Ambassador Bowles. The Government feels that it should be able to prevent or punish publication of "objectionable matter." But it is hard to see what advantage India now has over pre-independence British-ruled India with respect to freedom of speech and expression, and the fears of the bill's opponents that it may in the future come to be used repressively by an overzealous executive seem valid. Responsibility of the press, being based upon public standards of judgment and therefore of slow growth, seems likely to be a production of patience in any country, including India, and not capable of creation by a law which the entire press opposes and with which it is therefore unlikely to coöperate.

14. Population, Production, and the Good Life

Commentators have disagreed loudly on whether or not the India-Pakistan subcontinent is overpopulated. Nationalists during the struggle for independence often claimed that it could support a greater population if it reformed its agricultural structure and acquired a better industrial development than that permitted under the British imperialism. In such circumstances it could accommodate a vastly increased population on the present scale of living or a moderately increased one on an improved scale. Communist-oriented writers took a similar line. But defenders of British rule pointed out that mere increase of production would not be the answer. In the past century any such gain had always been absorbed by an increase in the population, which bred up to the full capacity of the greater production to give support on a subsistence basis. Areas newly opened to agriculture by irrigation were promptly filled with settlers who were shortly living no better than before they migrated from their old homes. Newly created industry led to the formation in cities of labor colonies, whose members lived in the most desolate poverty. The end result was not an advance of living standards, only a multiplication of the millions submerged in want.

The argument about overpopulation got nowhere, because the subject was not viewed in the whole except by a small number of sociologists and economists, whose misgivings seemed like whispers against the roaring blasts of political propaganda and rejoinder. But from not long before independence the pressing evils of the population problem have rudely crashed into the consciousness of politicians, who had formerly been only critics without authority but have now become responsible administrators.

The rapid expansion of the population is a justifiable reason for alarm. In the subcontinent it seems to have grown by more than 48 million or 12.3 per cent in the decade 1941–1951. This was a lower rate than that of 1931–1941, which was about 15 per cent, while in the half-century 1901–1951 the increase was 153 million, about 54 per cent. For an area with high standards of living and a rapidly expanding industrialism such rates would not be excessive, and the subcontinent's average year-to-year rate of gain is lower than that of Europe and North America and is less than the world average. But for an agricultural region with a long period of historic occupation it is ominous. It is figured by Kingsley Davis that, at the present rate of increase, the subcontinent is likely to have in the year 2005 a total of 840 million, more than one-third of the world's present estimated population.

Since there has been no corresponding increase of food production and no growth of industry to finance importation of food, the average individual is more poorly fed now than in 1901. Housing and clothing conditions, too, have deteriorated. Individual poverty is, in fact, worse now than ever before in this century. Estimates of annual per capita national income in India and Pakistan are all admittedly unreliable, but any one of them, as Dr. V. K. R. V. Rao's estimate for 1931–1932 of Rs. 65 (then equivalent to about $19.50) for undivided India, or the United Nations' figures for 1949 (issued in 1950) of $57 for India and $51 for Pakistan, may be considered near enough the truth to indicate a grim situation. Even after allowing for the difficulty of translating these money figures into terms of real goods consumed, the reality is inconceivable to most Americans.

In relation to the food problem the Government of India's Planning Commission states that in India in 1950 the amount of cereal available per adult per day was 13.67 ounces, a quite insufficient allowance. By 1956 to maintain the same scale for the increased population India will need to import 7 million tons of cereals. On a scale of 16 ounces per day she would need to import almost 16 million tons. And this figuring does not allow for natural calamities or any other disaster like war, which would reduce crops. Besides solving this staggering problem of finding mere food, the subcontinent must increase production of commercial crops—cotton, jute, tea, tobacco—some of which it needs for local consumption, some for export.

Secondly, housing, sanitation, health services, are hopelessly inadequate and the death rate is high. In spite of the fact that many of the usual population controls, such as internal war, famine, and pestilence, have been checked during the past century and a half, the rate still remains one of the highest in the world. For the decade 1931–1941 Kingsley Davis figures it at 31.2 per 1000, which, though high, is nevertheless a reduction from that of previous decades. The decline is in itself a cause of satisfaction, but it also carries an obvious threat when viewed in relation to the food supply. So many people living in so much misery and yet steadily increasing in number are a menace, not only to the progress of their own nations but to world stability and peace as well.

The crudest manifestation of the subcontinent's population and food problem has been its repeated appeals in the past decade for help in finding food. Concretely this has meant procuring food grains, which make up the bulk of the subcontinent's diet. The first occasion was in 1943 before India was partitioned, when a famine in Bengal was estimated to have killed three million persons. In 1945–1946 natural calamities—two droughts and a tidal wave—produced serious food shortages and led India to seek help from abroad. In 1949, at the time of another food crisis, the Government of the new India was again in difficulty. In 1950–1951, when there was still another desperate shortage after droughts and floods in 1950, India asked America for four million tons of wheat, and after prolonged discussion Congress approved a long-term low-interest loan of $190 million for purchases as needed up to that total tonnage. Another famine, caused by drought, is forecast for 1952, worse than that of 1951, and calling for imports of 5,000,000 tons of grains.

Besides producing poverty, semistarvation, a high mortality rate, and a low life expectancy, the large population and insufficient production preclude adequate expenditure on education and help to create group rivalries that prevent united action to achieve national ends. Both nations have in consequence a serious basic problem. India through its Planning Commission has drawn up and is now considering the embracing over-all economic and social five-year plan previously mentioned; Pakistan has so far presented no comparable plan.

To meet its needs India plans to increase both its agricultural and its industrial production and at the same time take such steps that the increase will produce social gains for its citizens and not be unprofitably swallowed up by a mere increase of population. This double aim seems to require a rapid rate of economic advance and an accompanying check upon the rate of population increase.

One phase of India's campaign is a direct attack upon the birth rate. This has two parts. The first is to create a desire for higher standards of living, on the general theory that poverty, rather than prosperity, leads to increase of population. There are many aspects of the national life which, when improved, may be expected to have that effect. With better health, better education, more material comforts, more intellectual interests, Indians will, like Americans and Europeans, themselves automatically check the birth rate.

The second part is the direct spreading of information about birth control. The Planning Commission had a Panel on Health Programmes, which through a Subcommittee on Population and Family Planning recommended that the state provide facilities for sterilization on medical grounds, furnish advice on contraception on medical, social, and economic grounds, and establish research centers to study family limitation and the means of providing inexpensive, safe, and efficacious birth control through contraceptives or otherwise. It is possible that this program can be executed in India without having to overcome marked religious opposition. Hinduism and Islam, though both condemn abortion, seem to have no Scriptural injunction against contraception, and neither has developed an organization to oppose it. Each, however, endorses the birth of many children. Hinduism does so to guarantee that a man has a son to perform the prescribed death rites for him, his father, and his grandfather, while both regard many children as an assurance of lineage and of support in old age in an environment where the mortality rate is high. Each community has also a great deal of social inertia which a birth control program would have to meet. The subcontinent, since it lives by an agricultural economy, has the usual attitude of a peasantry, which looks upon offspring as an immediate aid to the family by furnishing additional labor and does not see the long-term implications.

The Government of India began an experiment in the winter of 1951–1952 in coöperation with the World Health Organization employing the "safe period" method, which, since it involves part abstinence, would to that degree be consonant with Gandhi's attitude on sex. Pakistan, perhaps temporarily lulled by the fact of its better food supply, is less alarmed, but the crisis for it too cannot be far distant.

In a program to increase production the first point of attack has to be the agrarian problem. Here it is necessary to find more acreage for crops, introduce improved farming techniques, promote good animal husbandry, develop irrigation and other aids, eliminate the evils of the land tenure system, give the villages a better standard of living, encourage the peasantry to develop healthy political activity.

There seems to be only a limited possibility of increasing the cultivated acreage by use of present farming methods. In the period from 1920 to 1941 the net acreage sown in what was then British India, that is, the subcontinent excluding the Indian States, increased only from 197.3 million acres to 214 million acres, that is, by about 8.5 per cent. The waste land cultivable by current methods was by 1941 almost all used up; some further expansion through irrigation has been possible since and more is in prospect, but nothing that would be commensurate with the growth of population. India and Pakistan both have large areas not under cultivation because they lack water or have soil of unsuitable composition or have been overgrown with the deep-rooted destructive Kans grass, or are otherwise inarable. Some land once arable is now useless because of the advance of the Rajasthan desert into East Punjab. The need then is to develop methods for utilizing inarable land and so increase the productive area. India claims (1952) that by the use of modern resources it can reclaim 68 million acres of waste land. In its five-year plan (1951–1956) it proposes to reclaim by irrigation 8.8 million acres (and nearly 8 million more after 1956), restore 4 million acres of fallow land to cultivation, and reclaim 1.5 million acres with the aid of tractors.

Further, the land has been deteriorating under heavy usage. In 1949–1950 the area under cereals in India was 183.8 million acres; during the years 1936–1937 and 1938–1939 it was, in the corresponding region, only 167 million acres. Yet the production of cereals in 1949–1950 fell to 44.2 million tons from an annual average of 46.1 million tons in the earlier period.

In part the subcontinent's low agricultural productivity comes from uneconomic distribution of the land and inferior farming practices. Holdings are small and often fragmented. The average acreage used by the individual cultivator declined from 2.23 acres in 1891–1892 to 1.90 in 1939–1940, and this generally consists of tiny scattered parcels. Considerable soil deterioration has taken place through erosion, deforestation, overgrazing, waterlogging in irrigated areas. Cow dung, which is abundant and would be the subcontinent's source of natural fertilizer, would repair some of the damage, but it is instead mixed with straw and used for cooking fuel, which otherwise would be insufficient. Hence, crop yield per acre is low: rice (1240 lbs.) at about $\frac{4}{7}$ that in the United States (2185 lbs.), wheat (660 lbs.) at about $\frac{4}{5}$ (812 lbs.), cotton (96 lbs.) at about $\frac{2}{5}$ (245 lbs.). Though the total production in the twelve basic crops of the sub-continent rose in the twenty-year period 1901–1921, it declined in the next twenty-year period (that is, the years 1920/21 to 1940/41). The peak which it reached in 1920/21 was never equaled in any of the succeeding years.

Agricultural production can be increased, but a large-scale plan for that purpose needs to be more fundamental in its approach than any so far tried. A Grow More Food Campaign, based on a declaration in 1949 of self-sufficiency in 1951, has been inadequate. Nor have price incentives been effective. The Planning Commission has designated production targets for food and commercial crops to be achieved by 1955–1956, including both immediate and long-term objectives and requiring government support and mobilization of the village population. It expects that during the period 1951–1956 India will raise her annual food crop yield by 7.2 million tons and her commercial crops accordingly. Scientific experiments conducted in the past few years under the Government of India, and with American technical assistance, as at Etawah and Faridabad, have produced encouraging results. In some cases crop yields were reported as 30 to 40 per cent more than they had been before through the use of fertilizer, good seeds, simple machinery adapted to Indian conditions, control of insects and diseases, and other modern agricultural helps. The Indian Government believes that with the expenditure of larger funds than at present in sight it could greatly exceed the Planning Commission's estimates.

An integral part of an agricultural development plan has to be improvement in animal husbandry. Experiments in breeding and feeding have been made over a period of years by both governmental and private agencies and notable results have been obtained, but a way is needed to apply them on a general scale. The magnitude of the problem is illustrated by the fact that India produces about 750 pedigreed bulls a year and by the present breeding methods could use a million. Artificial insemination, so common in the United States, is scarcely practiced there. The removal of useless cattle is complicated by the ancient Hindu religious prepossession of their inviolability, which is now enshrined in the new Constitution.

Another item recognized as a necessary part of an agricultural development program is encouragement of rural cottage industries. The peasantry have certain off seasons when they could profitably engage in weaving, leather- and woodworking, and other occupations to supply needed articles. Such occupations could also provide employment for some of the population likely to be released as agricultural methods improve. Gandhi vigorously advocated cottage industry, but an effective program requires organization to give instruction, provide raw materials, furnish credit and financing, and take care of marketing.

The experimental agricultural projects at Etawah, Faridabad, and elsewhere have included both animal husbandry and cottage industry as integral features. They have in addition advanced village education, improved public health, and initiated community social projects such as adult education and amusements. These various undertakings stimulate peasant interest, raise his morale, and give him a goal of higher standards of living. Such programs can help, in the words of the Planning Commission, "to change the character of Indian agriculture from subsistence farming to economic farming." They can go further and give the village something of the better life. Many such projects have been launched or are planned, frequently with the aid of public or private funds from the United States.

Increase of yield and inculcation of social incentive, however, are not enough. There is another vital side to the agrarian problem, which is to reform the system of land tenure and remove peasant indebtedness. As peasant landholders were crowded out by the change in the system of tenure instituted by the British in the eighteenth and early nineteenth centuries and village artisans were forced out of their occupations by the influx of foreign machine-manufactured articles, both classes fell back on the land for support, and the number of landless laborers rose. It was 14 per cent of all cultivators in 1881; in 1931, the last census year for which such figures were collected, it was 38 per cent. It is presumably much higher now; some economists have estimated it at over 50 per cent. The primary problem of tenancy is compounded in many places to that of subtenancy. The landlord or proprietor who pays the taxes to the Government, especially in areas where land ownership lies with a landlord rather than the peasant, frequently does not deal directly with the cultivator but may be separated from him by a number of subproprietors. In Bengal cases have been reported by a Government Commission of as many as seventeen echelons from tiller to landowner.

With the shift in land ownership has gone a great increase in peasant indebtedness. Often the landowner is the moneylender. So dear has the land become and so cheap the worth of a peasant's labor that the peasantry, whether owner or tenant, is heavily encumbered with debt, on which, because a peasant has only low-grade security to offer, the interest rates are high. Studies made in limited areas of relatively high productivity and prosperity—Gujarat (1930), the Punjab (1925), United Provinces (1932)—have shown that somewhere around two-thirds to three-fourths of agricultural families are in debt and the size of the debt varies from about three-fifths of the annual income to 110 per cent of it; or, as M. L. Darling puts it, about three times the annual *net* income. In the Punjab, he noted, the rural indebtedness was more than seventeen times the land revenue of the province. Conditions are thought to be worse now. Interest rates ranged from 9 to 300 per cent. Coöperative credit societies have not been able to counteract the evil; the peasants who form a society can provide only meager capital to operate it, and the society cannot afford to accept any but good risks.

One of the results of the system of land tenure is that the basic payment which the peasantry makes, whether for tax or rent or both, is excessive in its time and place. Land hunger following the changes in the tenure system made in the nineteenth century induced peasants to overbid for the use of land, and landowners took full advantage of them. The British introduced regulatory Tenancy Acts. Nevertheless, in dealings with landlords (zamindari system), peasants were paying out in the twentieth century for revenue or other charges connected with use of the land, "from a maximum of one-fifth or one-sixth down to one-tenth or less of the gross produce," says W. H. Moreland, a profound student of the subject, and in the case of direct dealings with officials (ryotwari system) they were paying "between one-eighth and one-twelfth of the gross produce." This condition left the peasant impoverished, and he grew more so as the pressure upon the land continued to increase. In successive decades of the twentieth century the landowner in one way or another got more and more of the crop. The Planning Commission says that "in several parts of the country today as much as one-half of the produce goes to the landlord. He makes no return to the peasants in the shape of improvements; he deals with them mercilessly in auctioning his lands for rental; he confuses his accounts so as to get more than is due; he becomes a moneylender charging excessive interest." Hence the peasant's margin of profit for "better farming" and "better living" has steadily shrunk until, as we have seen above, he is now practicing poorer farming and enduring poorer living than his ancestors in the second half of the nineteenth century.

Agrarian reform got its greatest impetus when the peasants themselves began to form associations for their advancement. A number of peasant societies came into existence from about 1920, especially in the heavily settled regions of Bengal, Bihar, the United Provinces, and the Punjab, that is, in the highly productive and densely populated northern plain. Here the landlord system of tenure prevailed. The reform organizations went by various names, of which one of the most widely used was Kisan Sabha ("Peasants' Association"), while another was Krishak Proja ("Agriculturist Masses"). Their purpose was to alter the tenure system and reduce peasant indebtedness. They hoped to get relief through reduction in the amount of rent paid or abolition of landlordism and reversion of the land to peasant proprietorship. They wanted alleviation or removal of the landlord's right of eviction and establishment of coöperative credit and marketing systems.

When Congress launched its first Non-Coöperation Campaign, Gandhi, who was deeply concerned by peasant problems, won over the existing peasant organizations. It was a kind of paradox for him to do so, for Congress was getting its financial support and administrative direction from the middle classes, who were likely to be landowners. At that time Congress had no constructive policy on either agrarian or industrial labor problems. Gandhi's own attitude was that no one class should benefit at the expense of another but all should unselfishly work together. Landlords and industrialists, peasants and workers should not treat each other as enemies but should practice mutual forbearance and tolerance. The one should not withhold rent or go on strikes; the other should provide good living and working conditions, take only a just amount in rent, and pay fair wages. Under the application of this teaching the landlords lost nothing and the peasants gained nothing.

Other elements in the Congress, however, headed by Nehru, felt that a stronger Congress policy was needed for effecting agrarian reform. They were spurred on too in the late 1920's when the Communists sought political leadership of the peasants and workers. The "Draft Program of Action of the Communist Party of India" published late in 1930 included a section on "Peasant Demands," which called for confiscation without compensation of all lands and estates, forests, and pastures of the native princes, landlords, moneylenders, and the British Government, and the transference to peasant committees for use by the toiling masses of the peasantry . . . immediate confiscation of all plantations . . . immediate nationalization of the whole system of irrigation, complete cancellation of all indebtedness and taxes . . . the peasantry and agricultural proletariat to engage in all kinds of political demonstrations, and collective refusal to pay taxes and dues . . . refusal to pay rent . . . refusal to pay debts and arrears to government, the landlords, and the moneylenders in any form whatsoever . . .

This sweeping program was a challenge to both Government and Congress.

When Congress as a whole still would not adopt a clear agrarian program, a number of liberal and left-wing Congress members in 1934 formed the Congress Socialist Party. Functioning as a group within Congress, this subparty coöperated with the peasant associations, for a time controlled them, and urged Congress to admit them as a unit, but the more conservative elements in Congress defeated this.

In 1936, when the first elections under the 1935 Constitution were coming up, many of the separate peasant groups came together as the All-India Kisan Sabha. This adopted a resolution stating, "The Kisan movement stands for the achievement of ultimate economic and political power for the producing masses through its active participation in the national struggle for winning complete independence," and demanded a series of reforms including abolition of landlordism, cancellation of arrears of debt, rent reduction, and many others similar to Communist Party demands. It also adopted the red flag, but not the hammer and sickle, as its emblem.

At about the same time (1936), in connection with the same forthcoming elections, Nehru and his associates persuaded Congress to include in its election Manifesto a statement which, as Nehru has described it in his *Unity of India,* advocated "a reform of the system of land tenure and revenue and rent, and an equitable adjustment of the burden on agricultural land, giving immediate relief to the smaller peasantry by a substantial reduction of agricultural rent and revenue now paid by them and exempting uneconomic holdings from payment of rent and revenue."

This was a commitment, but when Congress set up its ministries in 1937 it was slow in fulfilling it. It did, however, introduce legislation which effected some reforms in tenancy, limited the rights of landlords, and abolished forced labor. These were still far from satisfying the peasantry. Between 1942 and 1944, when the British were suppressing the Congress by jailing its leaders but letting the Communist Party have free rein, communists gained control of the Kisan Sabhas.

After independence and partition Congress again took up the agrarian question and had acts passed in many states (especially in Uttar Pradesh, Bombay, Madhya Pradesh) which were designed to effect further reforms. They included provisions for recompensing the ousted landlords, usually through payments by the peasants who were getting the land, limitation upon the size of future acquisitions (50 acres in Bombay, 30 in Uttar Pradesh), restrictions upon the eviction of tenants-at-will. Some provisions have been severely criticized, especially that requiring compensation of the landlords by the tenants, who have no resources in sight for doing so. In Pakistan some agrarian legislation, similarly ameliorative, has been enacted in the Punjab.

The Indian Planning Commission recommends complete elimination of the variety of landlordism known as zamindari, and in ryotwari areas proposes a careful definition of tenant rights for a number of purposes. These are to prevent eviction except for cause, to enable a tenant to make improvements at the landlord's expense, to define the minimum leasehold period, to grant tenants the right of purchasing the land they cultivate at prices fixed by revenue courts, and to limit the amount of land anyone may acquire in the future.

The ultimate goal of the scheme is to be Village Coöperative Management. The entire holdings of a village are to be treated as a single farm, but individual owners are to receive annual harvest dividends according to the extent of their ownership. Workers are to receive compensation according to the amount of work they contribute. A management body is to assign cultivation to individual families or groups of families, working on blocks of land of appropriate size, as local circumstances may suggest. Such coöperative village management is to be available to any village on demand made by two-thirds of the owners or permanent tenants holding not less than one-half the cultivated area of the village, whereupon the system will apply to the entire area of the village including the holdings of the minority.

On the way to achieving this ultimate goal, the Planning Commission recommends as a program for immediate action, the founding of Village Production Councils, the establishment of Registered Farms, and the promotion of Coöperative Farming Societies. The Village Production Councils, organized to serve the entire village community, would frame production programs and budgets, be the channel for Government assistance, arrange for buying new land under cultivation, set minimum standards of tillage, develop devices, such as prizes, for stimulating production, promote community enterprises, help secure raw materials for village artisans, assist in the procurement and sale of surplus food grains. A Registered Farm would be of a prescribed size, should adhere to certain standards of efficiency, varying in different areas, should sell surplus grain to the Government, and should insure fair wages and good working conditions. The Government would provide technical advice, supplies, and other forms of aid. Coöperative Farming Societies would be used as a step toward creation of Registered Farms and would be protected by special legislation. This program involves consolidation of fragmented landholdings, education of the peasantry in improved farming techniques, protection of landless agricultural laborers.

Closely allied to the agrarian problem is the development of irrigation and power schemes, somewhat like our Tennessee Valley Authority. In undivided India about 24 per cent of the total cultivated area was irrigated (72 million acres out of 298). Since irrigation is the surest way of providing water, it needs to be extended. Many multiple-purpose projects, large and small, have been considered for utilizing the rivers, and the Government of India is developing four: the Bhakra-Nangal Project on the Sutlej River in the northeastern Punjab; the Mahanadi Project (Hirakud Dam) in Orissa; the Damodar Valley Corporation scheme in Bihar; and the Tungabhadra Project (Harike) for Madras and Hyderabad. These are to be completed in 1955 and 1956. Their total cost is to be Rs. 2,871,000,000 ($574,200,000); and they are to irrigate about 6,335,000 acres and generate about 930,000 kilowatts of power. The various states have further projects, great and small, under way and many more in planning (all together about 200) to cost a total of Rs. 4,472,800,000 ($894,530,000), and to irrigate 10,166,000 acres and generate 1,000,000 kilowatts of power. Because competition is so severe among all kinds of projects seeking any of the country's limited financing, it is exceedingly doubtful that many of these can be undertaken and completed. It is significant, however, that they are based upon need and if effected would contribute valuably to the country's economy.

Pakistan in its part in the Colombo Plan aims primarily at agricultural development. It has had an Agricultural Enquiry Committee at work under Lord Boyd Orr to deal with soil erosion, waterlogging, and other problems. It has provided for a number of agricultural developments and agricultural education, financing, coöperation, and marketing. Under the Colombo Plan it has two large irrigation and power schemes. One is located about a hundred miles from the mouth of the Indus, and is to irrigate about three million acres. In West Punjab is a scheme centered at Rasul to irrigate another 700,000 acres by means of 1800 tube wells electrically operated by a new hydroelectric plant. This same plant is to be used for draining water from areas already irrigated and now waterlogged. There are a number of smaller schemes. The Ganges-Kobadak Development Project in the Khulna district, East Bengal, would prepare more than two million acres for irrigation, generate power, facilitate navigation, and assist food control. All projects taken together are, if financed and successful, to increase agricultural production by more than one-third, with emphasis on food and other crops, oil seeds, fruits, sugar cane, vegetables, cotton, cereals, pulses, jute. Other power plants, not used for agriculture, are planned in both Eastern and Western Pakistan to produce 280,000 kilowatts. Pakistan obtained a loan of $27.2 million from the World Bank in March 1952, for rehabilitating and modernizing her railways.

Forest conservation, development of use of forest products, land utilization, soil conservation, checking of desiccation, are other important problems in the subcontinent.

The extension of fisheries—fresh, brackish, and marine—could increase the food resources. It has been estimated that the present consumption is less than 3.5 pounds per capita a year, as against 16 in Ceylon and 70 in Burma. The fishermen would have to be organized and helped to obtain supplies and market the catch.

The extraction of the subcontinent's mineral resources, most of which lie in India, needs development. This country now produces coal, iron ore, manganese ore, mica, gold, ilmenite, and building materials, and has deposits of bauxite, industrial clays, steatite, chromite, atomic energy minerals, refractory minerals, and abrasives. For any large industrial production these would need to be supplemented by imports of sulphur, copper, tin, nickel, lead, zinc, graphite, cobalt, mercury, and liquid fuels. The Indian mining industry is poorly organized and methods are antiquated and uneconomic. Labor usually has the most backward of working conditions.

Industrial development has to proceed side by side with agricultural. Almost all the subcontinent's existing industry is located in India, and it is weak and lopsided, producing consumers' goods, hardly any producers' goods. Its greatest strength is in cotton textiles, where it has a capacity of 1.65 billion pounds of yarn and 4.72 billion yards of cloth annually (production of 4.084 billion yards in 1951, supplemented by about half as much hand-loom manufacture), and in jute. The two industries together have about 500 mills and employ about a million workers. It has an annual production of finished steel of about one million or more tons (1,064,000 in 1951), some ordnance plants, various cement (3.1 million tons in 1951), sugar (690,000 tons in 1951), paper, soap, matches, and some small production of power alcohol (5.6 million bulk gallons in 1951), chemicals, nonferrous metals, bicycles, radios, automobile bodies, electric fans, domestic appliances. India raises about 30 million tons of coal annually (34 million in 1951). There is a shipbuilding yard at Vizagapatam. Since the war India has made the first beginnings in manufacturing machine tools, Diesel engines, textile machinery, locomotives. By defining "industry" liberally it may possibly be said to employ 2.5 million persons, a better figure would be 2 million.

The Indian Planning Commission sees, as objectives of industrial development, production of the tools and materials needed for agriculture, irrigation, and power; increase of the supply of consumers' goods, enlargement of heavy industries (pig iron, steel, heavy chemicals, and others), and the filling in of gaps in the existing industrial structure. The supply of raw materials needs to be increased—this is in part a function of an agricultural program. These aims are to be furthered by the Industries (Development and Control) Bill 1949, enacted in October 1951. At the same time that controls and stimulants are being applied to big business, the Planning Commission would also have small-scale industries encouraged and influenced to work in coördination with large-scale industry. For the purpose of industrial expansion India sought (October 1952) a loan of $40 million from the International Bank for Reconstruction and Development to expand its steel production by 600,000 tons annually, and has eased its terms for investment of foreign capital.

Though Pakistan has published no over-all, coördinated, and detailed plan of industrial development, it has sought funds under the Colombo Plan to assist in expanding its cotton textile manufactures from the present 100 million yards a year to 450 million in the near future and 1.35 billion in 1957, in building six jute mills, so as to gain some degree of independence from India in jute manufacturing, and a paper mill.

The railways of the subcontinent need extensive rehabilitation. The highway system is rudimentary and can be tolerated only in a region where the bullock cart is the prevailing form of rural transport. Both nations need and plan port development. India wants to enlarge and improve existing ports and build two new ones in Kathiawar. Karachi, the only port in Western Pakistan, now badly congested, needs improvements. Chittagong, the only port in Eastern Pakistan at the time of partition, able then to handle 500,000 to 600,000 tons annually, is said to be capable of enlargement to handle several million tons; a new small port named Chulna was opened in the winter of 1951–1952. Neither country has much shipping. India would like to increase its present tonnage of 377,500 to 2,000,-000. Civil aviation is well established in both but now needs rehabilitation and extension.

Just as industrial production in the subcontinent is far below needs or potentialities, so the condition of industrial labor is badly substandard. It is small in numbers, poorly paid, compelled to accept inferior working conditions, provided few if any chances for training, ill-housed and fed, and inefficient. As organized at present it follows political rather than economic lines, though with diverse political allegiance. Its personnel is not drawn from a settled industrial population but chiefly from agricultural workers, usually landless and belonging to the depressed castes, who at times of seasonal unemployment or other economic distress migrate to urban areas for temporary jobs. It uses many women and children. Male workers often leave their families behind in the villages and return to them when conditions improve. Turnover is high, unit productivity low.

According to surveys made before the war, about one-half (46 to 49 per cent) of the worker's wages went for food; in the United States at that time the percentage was about 38. Now that the wholesale price index in India has been steadily rising until it stands (1951) at about 4½ times that of 1939, and wages have not advanced correspondingly, the percentage the Indian worker spends is probably more. Many families live in perpetual debt. There is a statutory limitation of 54 working hours to the week; in certain seasonal factories 60 hours are allowed. Prewar surveys in industrial cities revealed wretched living conditions. Most industrial cities now have labor camps. The evils of urban life have fallen upon industrial workers, and they are considered to be even worse now than before the war.

As in agriculture the landlords are an obstacle to necessary tenancy reform, so in the opinion of the liberal wing of Congress and the Socialist Party, to say nothing of the Communist Party, the industrial owners are the first obstruction to social justice. They exact excessive profits from their industry—a mere ten per cent for dividends is scorned—are slow to undertake new industry, being shy of any industry that may be nationalized, and pursue an arbitrary and inconsiderate labor policy. Labor has been irregular and undisciplined, but in view of its lack of education and opportunity to live the good life it can hardly be assigned the same responsibility that belongs to ownership.

The Government of India has endeavored through the Ministry of Labour to formulate and activate a reform program, as by the Factories Act 1948, the Mines Act, the Plantation Bill 1951, but these need vigorous enforcement to accomplish their purpose. The new Constitution explicitly recognizes workers' rights; the problem remains to enact effective implementing legislation. Labor conditions being what they are, it is no wonder that the subcontinent has had a good deal of industrial dispute and that political parties have endeavored to get control of the labor organizations.

Trade unionism began in India about 1920, though before that time there had been a few strikes and as early as 1887 the Indian National Congress had recognized that India had labor problems to solve. In 1918 the Madras Textile Union was formed and Gandhi led a non-violent strike of textile workers in Ahmedabad, which was successful and resulted in the birth of the Ahmedabad Textile Labor Association. Though Gandhi rejected the class struggle in favor of coöperative solution of problems, Indian trade unionism has not accepted this principle generally. In 1920 the All-India Trade Union Congress (AITUC) was formed with the coöperation of Congress, which made use of it in the First Non-Coöperation Movement (1920–1922), and several leading Congressmen at various times in its early years held its presidency—J. Nehru, C. R. Das, Subhas Chandra Bose. But it was dissatisfied when Gandhi and Congress called off the Non-Coöperation campaign in 1922 with objectives unattained. The communists, who had been active in the Indian labor movement since 1920, in 1927 tried and in 1929 succeeded in getting control of the AITUC. Afterwards in 1931 they lost control and in the 1937 provincial elections Congress won a majority of the seats reserved for labor. Labor, however, was disappointed with its few gains under the Congress ministries in 1937–1939, and in 1942, when the Congress leaders were in detention and the communists at large, the latter again won so much power in the AITUC as practically to control it and they still do.

Various splits and realignments have occurred in the labor organizations since 1929 and besides the AITUC there are now three other important labor organizations in India. Of these the Indian National Trade Union Congress (INTUC), founded in 1947, is formally an independent body but it was organized under Congress leadership by Vallabhbhai Patel and Acharya Kripalani. The INTUC accepts the Gandhian principle of coöperation between management and labor and a certain degree of Government leadership. In return the Government nominates members of it to the International Labor Organization, considering it the most representative Indian labor group.

In 1948 the Hind Mazdoor Sabha (Indian Labor Association, HMS) was founded chiefly at the inspiration of the Socialist Party, which is an independent successor to the (former) Congress Socialist Party and is headed by Jaiprakash Narain. Another labor organization was founded in 1949 under the name United Trades Union Congress (UTUC) by certain non-party Socialists, including Professor K. T. Shah, the well-known economist.

There is also an All-India Railwaymen's Federation (AIRF), which is not a trade union congress, but a federation of unions aligned with various parties; its most influential element seems to be the Socialist.

The membership of the four trades union Congresses is hard to determine, since requirements are loose and the figures which each group issues are challenged by its rivals. In March and May 1949, the Calcutta *Statesman* gave the following figures, which seem high, perhaps including seasonal drifting workers:

Organization	Number of Members	Number of Affiliated Unions
INTUC	986,983	707
AITUC	679,143	734
HMS	618,802	380
UTUC	347,428	236
Total	2,632,356	2,057

Trades unions in India are poorly financed and provide almost no hardship benefits for workers. They are set up by industry or locality, rather than by craft, and get much of their direction from middle-class leaders. Nevertheless they have promoted labor's sense of solidarity and have organized large strikes, as in the Bombay textile industry in 1928 and 1950.

In Pakistan trade unionism is little developed because industry is small and the workers few. One organization is the Pakistan Trade Unions Congress, communist-controlled, whose president until his arrest on charges of complicity in a revolutionary conspiracy case, March 1951, was Faiz Ahmed Faiz, editor of the *Pakistan Times* (Lahore). Another is the non-communist All-Pakistan Confederation of Labour organized in 1950 by the merger of two already existing labor organizations.

The improvement of living conditions in India and Pakistan, whether rural or urban, requires a great increase in low-cost housing. The total task of providing adequate housing would take so much in building materials, architectural designing, city and town planning, and financing that it can be accomplished only by minute and slow stages. All that either the central or the state governments can hope to do in a five- or ten-year period is to point a way. Meanwhile the underprivileged need social welfare work on an embracing scale, little of which can be realized or even planned.

Public health is another general problem of overwhelming size. Throughout India and Pakistan at present undernourishment is widespread due to insufficient or inferior (such as rice) diet, accentuated by frequent food adulteration. Less than 30 of the 58 cities with a population of 100,000 or more have sanitary sewage disposal systems; about a dozen more have part systems; all together about 3 per cent of the total population have sewer service. In 1946 the Health Survey and Development Committee (Bhore Committee) reported that only 6 per cent of the towns (a "town" is an urban area of 5000 or more population) had a protected water supply and this served only a fraction of the population of those towns. The situation now is generally thought to be worse. The same Committee reported that there was one physician for 6300 people, one nurse for 43,000, one midwife for 60,000. The Government of India's Planning Commission aims at one doctor to 2000, one nurse to 500, one midwife to 4000. There is heavy incidence of disease, high maternity and infant mortality. Industrial health is still a field which is almost virgin.

Modern scientific medical education is offered in only some 20 institutions in India and three in Pakistan. Drugs and surgical equipment are mostly imported. Meanwhile some states support schools and hospitals which teach and practice the antiquated traditional Hindu (Ayurvedic) and Muslim (Unani) systems of medicine, and in 1948 the Director of Public Health, Dr. Jivraj N. Mehta, in India, endorsed this policy on the theory that any system is better than none at all. In September 1950 the Health Ministers of India's States outlined a plan to put traditional medicine on a parity with western medicine. Vital statistics in the subcontinent are not systematically collected and are unreliable.

In the quest for the good life both nations have a special problem concerning the status of women. This affects less than half of the population, for there is a general sex disparity in the subcontinent in favor of males (1000 to 934, according to the 1941 census), as contrasted with the disparity in favor of females in "advanced" countries. Of women of reproductive age in the subcontinent an unusually high percentage is married or widowed; less than 5 per cent are unmarried. Both the Hindu and the Muslim communities traditionally impose disabilities upon women, but of different sorts, and both give them religious sanction.

Hindu traditional law permits plural marriage for males, though financial considerations usually make it impracticable. A Hindu woman, however, may marry only once, and after her husband's death must remain a widow, and be subject to lowered status in the family and constricted social privileges. Since a Hindu marriage is a religious sacrament and not a contract, divorce is permitted to neither party, and a husband may not discontinue to support a wife.

Among Hindus child marriage is common. Some ancient legal authorities required marriage of girls before first menstruation. Such a marriage relieves a family of the need to support a daughter and gives the husband's family her maximum service in raising children and so perpetuating the line. The traditional Hindu joint family system, by which all males share the family income, encourages early marriage of sons. The young husband does not need to earn the support of his wife and children; the family provides it as an accepted obligation.

Though Muslim traditional practice encourages veiling and seclusion of women, it does not regard marriage as a sacrament and therefore allows divorce and remarriage for both sexes. It also allows polygamy for men. Islamic law permits four wives at once—in the India-Pakistan subcontinent Muslim public opinion disapproves the practice, though for centuries and down to within the past two decades Muslims of some prominence have published heated defenses of polygamy. A Muslim woman, however, may have only one husband at a time.

Legally a Hindu woman's position is inferior to man's. By traditional Hindu law a woman does not share in the inheritance of family property. The Hindu joint family system is coparcenary; property belongs to the family, but that means to the males, and inheritance is by survivorship, not by succession. Each male of the family has a right in it by birth. When a woman marries, she enters the family of her husband and departs from her father's family, having no property rights in either. She has property rights only under certain conditions and only to certain kinds of property, specifically her dowry. These various provisions, codified by Brahmans, apply to only a portion of the Hindu community. Many other parts of it permit divorce, remarriage of widows, and sometimes female inheritance of property, though there has been a constant tendency for groups coming into the Hindu system or rising in it to accept a Brahmanical code.

Something was done to improve women's status in pre-independence times by nationalism. One of its impressive features was the participation of women from the time of the First Non-Coöperation Movement (1920–1922) when they were arrested by thousands. Muslim women took less part in public affairs than did Hindu women, yet in the 1930's, and since, a few have been politically prominent. In neither country is the right of suffrage a sex perquisite—votes for women became a reality in the different provinces by legislation first in Madras and Bombay in 1921. Since independence, India especially has had women holding high public office—the Minister for Health is a woman (Rajkumari Amritlal Kaur) and so was for long the tenant of India's ambassadorship to the United States (Madame Vijaya Lakshmi Pandit).

Islamic law, not recognizing the joint male family, permits wives and daughters to inherit property. Among Muslims in the subcontinent segregation of women is common, though nowadays many outstanding Muslim leaders oppose or ignore it as being intellectually narrowing and physically harmful. A conspicuous example was the late Prime Minister of Pakistan, Liaquat Ali Khan, whose Begum ("Lady") has exercised the same freedom in her country that Hindu women leaders do in India.

Various kinds of reform measures have been adopted or are contemplated. In undivided India an Age of Consent Bill (Sarda Bill) was enacted in 1930 but for lack of proper implementing provisions and the support of public opinion could not be enforced. A good many years before independence, advanced Hindu opinion was in favor of revising and codifying the traditional Hindu Laws concerning marriage, divorce, succession to property. The Central Legislature adopted a Hindu Women's Rights to Property Act in 1937, and in 1941 a legislative committee headed by Sir B. N. Rau (later head of India's permanent delegation to the United Nations) was appointed to consider wider reform of Hindu law. After some years of study and investigation in all parts of India, it recommended a wide program which dealt with intestate and testamentary succession, marriage and divorce, minority and guardianship, and adoption. It provided for inheritance by daughters and control by wives and daughters of their inheritance, admitted civil marriage, prohibited either sacramental or civil marriage if either spouse were alive (this would compel monogamy), recommended divorce under certain conditions (adultery or insanity) on the initiative of either husband or wife.

The present Government of India has before the Parliament a Hindu Code Bill embodying these recommendations. Conservative Hindu opinion is against the reforms, organizes hostile meetings, inspires speeches and press articles, and instigates protest demonstrations by women before Parliament, sometimes extending over weeks. Within the Government of India some ministers doubt the bill's justification, certainly its political expediency. In September 1951, Parliament adopted as a separate bill the clause saying that the Hindu Code Bill should apply to Hindus, Buddhists, Jains, Sikhs— the religions that are indigenous to India—but the rest of it was temporarily shelved.

Solution of the subcontinent's social and economic problems requires large expenditure of money, that is, large for India and Pakistan. The Government of India has an annual ordinary revenue of only about $900,000,000, Pakistan of about $371,100,000. These sums are an index of the small resources of the two countries. Neither nation can raise from its own resources the amount to do much more than hold its own in a worsening situation. Each, therefore, is seeking outside aid. Under the Colombo Plan India expects to use about $3.5 billion, Pakistan about $760 million. The Government of India's Planning Commission in its Draft Outline proposes the use of not only the funds available under the Colombo Plan, but also much more. The Five-Year Plan is in two parts, and the total amount to be spent in five years is Rs. 1793 crores ($3.77 billion). Of this total, Rs. 1493 crores ($3.14 billion) the Commission says must certainly be spent. It is to go chiefly for projects already started, and

takes into account the resources that can be raised internally through taxation and borrowing, external assistance which has already been offered to India and which is likely to be available in this period for financing the Plan, and the possibility of being compelled to resort to deficit financing to the extent of about Rs. 290 crores ($609 million), if no further foreign assistance is forthcoming.

This part of the Plan, the Commission says, "will barely restore the prewar availability of essential consumer goods by the end of 1955–1956." It will exhaust all the resources which India has in sight. But the Planning Commission points out that "to ensure a balanced and sustained utilization of the technical organization built up in connection with the various projects included in the first part," the second part of the Plan should be implemented costing Rs. 300 crores ($620 million). This would require additional financing, not yet in sight, that would have to be supplied from outside. If Pakistan evolves an over-all plan for development, it too will need to look outside its own resources for assistance.

Failing outside assistance both India and Pakistan seem unlikely to emerge from their present critical situation. They will constitute an area where democratization has to overcome the most severe economic and social handicaps and will be countries whose people, if disappointed in not achieving the good life by constitutional evolution, may become receptive to counsels of desperation and violence.

15. Foreign Affairs

The most important foreign relations of India and Pakistan are those with each other. These have been discussed earlier in this book. Associated with these are relations with Afghanistan, which are most strongly influenced by the aspirations of many Pashtu-speaking people to become a nation called Pakhtunistan "Land of the Pathans." These inhabit an area consisting of eastern Afghanistan, the western part of the North-West Frontier Province in Pakistan, and the no-man's land between the two. Such a nation would presumably incline more to Afghanistan than to Pakistan, which latter claims that Afghanistan supports the movement. This quarrel and a border dispute caused Pakistan in 1949 to recall its Ambassador from Kabul. The political aspects of the situation are heightened by the irritation which Afghanistan feels in having to get imports through Pakistan by way of Karachi, its nearest seaport. India and Afghanistan, being on opposite sides of Pakistan and both having quarrels with it, are drawn together in this connection.

Affecting matters strongly domestic in character have been the negotiations of India with Portugal and France concerning their possessions in India. Each of these European nations has small establishments inherited from the sixteenth and eighteenth centuries. France has relinquished Chandernagore (in modern times a suburb of Calcutta) but retains four other possessions, of which the most important is Pondicherry, an inferior port about a hundred miles south of Madras, through which there is a certain amount of smuggling. Portugal holds Goa about 250 miles south of Bombay, and Daman, about 100 miles north of Bombay, and the small island and port of Diu, at the southern tip of the peninsula of Kathiawar. Goa, too, has been a center of smuggling. The area of the French and Portuguese holdings is small and the total population only about a million, but India wants to eliminate all foreign ownership of any Indian territory. The negotiations with Portugal especially have been tart. On November 1, 1952, B. Shiva Rao, India's representative in the Trusteeship Committee of the General Assembly of the United Nations, reviewed the situation in firm language before the Committee and quoted Nehru's declaration that these French and Portuguese possessions "must inevitably belong" to India.

An important category of foreign relations concerns India and Pakistan as members of the British Commonwealth of Nations. This includes questions of relationship with the United Kingdom as the core of the Commonwealth and relations with other members nations.

During the latter phases of the nationalist struggle Congress more than once formally committed itself to severing its political tie with Britain when it should win power. There were, of course, bound to be certain disadvantages in such an action. India would lose protection from the British Navy and the trade preferences it enjoyed with other Commonwealth members. Some Congressmen conceded these points, but Congress as a whole felt that other features of the British association, which it considered offensive, should be decisive. It wanted to eliminate every form of foreign domination and even the appearance of it. It was influenced also by the general Indian resentment against racial discrimination based upon color which humiliated Indians in South Africa, Canada, Australia, New Zealand.

It is possible that, if India had obtained Dominion Status as a single unpartitioned nation, it would have exercised its right to secede. At the time of independence and partition, when the costly results of partition were only dimly perceived and nationalist resentment still flamed high, most politically conscious persons in the subcontinent thought that of the two new Dominions India at least would leave the Commonwealth. Without doubt, most of the British public thought so, too. There was less apprehension in Britain concerning Pakistan, whose weaker position made her less likely to break away. Severance of relations by India was sure to be a serious blow to the Commonwealth. It would deprive the Commonwealth of nearly two-thirds of its population and a large part of its area, diminish its economic power, and impair its prestige in Asia and the world. During the first year of Dominion Status there seemed to be an omen in the decision of Burma, which formally severed all ties with the Commonwealth when it became a republic early in 1948. One of the first resolutions of the India Constituent Assembly preparatory to framing a Constitution, taken on January 22, 1947, six months before the British Parliament had passed the Indian Independence Act and while the Assembly still expected India to be an undivided nation, had asserted that India was to become an "independent sovereign republic." The situation was still delicate after independence and partition. Britain deplored the prospect of secession, but could only state, as it had stated previously in the Cabinet Mission's proposals in 1946, that it hoped the two new nations would maintain the connection.

After partition, in the case of India, it seems to have been Prime Minister Nehru who devised a solution continuing the association. In a Conference of the eight Commonwealth Prime Ministers, April 1949, he agreed to a declaration, ratified by the Indian Constituent Assembly in May, containing the words:

The Government of India have informed the other Governments of the Commonwealth of the intention of the Indian people that, under the new Constitution which is about to be adopted, India shall become a sovereign independent republic. The Government of India have, however, declared and affirmed India's desire to continue her full membership of the Commonwealth of Nations and her acceptance of the King as the symbol of the free association of its independent member nations and, as such, the head of the Commonwealth.

This decision was a matter of great gratification to all the rest of the Commonwealth. It was a relief to all parties in Britain, and Conservatives and Liberals, as well as Laborites, had worked to achieve it. Though India has not been satisfied with the British attitude on Kashmir, Britain and the British generally stand well with Indians today.

Pakistan has not redefined its position since receiving Dominion Status, and may not do so at all, since in various public statements high Government officials have expressed their country's satisfaction with the present relationship. For example, the late Prime Minister Liaquat Ali Khan, speaking before the Canadian House of Parliament on May 31, 1950, said:

If the Commonwealth does nothing more than give the world a lead in establishing the brotherhood of man, irrespective of race, creed or colour, it will still have made a notable contribution to the cause of human welfare . . . the Commonwealth has great opportunities for raising the hopes of mankind by outlawing war and aggression and the use of coercion as a method of settling disputes amongst its own members. We sincerely believe that in this way the free association of free nations can set the world an inspiring example and can give greater reality and efficiency not only to itself but also to the charter of the United Nations, to whose aims we are all pledged and whose success we all pray for.

There is a certain amount of anti-British sentiment in Pakistan, partly resulting from dissatisfaction with the Radcliffe Award demarcating the partition line and partly created by a feeling that Britain has not stood strongly enough at Pakistan's side in the disputes with India before the United Nations. A disappointing final solution concerning Kashmir could lead to agitation for secession from the Commonwealth. Britain's disputes with other Islamic nations—Iran, Egypt, Iraq—might intensify the situation because Pakistan has strong sympathy for them as Muslim kin.

In the relations of India and Pakistan with other Commonwealth states the thorniest issues have concerned the treatment of emigrants from the subcontinent and their descendants. There are somewhere around three million such persons in Ceylon, Malaya, Fiji, Mauritius, Jamaica, Trinidad, British Guiana, Kenya, Tanganyika, Uganda, Zanzibar, and the Union of South Africa. In Fiji, Trinidad, and British Guiana Indians constitute from one-third to nearly half of the population, in Mauritius about two-thirds. There are negligible numbers in Canada, Australia, and New Zealand, but the smallness of the numbers is the result only of strict exclusion policies (modified in Canada in 1950 to permit a small number of immigrants). A million more live in Burma, which was a member of the Commonwealth until 1948, and the status of Indians there was also a Commonwealth problem.

Indians first went to most of these regions as unskilled cheap labor, eagerly desired in undeveloped areas, such as South Africa (especially Natal) and the British West Indies. Often they went under indenture, being recruited from uneducated and economically underprivileged groups. They had low standards of living and were looked down upon in their new homes. When their terms of service were completed, they usually remained in the country, having few or no ties to draw them back to India. They did not, however, become assimilated. They retained an Indian language as their speech, adhered to their native religion, married almost exclusively among themselves, and observed many of their traditional social practices. Sometimes they were joined by other Indians, who came unbound by indenture, to make their living either as laborers or traders. A few

Indians came for the professions, mostly for law; Gandhi won his first fame in South Africa by championing the cause of his fellow Indians.

In most colonies and Dominions, Indians have been and still are subjected to disabilities of domicile, which make them second-class citizens. These include denial or elaborate restriction of franchise, limitation upon ownership of property and rights of trading, restriction of intermarriage with non-Indians, segregation of residence on "sanitary" grounds without any accompanying provision of "sanitary" facilities, denial or severe limitation of entry to public eating and amusement places frequented by "whites"—in short, some form or other of legal Jim-Crowism.

The Indians abroad looked back to the Government of India for protection of their civil rights and the Government of pre-independence undivided India accepted the responsibility. One might say that Indians living in foreign countries, even unto the third and fourth generation, are still looked upon as Indians. In their interest the Government of India conducted negotiations, frequently unprofitable, with the Dominions and the British Colonial Office. The reaction in India was resentment, especially toward the Dominions, where color prejudice was a factor. In the then colonies or possessions where the population, like that of India, was dark-skinned, agreements were worked out to protect Indian laborers and at the same time to control emigration from India within limits satisfactory to the receiving countries. Some of these agreements have at times proved insufficient, for example, that with Ceylon in April 1952, when new voting regulations were adopted which were going to operate to disenfranchise most of the resident Indians entitled to vote.

The Dominions and colonies which have higher living standards than India's have wanted protection from India's inexhaustible reservoir of unskilled, undernourished, cheap labor, and many Indians and Pakistanis have seen justice in this desire. They have also concluded that protection of their countries' own good name abroad requires control of emigration. Hence they have modified their bitterness at being excluded as a group. They remain firm, however, in demanding just civil status for Indians legally in Commonwealth states. In recent years, therefore, they have fought hard in the United Nations for a wide-extending code of human rights.

The one really bitter quarrel today is with the Union of South

Africa, where the Boers have been more race-conscious than the British. This Dominion has a long history of discrimination against Indians. The latest development came on March 31, 1951, when the Union put into operation a Group Areas Act, imposing segregation and a series of other restrictions. By it no one may live, acquire property, or conduct business in any area except one designated for his own racial group. India and Pakistan had already objected to this law and had laid a complaint before the United Nations General Assembly. The latter body, on December 2, 1950, had adopted a resolution proposing a round-table conference between them and the Union of South Africa and the establishment of a three-member commission to assist the negotiations. South Africa opposed the resolution while it was in debate, and in the sequel brusquely rejected the proposals as constituting "intervention in a matter essentially within the Union's domestic jurisdiction." In January 1952 India and some other Asian nations introduced a resolution in the United Nations condemning segregation as contrary to the United Nations Charter and its Declaration of Human Rights. When the General Assembly convened in the autumn of 1952 India again pressed the issue before the Special Political Committee, and Asian, Arab, and Latin-American nations joined her in a resolution calling for a United Nations commission to look into *apartheid* (race segregation) in South Africa.

Race discrimination in South Africa and exclusion policies in other Dominions could imperil Commonwealth solidarity and help create a future intra-Asian alignment that might disrupt it. If the Commonwealth is to continue, those members in which the rulership is white will have to gain and hold the confidence of those where the population is dark. The nationalist revolutions of Asia, some achieved and some still in progress, demand the removal of racism.

Membership in the Commonwealth is already felt by many thoughtful Indians and Pakistanis to be of less importance than association with other Asian nations. With the latter, they argue, India and Pakistan have the prospect of more productive commercial relations than with Commonwealth areas. With them, too, they have more mutual understanding because they have similar problems to solve and a similar dearth of resources to use in the solution. They also have a common affinity in that they themselves are Asians and constitute a group which is marked off from white-skinned western groups.

To appreciate the position of India and Pakistan in respect to their Asian relations it is necessary to recall two important features of their recent history and present internal situation which influence thinking on foreign relations. The first is the pressing poverty and population problem, which demands each nation's primary attention and the use in attacking it of all available material resources. The two nations cannot afford to dissipate any of their resources in unproductive expenditure, as for war; they are already economically overstrained because of their quarrel with each other. They have, therefore, in their dealings with other Asian nations the fundamental and compelling motive of maintaining peace between themselves and those nations and between those nations and European and American nations. For India and Pakistan with their weak economies, involvement in war would bring obliteration of the very basis of life. Neither nation would be likely to survive in its present form, but would have to be recreated, in what terms it would be impossible to foresee.

Secondly, because they have themselves only recently emerged from a colonial status and their people are still somewhat unassured of the intentions of the western industrialized powers, they are keenly sensitive to any infringement upon the independence of all Asian nations. Asian nations, they maintain, when in dispute with one another, should reach a settlement without interference from western nations and in such a dispute other Asian nations are the most interested external parties and should be the natural go-betweens and arbiters. This assertion of intra-Asian autonomy is buttressed by resentment of western racism and an unswerving promotion of their own modernizing economic, political, and social revolution. It is not accompanied, however, by general Asian solidarity; rather, disputes and jealousies exist among the various Asian nations.

The feeling against western imperialism explains the lukewarm support which India gave the western powers against the Japanese when the latter had occupied Indonesia, Indo-China, Siam, Malaya, and Burma, had bombed Calcutta, and stood poised at the Burma frontier to invade eastern India. Similarly, after the war was over, westerners were astounded at the intense sentiment which arose in India on behalf of those Indians who had collaborated with the Japanese in Malaya and Burma to form the Indian National Army, and which forced the Government to abandon the prosecution of that army's leaders for treason. To Indians there was after all not much difference between imperialist Japanese and imperialist westerners. What India's eyes were fixed upon was the common element of both, namely, the imperialism.

The conviction that Asian nations should work together for common international aims led India to convene the Asian Relations Conference in New Delhi during March and April 1947 (before partition). Twenty-eight countries participated, from the Near East, Southern Asia, Southeastern Asia, Central Asia, and the Far East. Some of these were Asian republics belonging to the Soviet Union. At the Conference, the topics discussed were national movements for freedom, national problems and inter-Asian migration, transition from colonial to national economy, agricultural reconstruction and industrial development, labor problems and social services, cultural problems, the status of women and women's movements. In connection with the Conference there was an inter-Asian art exhibition, a science exhibition, and an archaeological exhibition. On the conclusion of the Conference an Asian relations organization was set up to provide for future meetings. At the Conference it was clear that these Asian nations felt that they had common interests of political, economic, and intellectual development, and faced social problems which required united action. It was also clear that these Asian countries felt that they must preserve their Asian independence against any political or economic encroachment from the west. Some years later, India, Pakistan, and other Asian nations created the Asian-Arab bloc, which has become a strong force in the United Nations. But neither the Asian Relations Conference nor the Asian-Arab bloc has shown the existence of Asian solidarity or created a "third force" in international affairs, which some observers feared. Nor has either shown that India is dominant in Asian affairs or wishful to become so.

In their relations with other Asian nations, India and Pakistan, subject to the conditions already mentioned, tend to cast their glances in opposite geographical directions. Though each has a concern with all of Asia, India looks more toward Southeast Asia and the Far East, while Pakistan looks prevailingly toward the Near and Middle East. This divergence has a basis in history. From India's indigenous traditional culture, much of religion, literature, drama, language, folklore, script, architecture, sculpture, dance, family, personal and place names, and law has gone out by sea to Burma, Siam, Malaya, Cambodia, and Indonesia, even to Vietnam. By land it has gone to Central Asia. It was carried by colonizers and merchants and occasionally by conquerors. From some of these areas items have gone still farther, by sea from Southeast Asia to the Philippines and the Pacific, by land from Central Asia to China and Korea, and from these last regions still farther by sea to Japan. India has been one of the great contributors to civilization in Southeast Asia and the Far East, and is well aware of her contributions. Those regions on their side are aware of their borrowing, and ties have therefore been created and are recognized. The new nation of India, where nationality has had the indigenous Indian culture as its matrix, stands now as friend and kin to them, somewhat as Europe does to the Americas.

Pakistan, as a Muslim nation adhering in large measure to a non-indigenous culture, looks back to the lands where Islam was born and became great. This is natural enough. Indian Islam has an uneasy stance in the subcontinent and seeks to steady itself by leaning upon the Muslim west. Part of the motivation is a still larger desire to see all Islamic nations working together. When a Conference of Muslim divines from all Islam was held in Karachi in February 1952, Prime Minister Khwaja Nazimuddin said that Pakistan's "existence has brought the unification of the Muslim world and the cohesion of the *Millat* (Faith) within the pale of possibility." Shortly afterwards Pakistan proposed a conference in Karachi of the Prime Ministers of twelve Muslim countries (Afghanistan, Egypt, Indonesia, Iran, Iraq, Jordan, Lebanon, Libya, Saudi Arabia, Syria, Turkey, and Yemen) besides itself. The purpose would be to consult on questions of common interest. Today Pakistan seeks to be a part of Western Asia, though itself uncherished by the classical lands of Islam. Hence it would forget geography and normal economic relations, ignore the natural associations it should have with India, and cultivate instead new links with other Islamic nations, supplementing the existing connections of spiritual culture with fragile transmontane threads of political and economic intercourse.

India's relations with the nations of Southeast Asia have been basically determined by the attitudes mentioned above. The war was hardly over before the Indian National Congress, through its Working Committee, adopted (September 21, 1945) a resolution asking for freedom from "imperialist domination" of India, Burma, Malaya, Indo-China, and Indonesia.

The first reference of this outside India was to Indonesia. To Indian leaders there was only one just solution of that situation. That was that the Indonesians themselves should prescribe their own form of government and should not be compelled to accept any arrangement which would perpetuate Dutch control. From the time when Nehru and the other nationalist political leaders of India had been released from jail on June 15, 1945, and had shortly afterwards paid visits to Indonesia and Singapore, they had been indicating that they expected Indonesia to be self-governing, now that the Dutch had been expelled and an Indonesian Republic had come into existence. They were disappointed that the British had condoned, even helped, the restoration of Dutch power in Java. In 1947, when the Dutch failed to adhere to the terms of agreements they had made with the Indonesian republic, the Indians again expressed their keen disapproval.

After the Dutch in December 1948, in a "police action," moved by force of arms against Djokjakarta, then the capital of the Republic of Indonesia, and put President Soekarno and other leaders in detention, India convened a Conference on Indonesia (sometimes called the second Asian Relations Conference). It consisted of representatives from fifteen nations (Afghanistan, Australia, Burma, Ceylon, Egypt, Ethiopia, India, Iran, Iraq, Lebanon, Pakistan, the Philippines, Saudi Arabia, Syria, and Yemen) with observers from four others (China, Nepal, New Zealand, Thailand). No constituents of the Soviet Union were invited. In issuing the call to the Conference Nehru had spoken of the Dutch attack on the Indonesian Republic as "the most naked and unabashed aggression," and in opening the Conference he remarked, "Asia, too long submissive and dependent and a plaything of other countries, will no longer brook any interference with her freedom." Three days after its organization, the Conference adopted a series of drastic resolutions which it presented to the Security Council, and following the Conference some of the nations (Burma, Ceylon, India, Pakistan, and Saudi Arabia) represented at it imposed sanctions against the Dutch by denying facilities of transit by land, sea, or air. The immediate subsequent action of the Security Council was disappointing to India and the other participants; nevertheless, the final winning of Indonesian independence, by the terms of an agreement with the Netherlands on November 2, 1949, may be considered a result in part of this united stand by Asian nations.

India and Pakistan have not taken so forceful an attitude with respect to the Viet Minh League's nationalist movement in Indo-

China. Nehru said specifically in March 1950, ". . . in regard to Indo-China we have not interfered in any way and we intend keeping apart." He gave as his reason that countries emerging from colonialism do not like outside interference. Neither has India tried to interfere in the anti-British Communist-controlled movement in Malaya. Yet both movements have received considerable sympathy from Indians and Pakistanis. The Bao Dai government is widely viewed in the press as a French tool and the British methods of suppression in Malaya are usually condemned as harsh and anti-democratic. In each case there has been nothing equivocal about the attitude toward the position of the western nations in the dispute. Both the French and the British positions are considered indefensible by Indian, and to a less extent Pakistani, public opinion generally, as expressed in newspapers, editorials, and many speeches of political and cultural leaders.

With Burma India has consistently maintained good relations, standing today in the position of Burma's best friend. She has promoted economic aid to Burma for recovery from wartime losses during the Japanese occupation, and has offered to mediate between the government and the various unreconciled groups that have kept Burma's politics in violent confusion. India's leaders have been conspicuously friendly on such occasions as Burma's assumption of independence, and the prestige of India and Nehru is high there. Burma's policy of nationalizing its industries has been congenial to Nehru, and he and the leaders of the Burma government have had much in common. The troublesome issue of Indians in Burma and the restoration of property rights to the Indian moneylenders, who owned vast areas of Burma rice land before the war but were dispossessed by the Burmans during the war, have not impaired the generally good relationship.

Pakistan has had a less amiable relationship with Burma. Rice-smuggling from Burma into Eastern Pakistan has created friction; and so too the aspirations of the Muslim community which lives on the Arakan coast and speaks a kind of Hindustani. This community feels itself insufficiently represented in Burma government affairs, considers itself discriminated against by the majority Buddhist community—as did the Muslims of India in relation to the Hindus—and some of its members have indicated a desire to be a part of Pakistan. But the Pakistan government has stood apart from this situation. Another aspect of the same situation, however, has been that

Arakan Muslims have emigrated into Pakistan. It is claimed by the Pakistan Government that during the period 1949–1951 nearly a quarter of a million entered East Bengal, many carrying modern weapons supplied by communists, and the Pakistan government in December 1951 asked Burma to stop the movement and repatriate those already entered.

With Thailand (Siam), India's relations have been correct rather than cordial. Siam, under Marshal Pibul Songgram as Premier, supports a political ideology not congenial to Nehru, and when Nehru called the Conference on Indonesia in January 1949, Thailand at first refused to attend and later was represented only as an observer. If there were to be western pressure on Thailand, as by the French and British in the nineteenth century and by the British at the conclusion of the second World War, the two countries would doubtless be drawn close together. Pakistan and Thailand have no relations of particular significance.

Toward Japan the Indian attitude since the war has not been one of animosity. Indians still have considerable admiration for the Japanese as the first Asian people of modern times to defeat a western power. Subhash Chandra Bose, who fled India, then collaborated with the Japanese, and was "Leader" of the Japanese-organized Indian National Army in Singapore and Burma, was widely popular in his native Bengal and other parts of India as well. In September 1951, when the Japanese peace treaty was signed in San Francisco, India stayed away. India's feeling against western control of Asian nations brought her to protest that the treaty limited Japan's freedom to make its own defense arrangements and deprived it of territory, the Ryuku and Bonin Islands, whose people have strong historic affinities with Japan. India later separately terminated her war with Japan, formally signing a treaty in June, 1952.

India's solicitude for Japan on general Asian nationalist grounds outweighs apparently the potential economic rivalry between the two countries. Before the war Japan had large markets in Southeast Asia and her cotton textile industry sent its products not only there but to India as well, which protected itself by imposing prohibitive import duties. When the United States began to rebuild Japanese economy, Indian industry was alarmed lest its own aspirations to win the Southeast Asia market some day would be thwarted. It even feared that Japanese industry might again raid the Indian market. Yet the government and the newspapers and public opinion were practically unanimous in opposition to the treaty. In Pakistan there was also doubt about the treaty, but not enough to sway the government, which gave it hearty endorsement at San Francisco. To Pakistan the case of Japan was hardly worth a quarrel with western nations when the issue of Kashmir, much more important to her, was still undecided. Pakistan had been developing its trade with Japan, which helps to replace its diminished trade with India.

India's relations with the People's Government of China are again based upon the principle that as an Asian nation and the world's most populous nation, China should have all the status enjoyed by any western nation. This consideration overrides for India any existing or possible future conflict with China. Territorially, this means, first, the vigorous military and economic advance of Communist China into Tibet, over which China has long claimed suzerainty. Second is the reassertion of the ancient Chinese claim to parts of northern Burma and a corner of Assam, as in maps published in 1951. Third, the communist government might even reassert China's ancient claim to part of Kashmir.

In the economic development of Southeast Asia, India and China are natural rivals. There are large groups of both Indians and Chinese in Malaya, and representatives of both in Burma, where the Indians are much the more numerous, and in Thailand, Indo-China, and Indonesia, where the Chinese have by far the greater number. Whichever country, India or China, succeeds in developing modern industry would look to Southeast Asia as a market, and would have to compete with the other. Militarily, neither nation could unconcernedly see the other establish bases there.

Such considerations, however, are put in second place by India. The Indian view, as expressed by Nehru, is that China, after passing through a great revolution, has freely chosen its present government. This is a fact, he has maintained, that should be faced, and India was therefore the second nation outside the Russian orbit and Yugoslavia to give China recognition (the first was Burma on December 17, 1949; then India on December 30, 1949; Pakistan on January 4, 1950; Ceylon and the United Kingdom on January 6, 1950). India has maintained an active embassy in Peking; has continuously advocated admission of China to the United Nations since July 1950; opposed the branding of China as an aggressor in January 1951; led the Asian-Arab group in seeking reconciliation of the United Nations and China; regretted that communist China was not represented at the Japanese peace treaty in San Francisco; and has repeatedly requested the United Nations to take up the question of Formosa, which it has stated should be put under the existing China government.

This has all been done in spite of ancient close relations between the Kuomintang and the Indian National Congress, Chiang Kai-shek and Nehru, dating from 1925. At that time Congress supported the Kuomintang and with it Chiang as leader of a unified China. During the time of Japanese aggression on China in the 1930's Congress continued to support Chiang's government, and in August 1939 Nehru visited him in Chungking. Early in 1942 Chiang visited India seeking India's support for the war and aid for China against Japan, and an endorsement of his own unsteady government. Nehru, writing in jail in 1944, characterized the visit as "a great event in India," and he and other nationalist leaders considered that through it "the bonds that tied India and China grew stronger." But Nehru's primary desire respecting China was to see it united and strong, and when Chiang's government could not make it so, but the communists under Mao Tse-tung and Chou En-lai could, he supported the latter.

Another point that interests India in regard to China is the program of agricultural, social, and administrative reform of the new China government. China's most basic problem is the agrarian, as is also India's, and the communist government has focused its attention upon it. This has been the most significant feature of the new Chinese revolution in Indian eyes, not the degree of affiliation with the U.S.S.R., which India minimizes. India does not expect China to become a Russian tool or to become like Russia. Even Indian industrialists are not alarmed. G. D. Birla, one of the most influential of them, said (November 1951), "Our knowledge of the Chinese makes us believe they can never become narrow-type communists. We know that the Chinese capitalists in Malaya, Siam, and Burma take the side of the Chinese government, which strengthens us in this belief. Therefore we hope that through our friendship China will play an important role for world peace." China has been popular in India, and the two nations have exchanged cultural missions. China offered to sell grain to India to help during the 1951 shortage, but was able to ship only a very small amount. In May 1952 China agreed to sell India 100,000 tons of rice.

In spite of all this friendliness, India has not been free of apprehension about her Himalayan border. When China, after various preliminary threatening announcements and moves in 1950, invaded Tibet in October 1950, India formally protested, but the Chinese government stated flatly that "Tibet is an integral part of Chinese territory," called relations between itself and Tibet "a domestic problem of the People's Republic of China," and brusquely rejected the Indian protest. The late Deputy Prime Minister Vallabhbhai Patel called the Chinese move "aggression," but had no way to check it. India did, however, in December 1950, hasten to execute a treaty with the small Himalayan state of Sikkim, which it had occupied in June 1949, to prevent "bloodshed," gaining the right to conduct Sikkim's defense. It has also taken a strong part in Nepal's affairs, 1950–1952. This sovereign state is strategically located for a length of about 500 miles in the Himalayas bordering Tibet. In building up its defenses India stimulated reconstitution of the Nepal government and sent troops across the border to quell local uprisings. Nepalese politics, once the reconstitution was effected, have revolved chiefly around the issue of pro-Indianism versus pro-Chinese communism. India has also become concerned about the security of the Himalayan state Bhutan. India cannot help being suspicious of China, though in the larger interests of Asian solidarity against non-Asians it may play its apprehensions down.

Pakistan has been less wholehearted in supporting China, though popular sympathy for the new China government has appeared to be strong. It has generally acted with India on this matter before the United Nations, and like India has had an intense interest in China's agrarian reforms.

At the time of the Korean crisis, both India and Pakistan were slow in endorsing the first United Nations resolution of June 25, 1950, though eventually they both did. Neither nation has contributed troops, though India has sent a medical unit. In October 1950, India opposed the Security Council's resolution to cross the 38th parallel, and issued a warning on the basis of communications from K. M. Panikkar, its ambassador in Peking, that the crossing would bring China into the conflict. The United States newspapers seemed rather generally to consider this a bluff, having no real conception of the feeling in China. Later, in December, India besought China not to cross the 38th parallel when its forces were advancing southward. Throughout the Korean affair, India has offered its services as mediator, hoping to produce that peace which it regards not only as the world's major goal but also as its own first need in international affairs. The latest move in this connection came in November 1952 when India, seeking to break the deadlock in the armistice negotiations, offered a compromise solution of the decisive problem of repatriating prisoners of war. While the Western powers were discussing this, Russia flatly and harshly rejected it, and shortly afterward China, too, rejected it. In doing so, both nations seemed to risk a diplomatic defeat in non-communist Asia.

While India has conducted the more significant of the subcontinent's relations with Asian regions to the north and east, Pakistan has felt the deeper concern about those to the west. Both, however, disapproved the formation of Israel, though for different reasons. Pakistan, being a Muslim state created to affirm Muslim integrity as a nation, sided on religious grounds with its Arab fellow Muslims. India, whose leaders had fought the partition of the old India, objected to the partition of Palestine on principle. Nehru stated at the Asian Relations Conference (March 1947) that the people of India regarded Palestine as an essentially Arab region. India was one of the countries sponsoring the minority report of the United Nations Special Committee on Palestine (September 1947) which recommended a federation of Arab and Jewish states, wherein the Arab states were bound to be dominant, rather than partition. India at last recognized Israel on September 18, 1950, but only after three Islamic countries had recognized it—Turkey, Indonesia, and Iran. Pakistan continued not to recognize it, and as recently as March 21, 1952, Sir Mohammed Zafrullah Khan, Pakistan's Foreign Minister, reiterated his country's support of the Arab states' demands concerning Israel.

Pakistan's policy of cultivating pan-Islamic friendship—possibly expecting to become the leader in such a group—has progressed well enough with all Islamic countries except Afghanistan and the Hashimite kingdom of Jordan. As Pakistan's Foreign Minister, Sir Zafrullah Khan, claimed of his nation (August 18, 1951), "It has served actively . . . in the cause of independence of Indonesia, Libya, Eritrea, and Somaliland." Though none of these nations has many ties with Pakistan other than the cultural, promotion of Muslim culture, as the late Prime Minister Liaquat Ali Khan said in Washington May 4, 1950, is one of Pakistan's national aims and ranks second only to the integrity of the state itself. After Liaquat's assassination his successor Khwaja Nazimmudin, the new premier, said

(October 21, 1951), "Islam is a body, and the Muslim states represent the limbs of this body. Pain inflicted on any one part of the body gives pain and anguish to the whole body."

Pakistan's closest cultural ties are with Iran, which has been the chief channel of Islam into the India-Pakistan subcontinent, giving it much of specifically Iranian art, literature, script, vocabulary, social customs, dress, as well as transmitting Arabic Muslim religion and law. The two nations have exchanged cultural missions and executed the usual treaty of friendship and commerce, and the Shah paid a good-will visit to Pakistan early in 1950 (at exactly the time when Iran was recognizing Israel).

With Turkey, Pakistan's relations are correct and friendly, but hardly go beyond that point into active association. Pakistan admires Turkish achievement, and Turkey respects Pakistan. The two have executed the usual treaty, but economic and political ties are few and unimportant. Turkey, as the most secular of Islamic states in the Near and Middle East, is possibly farther removed in spirit from Pakistan than any of the others and correspondingly closer to India.

When Iran, then Egypt, and then Iraq exploded against Britain in the summer and autumn of 1951, Pakistan found itself in an embarrassing situation. It had a policy of close friendship with those countries; at the same time their immediate actions were being prejudicial to its interests. Iran's abrogation of Britain's oil rights threatened Pakistan's essential oil supply. Egypt's effort to break the treaty concerning the Suez Canal could interfere with the flow of trade to Pakistan from the West. Further, Pakistan wants British support in the United Nations in its quarrel with India. Hence it has tried to soothe both sides. In a speech on the Egyptian situation on November 22, 1951, Prime Minister Nazimuddin spoke in many words of Muslim unity and international coöperation, but said nothing positive about ways of settling the Anglo-Egyptian dispute.

India's situation is not much clearer. Though it has no policy of unity with the Muslim countries on religious grounds, it sympathizes with their nationalism, which Nehru calls a "legitimate growth," and views the present actions as resistance to western imperialism in Asia. It also does not wish to offend the sensibilities of its large Muslim population. At the same time success of Iran and Egypt in the quarrel with Britain would threaten Indian economic interests and might imperil defense as well, since Egypt and the other Near

Eastern nations could never hold the Suez Canal if the Soviet Union should try to press forward to it and so cut off India's communications with the West.

Both nations were indignant when the question of Tunisia was not put on the Security Council's agenda in the spring of 1952. Each sympathized with Tunisian nationalism against the French. The two nations joined other Asian and Arab nations in September 1952 in calling upon the General Assembly of the United Nations to take up charges against France of misrule in Morocco.

What are the relations of India and Pakistan with the Soviet Union and what are their attitudes toward communism? It is basic in this connection that neither the people nor the governments of these countries have viewed the U.S.S.R. and communism with the same alarm and preoccupation that exist in the United States. The cold war has seemed to them a struggle between the two great powers for world superiority, while communism has been viewed as a political and social philosophy with features of possible application to their countries' ills. It becomes a menace in their eyes deserving suppression only when it employs violence. The attitude in each country toward the U.S.S.R., therefore, is rarely one of open or widespread hostility. In newspaper editorials and private conversation it may be one of sufferance and reserve, or of mild sympathy or approval, or of pronounced friendliness. Whenever Russia takes the side of an Asian nationalist movement against a western power, then Russia appears to people in India and Pakistan to be on the right side. When the question of Indonesia was before the Security Council, Russia's position in supporting the Indonesian Republic's demands was more satisfactory to both the governments and press of India and Pakistan than the American, which during a large part of the discussion seemed to them unduly favorable to the Netherlands.

Russia has seemed to these nations better qualified to appreciate their problems than any of the world's other great nations. They feel that Russia at the time of her revolution was in an economic state not greatly unlike theirs at present, while her progress since has not removed her too far from that earlier condition to grasp the character and importance of their own present problems. Russia's advance in a third of a century, with the accompanying improvement in public education and health and increase of world power, stimulates the Indians and Pakistanis to think there may be profitable lessons in Russian techniques. India and Pakistan feel, too, that racial discrimination does not exist in Russia, as in Western Europe and

America. Russia has also generally maintained a neutral position in India-Pakistan quarrels, though this seemed to break when Malik at the United Nations in January 1952 supported India on the Kashmir question.

The relations of Russia with both nations are helped by the communist propagandists throughout the villages and in the urban industrial centers. Those who make this unceasing day-to-day campaign are of the same economic and social groups as the villagers and industrial workers to whom they address it. They speak primarily of food, shelter, wages, that is, they deal with the basic question of poverty; then they relate these to political institutions. No other foreign power has such an approach to the people.

Though the Indian and Pakistani public gives a full hearing to Russian propaganda, the governments and the leaders have by stages been hardening against Russia. Indian communist activity since the elections has hastened this. Nehru's case is illustrative. In 1927 on the tenth anniversary of the Russian Revolution, he visited Moscow at the invitation of the Society for Cultural Relations with Foreign Countries. While there he wrote a number of newspaper articles and on his return published (1928) a book based on them, *Soviet Russia*. His position is summarized, when he says (page 54), ". . . the impressions I carried back with me from Moscow were very favourable and all my reading has confirmed these impressions, although there is much that I do not understand and much that I do not like or admire." A few years later in his autobiography, written in 1934–1935, while in jail, he wrote (*Toward Freedom,* page 348):

As these pages will show, I am very far from being a communist. My roots are still perhaps partly in the nineteenth century, and I have been too much influenced by the humanist liberal tradition to get out of it completely. This bourgeois background follows me about and is naturally a source of irritation to many communists. I dislike dogmatism, and the treatment of Karl Marx's writings or any other books as revealed scripture which cannot be challenged, and the regimentation and heresy hunts which seem to be a feature of modern communism.

A few more years later in *The Discovery of India,* written during 1942–1945, while again in jail, he said (page 528):

. . . I know that in India the Communist party is completely divorced from, and is ignorant of, the national traditions that fill the minds of the people. It believes that communism necessarily implies a contempt for the past. So far as it is concerned, the history of the world began in November 1917 and everything that preceded this was preparatory and leading up to it. Normally speaking, in a country like India with large numbers of people on the verge of starvation and the economic structure cracking up, communism should have a wide appeal. In a sense there is that vague appeal, but the Communist party cannot take advantage of it, because it has cut itself off from the spring of national sentiment and speaks in a language which finds no echo in the hearts of the people. It remains an energetic but small group with no real roots.

Five years later, in a statement of October 16, 1950, he said, "Most of them (countries in Asia) are opposed to totalitarianism as represented by either communism or fascism." On January 31, 1951, he stated that communists in India were "bent only on rebellion and armed rebellion at that." In an interview in March 1951 (N. Cousins, *Talks with Nehru*), he said, "In recent years . . . the communist tendency has come into conflict with the nationalist tendency in many countries—India, Indonesia, Burma, and some other countries . . . Today in India communism is definitely opposed to nationalism." That same year (October 18, 1951), in his presidential address to the Indian National Congress, he spoke of communism as follows, "Communism, for all its triumphs in many fields, crushes the free spirit of man. Democracy itself gradually succumbs to the new cult of force and violence." And on May 22, 1952, he remarked that India "will never pay the price that the Soviet Union and China have paid to achieve progress." He described the activities of the Communist Party of India as "counter-revolutionary and completely out of date."

When in the summer of 1952 several private communist organizations in the U.S.S.R. and China offered food for famine relief in India to be distributed through communist front organizations there, the Government of India refused the gift, insisting that it should be distributed only by itself or by the Indian Red Cross.

Both India and Pakistan have tried to maintain nonpartisanship toward the cold war, India especially. The latter country's policy is for independent action, often described in the West as "neutralism," motivated by a desire to avoid "entangling alliances." Even before partition, at the time of the Interim Government on August 31, 1946, Nehru voiced this policy as leader of the government. He affirmed it December 4, 1947, in his first full-dress statement of India's foreign policy after the attainment of independence:

We have proclaimed during the past year that we will not attach ourselves to any particular group. That has nothing to do with neutrality or anything else, or with passivity. If there is a big war there is no particular reason why we should jump into it. Nevertheless, it is a little difficult now-a-days in world wars to be neutral. We are not going to join a war if we can help it and we are going to join the side which is to our interest when the choice comes to it.

He went on to say that India wished to coöperate with both the United States and the U.S.S.R., but "neither of these big blocs looks with favor on us. They think we are undependable because we cannot be sent a writ to vote this way or that way." A little later, in April 1948, he said that he did not believe that there would be a third World War in the near future, that India wants to be friendly with every country and follow its own line of policy on every question that may arise.

It is widely felt in India that India has nothing to gain from a third World War and India's destiny would be better served if she could act as a peacemaker between the two great powers, provide a bridge between them. This type of thinking is official Government of India policy. Speaking before the Indian Parliament on March 8, 1949, Nehru said,

Nevertheless, it is true that the background of Europe is not completely the background of India or the world and there is absolutely no reason why we should be asked to choose between this ideology and the other in toto.

He added,

Our main stake in world affairs is peace, to see that there is racial equality and that people who are still subjugated should be free. For the rest we do not desire to interfere in world affairs and we do not desire that other people should interfere in our affairs. If, however, there is interference, whether military, political, or economic, we shall resist it.

This position is supported by almost all shades of Indian opinion. It seems inevitable that as the Communist Party becomes more prominent in India and Pakistan and comes into ever more violent conflict with their democratic governments, positive anti-communist sentiment will increase and the lines in that conflict will become more clearly defined. In consequence anti-Russian and pro-Russian sentiment will also be more sharply differentiated. In the circumstances the two nations will find it increasingly difficult to maintain a position of nonpartisanship in the cold war, and will be drawn closer to the West, with which they have most of their productive international relationships.

16. Relations with the United States

The official relations of the United States with undivided India began only during the second World War. Before then India's foreign affairs were handled by the British Foreign Office, while the United States maintained in India only a few consular offices, lightly manned, to care for trade relations and the interests of the few hundred American citizens living in the country. The officers, conforming to the usual practice of the United States foreign service, stayed only a brief period in India before being transferred to some other country. The State Department received and transmitted most of its political communications concerning India through the British Foreign Office in London or the British Embassy in Washington. It received also a few direct reports from its own officers on social, political, and general economic conditions.

Unofficial relations between the United States and the subcontinent were also poorly cultivated. Each side lacked a substantial body of knowledge about the other, each had only the slenderest tradition of careful study about the other; in each, scholars, experts, and competent journalists to interpret the other were scarce. Public attitudes of both, therefore, were chiefly based on ignorance and subject to rapid fluctuation.

For most Americans at that time India had an ill-defined interest as a land of romantic color, ancient splendor, present poverty, and varied religions, which latter were characterized as debased, curious, or profound, according to the commentators' prepossessions. It had an economic interest to a few Americans for its trade, though in this respect it was vastly more important to Great Britain. There were also Americans who knew that certain Indians with nationalist aspirations were seeking their country's freedom from Britain, but these Americans usually had little if any knowledge of the origins, aims, and problems of Indian nationalism, and their views were determined

almost entirely by either an unreasoning Anglophobia or an un-
inquiring Anglophilia.

American contacts with India had started before the American
Revolution through soldiers and seamen who had lived both in the
American colonies and in India. After the Revolution during the re-
mainder of the eighteenth century and the early part of the nineteenth
many American ships visited Indian ports, trading within the limits
permitted by the East India Company's monopoly. Some decades
later, when the clippers were sailing from Atlantic ports around
Cape Horn to the Far East, a few made the full passage to India, to
return with tea, spices, and other commodities for the American
market and often curios of wood, metal, ivory, textiles, and even
now and then a sculpture or miniature painting, such as can still
be found in old New England homes. The persons engaged in this
enterprise were realistic businessmen and knew about trading conditions, but they had little curiosity about India's intellectual life,
history, or politics. America learned nothing of India from them nor
did they leave any impression of America in India.

American missionaries started to go to India in 1810. The great development of American missions in India under Congregational,
Baptist, and Presbyterian missionary societies started in the 1830's;
many other denominations followed in succeeding decades. India was
a major field for Protestant missions, and the American public's con-
ceptions of India to a large extent were influenced by the reporting
of returned missionaries. This was not always happy. Too often
missionaries were ardently evangelistic, at the same time untrained in
the study of religion as a science, uninformed about either their own
or Indian religions, and unappreciative generally of the civilizations
existing in India. Such persons would be inclined to picture America's
superior economic culture as attributable to superior religion and
morality, thus confusing the material and the spiritual. Back in the
United States they disparaged India for poverty, lack of sanitation
and education, and addiction to religious notions which they regarded
as irrational and reprehensible, though most of them could be matched
in character, if not in specific form, in the United States. The higher
culture of India they did not know and could not describe. The reports of this type of missionary were not counterbalanced by the
reports of those educational and medical missionaries who had intellectual curiosity and endeavored to learn about India. On returning to America the latter were likely to speak with knowledge

and sympathy, but they did not get the audiences that the others did.

The intellectual side of Indian culture had an introduction to America through Emerson and the Transcendentalists, who had become acquainted with Indian thought in translations by European scholars. Emerson and his associates contributed Indian ideas to American thought, but in the successive generations of transmission Americans lost sight of the Indian source.

There was a very small number of distinguished American scholars in the nineteenth century who worked on India but never got a large public audience. Their field was the traditional language and culture and they held chairs in American universities, where they carried on research and taught their few students. The first was William Dwight Whitney (1827–1894) of Yale. Four others, whose activities bridged the nineteenth and twentieth centuries were: Charles Rockwell Lanman (1850–1941) of Harvard; Maurice Bloomfield (1855–1928) of Johns Hopkins; E. Washburn Hopkins (1857–1932) of Yale; and A. V. Williams Jackson (1862–1937) of Columbia. These five scholars together with their pupils in the twentieth century and a few additional scholars from abroad, such as Ananda K. Coomaraswamy (1877–1947) at the Museum of Fine Arts in Boston, established a distinguished tradition of productive humanistic scholarship concerning India. But the number of American institutions willing to shelter such work was small. Only eight universities maintained chairs of Sanskrit or Indic Studies in the interwar period—Harvard, Yale, Columbia, Princeton, Pennsylvania, Johns Hopkins, Chicago, California. Only one museum (Boston) had a full-time curator of Indian art.

The high achievements of American humanistic scholarship concerning India were not matched in the social sciences. Before the first World War there was scarcely an American economist, sociologist, modern historian, political scientist, geographer, anthropologist, who was trained in the Indian aspect of his science or knew his way around in it. In the interwar period a very small number of social scientists, less than a dozen all told, came to qualify as competent on India. The dearth was felt during the second World War, when government agencies needed social scientists to work on India and could find scarcely a handful. Since the war some American universities, aided by philanthropic foundations or other benefactors, have provided specialized training. Some other Americans by direct contact with India or Pakistan and Indian or Pakistani materials have trained themselves. There are now in American academic institutions, government agencies, journalism, and other miscellaneous kinds of occupations possibly sixty or seventy Americans, the number depending upon the strictness of the standards applied, with an authoritative knowledge of some one of the humanities, social sciences, medical, physical, or technical sciences in relation to India or Pakistan. A few foreigners also live in America who are qualified specialists on India or Pakistan, possibly fifteen or twenty, excluding official representatives of the two countries.

Indian visitors to the United States who presented India's best until recently have been few. Occasionally there were such distinguished guests as Tagore or the poetess and nationalist leader Sarojini Naidu. They did not draw large audiences. Besides such outstanding figures, other Indians came to the United States to present India on the propagandist or journalist level. Sometimes these were well versed in their own culture and disinterested, sometimes less well motivated. The most celebrated was Swami Vivekananda (born Narendranath Datta, 1862–1902), who was a kind of reverse missionary, one come from India to America. Following him has been a continuous stream of swamis, some of them worthy and dignified men preaching India's thought in the best tradition of devotion, courtesy, and tolerance. Others, however, have too often come to America for mercenary purposes masked by religion, preying upon the credulous and bringing ridicule and discredit upon India. Frequently the Indian who received the most public attention was some playboy prince, whose escapades made good newspaper copy.

Thoughtful books about India had small sale. E. M. Forster's *Passage to India* was read less for what it said about India than for its quality as a work of art. Gandhi was admired by a few Americans for his devotion to non-violence, which they hoped could be applied universally, but to most Americans who heard of him he was a curiosity whose notions seemed fantastic and costume ludicrous, though he was conceded to have a fascinating skill in twisting the lion's tail.

Of improperly qualified Americans who wrote on India for other Americans the most conspicuous was Katherine Mayo. Her sensational *Mother India* (1927) had a wide audience in the United States. It shocked Americans, aroused loathing of India, and discredited that country before tens of thousands who would never hear another presentation. It offended Indians grievously, inspired a number of retaliatory attacks on America, and probably did more to create ill feeling between India and America than any other book ever published.

From these different sources have developed various American stereotypes about India, some of them mutually contradictory, which appear in the remarks of legislators, editorial writers, columnists, public speakers, and thereafter lodge as accepted truth in the minds of numerous readers or listeners. A large number of Americans, therefore, have a picture of India as a land of meditating omphalopsychites, hypnotic swamis, naked ascetics, bejeweled princes of fabulous wealth and incomparable harems, gross superstition, bareskinned, poverty-stricken, famine-ridden masses, where everyone is a beggar and caste is more important than life, the countryside terrifying with Bengal tigers, the houses and fields infested with hooded serpents, a land where disease and depravity are rampant. It all adds up to an unreal and shoddy India, for which Americans might feel wonder, envy, pity, loathing, ridicule, patronage, the urge to charity, but not the sympathy born of knowledge that Indians are the same kind of beings as themselves, creators of civilizations deserving the highest respect, capable today of giving as well as receiving, a people with whom America should coöperate on terms of equality.

In India before World War II the sources of information about America were as unreliable as those about India in America. It is doubtful if there were as many Indians competent in any American field at that time as there were Americans competent in an Indian field, small as the latter number was. Few Indians had come to America except students, whose purpose was not to study American institutions but to acquire technical science. Back in India they interpreted America in terms of their personal experiences. If they had been successful in their studies, made agreeable social contacts, been able to live in something better than constricting poverty, and found good jobs on returning home, they would speak well of America. But if they had had unpleasant experiences because of their skin color, they might be soured. If it had been difficult for them to adjust to the western world, so different from their own, they might leave America confused, frustrated, unfriendly.

The few Americans in prewar India did not do much to create a favorable public impression. This was particularly the case with the more illiberal type of evangelistic missionary, which was contemptuous of India's civilization. Educational and medical missions, however, were better appreciated. Until the first World War American missionaries usually stood behind the British and opposed nationalism but this condition began to change in the interwar period, as did also the strong American home control over the Indian mission churches.

Every winter a few round-the-world shiploads of American tourists rushed through the country from Bombay or Calcutta to Banaras, Agra, Delhi, perhaps a few other cities, dispensing their dollars freely, showing little discrimination in their purchase of curios, and revealing small understanding of Indian architecture, sculpture, and ideas, but usually expressing friendliness to Indians personally. Unconsciously they served to confirm the frequent Indian opinion of Americans as good-humored over-age children with too much spending money.

Certain isolated instances of contact left strong impressions upon Indians. One was American relief during the famines of 1896–1900. Gandhi's sympathetic press in America at certain periods pleased Indians, who liked America accordingly. On the negative side was the United States exclusion law, which prohibited Indians from immigrating and acquiring citizenship. When the Supreme Court confirmed this in 1922, Indians were humiliated and puzzled, and called American democracy hypocrisy. Though Congress in 1946 passed the India Immigration and Naturalization Bill which mitigated the situation, the memory of the years of exclusion still rankles, and is associated in the Indian and Pakistani mind with color prejudice, or with any unpleasant experiences which an Indian, like Tagore, may have had in America, as when the West Coast immigration authorities were discourteous to him.

The stereotypes in India and Pakistan concerning America are, like ours concerning India, often false and conflicting. They begin with a cliché which contrasts the spiritual East, represented best by themselves, and the material West, whose foremost illustration they consider to be the United States. The dollar they speak of as our god, the safety-deposit box our soul. We are all rich, they think, beyond an Indian's dream and engrossed in getting richer. We disdain the teachings of India's religious thinkers; we give only lip-service to those of Western Asia whose names we celebrate. We boast of our great and well-built cities, our comforts of life, our high standard of living, the size, elegance, speed, efficiency of everything American—all of which, it is clear, they envy deeply. We are a young nation, crude, bouncing, full of the new graduate's self-conceit. Our city streets are assumed to swarm with feather-hooded wild Indians and gun-toting gangsters. We have no sex morals, no idealism, but we are easygoing, democratic in our behavior, and in the mood free spenders. American movies seem to them to confirm it all.

The United States and India began to have more and closer contacts during the second World War. In the years 1939–1941 President Roosevelt apparently saw that India was going to be important in the war, that the western democracies would need Indian physical and moral support, and that Britain was alienating India. In the summer of 1941, therefore, the United States agreed with India and Britain for exchange of diplomatic representatives. The United States placed a Commissioner with the rank of Minister in New Delhi and India sent an Agent General with the same rank to Washington, to act under the British Embassy. The American press, too, began to recognize the importance of Indian news, and in due time several large newspapers stationed full-time correspondents there; the most sustained service has been that of the *New York Times*.

After we entered the war in December 1941, the question of India created a delicate situation between the United States and Britain, or more specifically between Roosevelt and Churchill. The British War Cabinet either could not or would not satisfy Indian leaders so as to win their coöperation in the war effort. Churchill had a long record of anti-Indianism, which was now obstructing the Indian aspirations for self-rule. It does not appear what Roosevelt thought when Churchill denied that the Atlantic Charter of August 1941 presaged freedom for India, but it is known, from allusions in R. E. Sherwood's *Roosevelt and Hopkins,* that whenever throughout the war Roosevelt felt it opportune to do so he urged that steps be taken to settle the Indian question.

In the spring of 1942 President Roosevelt sent to India Colonel Louis Johnson (afterwards Secretary of War in 1949) as his personal representative with the rank of Ambassador. A technical mission headed by Henry F. Grady, formerly Assistant Secretary of State and in 1947–1948 first American Ambassador to India, was also dispatched to survey industrial potential for the war effort. Johnson was in India when the British War Cabinet's Mission headed by Sir Stafford Cripps arrived in March 1942, and he talked unofficially with many of the Indian leaders and with Cripps, creating the impression that Roosevelt hoped for a liberal political settlement. This gave America prestige in Indian eyes. When the Cripps Mission failed, however, the United States press was unreserved in denunciation of the Indian leaders for refusing the proposals and for failing to coöperate in the war. Like the lady in the Helen Hokinson cartoon of the period, it had become "tired of being patient with India." It assessed all Indian actions according to their assumed harm or good to American war purposes, and British propaganda contributed to producing this result. Indians resented the reaction as unfair in not taking Indian necessities into account and on their side judged the United States in relation to their nationalist aspirations rather than war strategy. At the same time a number of Indians saw the Grady Mission as an American effort to get a foot in the door so that after the war America could establish an economic imperialism over India to succeed that of the British which was obviously starting to decline.

Two factors, however, regained much of Indian goodwill for America. One was the strong democratic world leadership of Roosevelt expressed in his speeches, his policies, and his sponsorship of material aid to all the United Nations including India. He already had appeared to Indians before the war as a protector of the oppressed, a champion in our time of freedom and democracy. They hoped for much from him, and his prestige increased steadily as he threw America's resources unreservedly and successfully into the war. When he died, grief in India was general and sincere. Through him the United States acquired a stature in Indian minds never achieved before or since. Specifically much was due in this respect to the activities of William Phillips, Roosevelt's second personal representative in India, who served in New Delhi with the rank of Ambassador from December 1942 to 1943. He endeavored to bring the Government of India and the Indian political parties into a working relationship but without success, in part because of the Government of India's reluctance to let him be a go-between: it refused him permission to see Gandhi, who was then in detention. Phillips strongly urged Roosevelt to press for a settlement of the Indian problem, and his views, though not officially revealed, were well known and appreciated in India. Afterwards some of his correspondence, published by a journalistic leak, confirmed the Indian presumptions.

The second factor was the presence of American troops in India. The G.I.'s were liked for their informality and easy social relations with Indians, so different from those of the British whom the people had known, and they helped smooth out some of the old misconceptions about Americans. When the war ended American stock stood high. America was idealized as a nation, in fact overidealized.

After the war the Indian warmth toward America began to cool as we disappointed Indian expectations and criticized Indian actions. We got away to a bad start by giving our moral support to the re-establishment of Dutch and French rule in Indonesia and Indo-China, though our policy in the Philippines commanded high approval. The net result was equivocal; we both aroused and allayed suspicion that we had "imperialist" leanings ourselves and were supporting Western imperialism in general at the expense of Asian nations. The first major postwar disappointment in India came from our failure to provide capital for industrial expansion. During the latter war years Indian industry had begun to draft plans for postwar development. Indians thought their country an ideal field for investment, and expected to be besieged by offers of funds which they could accept on favorable terms. These were not forthcoming for a variety of reasons, including the unsettled political condition resulting from the Hindu-Muslim conflict, the still unresolved nationalist issue, and the disadvantageous terms which India prescribed for the entry of foreign capital. Many Indians were also disappointed that America did not help India recover her blocked sterling balances in London, which Britain was obviously in no position to make over with any rapidity.

During the final stages of the British-Indian and Hindu-Muslim settlements America played a part not very clear to the public, but one which seemed on the outside to imply that any settlement if only it avoided civil war would be satisfactory. Thus in February 1947 the Department of State welcomed the then expected federal solution for an undivided India, applauding the Labour Government's decision that month. But when in June the Labour Government reversed itself and announced that the solution would be by partition, the State Department applauded this too. It appeared to many Indians that America's primary interest was Anglo-American concord rather than India's welfare. America was promoting, they felt, its alliances in the Cold War, which had developed in 1946, rather than considering the needs of Asian nations. India—and after partition India and Pakistan—and the United States, each in its own way, thought its position unappreciated by the other.

Relations of the United States with India had reached a low point in the spring of 1951, but after Chester Bowles went as Ambassador they improved, until by May 1952 they had reached a high point. Not only was the Indian attitude toward the United States good, but also that in the United States was improving toward India. In the latter connection it was notable that in May Senator Owen Brewster had the Director of the Faridabad Development Project present his work before other Senators in Washington. In Pakistan attitudes have been generally good since independence except for critical moments when Pakistan has felt America biased against her on the Kashmir issue and discriminating against her on technical aid. Pakistan has got far less of this than has India. Aiding the favorable impression created by Ambassador Bowles in India, as well as that produced by Ambassador Avra M. Warren in Pakistan, was the visit of Mrs. Eleanor Roosevelt to the two countries in February and March 1952. Her own work in the United Nations, as well as the great esteem in Asia for President Roosevelt brought her a warm personal welcome and reminded India and Pakistan afresh of America's friendship as Roosevelt had expressed and implemented it.

The specific issues on which the United States has disagreed with India and Pakistan since they attained independence have already been mentioned in this book. Most of them have been Asian matters. First, was the independence of Indonesia. Second, has been admission of the People's Government of China to the United Nations and the body of related issues. Third is the action in Korea. Fourth, in regard to Indo-China, India has viewed with disquiet our support of the French and Bao Dai. Fifth, India would not sign the Japanese Peace Treaty in San Francisco, but Pakistan did. Sixth, both India and Pakistan long disagreed with the United States concerning Israel. Seventh, both countries but especially Pakistan resent the fact that America took a leading part in keeping the question of Tunisia from being put on the Security Council's agenda in April 1952, thereby supporting France. Last and most important has been the position, especially of India, on the Cold War, in which India, maintaining her independent or neutral position, has not sided for (or against) the United States.

Other foreign issues which could affect United States relations with India and Pakistan are the dispute between Egypt and Britain concerning control of the Suez Canal, the dispute between Iran and Britain concerning oil, and the question of treaty revisions between Iraq and Britain. In all these, American sympathies have lain with Britain, while Pakistan has leaned toward its fellow-Muslim countries. In connection with the dispute of India and Pakistan over the Jammu and Kashmir State, the press and public in each country charges the United States with favoring the other in the Security

Council. Finally, on India's requests for grain in 1951, Indian editorial writers and the Indian public generally found the United
States slow in responding and felt an unfriendly tone in the debate
in Congress and the comments in the press. The American attitude
has variously and vaguely been characterized by Indians and Pakistanis as "imperialist," color conscious, callous, selfish.

The reaction of the United States press, public, and government to
Indian and Pakistani expression on these various issues has been one
of annoyance, rising often to exasperation. Americans have been
peculiarly irked by a tone of self-righteousness in the remarks of
Indians, especially some by Nehru, and have resented the charge of
acting "imperialistically." Americans have pointed out inconsistencies
in Indian and Pakistani arguments. For example, there is no simple
struggle in progress between western colonialism and Asian democratic aspirations. Instead Asia itself is full of internal conflicts—
interregional strife in the Near East, in the Far East, even in South
Asia between India and Pakistan. With regard to Korea, India's
attitude of first supporting and then not supporting the United Nations is characterized as illogical and indefensible. Americans have
maintained that mere economic aid to Asia is not enough. The area
must become militarily strong and must forestall subversion lest as
it prospers it proves to be a power vacuum and a temptation to aggression by some powerful and expansionist neighbor, that is, the
U.S.S.R. And, finally, if countries wish aid from the United States,
they should do something in return.

Neither the Indians and Pakistanis nor Americans seem to grasp
the other's point of view. We consider our international motives
and policies clear and unexceptionable. We see the world engaged in
a gigantic ideological struggle and divided into the two camps of
Democracy versus Communism, of individual freedom versus suppression of individual rights, of liberty versus slavery, of the U.S.A.
and the other western democracies versus the U.S.S.R. and its
satellites (among whom we Americans, unlike Indians and Pakistanis,
normally list China). We are territorially unambitious, but regard
Russia as expansionistic and imperialistically minded. Everywhere
we want the aid of other nations. Of one that has not yet committed
itself we ask the direct questions: Are you for democracy or communism, for China or the United Nations, for the Soviet Union or
for the United States? In Asia we expect the Asians to be with us,
and we cannot understand hesitation or reservations.

Because America has not got simple and clear and favorable answers to these questions, many Americans have assumed India, and
to a less degree Pakistan, are on the other side, favor the U.S.S.R.
It has been common enough to hear Americans accuse Nehru and
India of being communist—"India has gone over to the Communists"
or "India is absent from the Japanese Peace Treaty Conference on
Russia's side." The American press freely administers reproofs to
India and Nehru; for example, the *New York Times* speaks of Nehru
as a "Lost Leader," permits itself "Plain Words to Indians," tells
Nehru he is "not being helpful." Most of the rest of the American
press pursues the same line, but in more unreserved language. The
Mutual Security Administrator in the present American administration once publicly called Nehru the man in the middle, and one of
the large American weeklies has spoken of him as "a political Peter
Pan." In Congress, a prominent legislator, angry over India's stand
on the Japanese peace treaty, once suggested that America stop the
promised shipments of wheat.

These irritated reactions indicate lack of acquaintance with reasons
held by India and Pakistan for their positions, and a failure to look
at America through Indian and Pakistani eyes. It should be recognized, first, that neither of the two countries nor any of its present
leaders is communist or pro-Russian. We should recall the basic
elements in their foreign policy, so often stated—their dread of war
and their desire to build up their own economies, their fear of renewed western colonialism, their deep feeling about race discrimination.

India and Pakistan and other countries in Asia, as Justice Douglas
has remarked, are engaged in a great social, economic, and political
revolution, which is the most important phase of their national life.
It is more important to them than the struggle between Western
democracy and Soviet communism and the character of political institutions. As Nehru has put it, "Where, let us say, people are starving the vote does not count." Neither country fears communist
economic and social ideas as such; some of those ideas, its people
think, may even be helpful in achieving economic advance; at least
they should be considered. India and Pakistan are apprehensive of
communism when it is violently aggressive within their borders and
when the communist nations, Russia and China, expand politically in
their direction. On this point Nehru said in March 1951: "Undoubtedly if, as has often happened recently, communism comes not

only as an economic doctrine but rather as an extension of imperialism . . . there is bound to be resistance to it, which resistance will grow." Communist violence and aggression the governments of these two nations resist. But help in reaching the good life they need desperately, and they will take it from whatever quarters they can get it.

In the light of their own interests and aspirations, how does the United States appear to India and Pakistan? It is, first of all, in this mid-twentieth century economically and militarily the world's leading nation and so the heritor of the British Empire. The sins of Britain which Indians complained about fifty or even ten years ago are now often ascribed to the United States, for it has all the potentialities of committing them. Britain was in India's view an imperialist power, upholding reactionary regimes, denying to India and other parts of Asia and Africa their democratic rights. America, too, despite its own opinion of itself, sometimes seems so to many Indians. They say America tolerated fascist aggression in Ethiopia in 1935 and in Spain in 1936–1938, Japanese aggression in China in the 1920's and 1930's, British and French imperialism in the Near East then and since. But the Indian National Congress during those various decades was in every case denouncing the aggressors and denouncing Britain for perpetrating or tolerating the aggression.

Secondly, we Americans appear to Indians and Pakistanis as race-conscious; they assail us perennially for our treatment of the Negro. In that same connection they point out too that when the atom bomb was employed at the end of the second World War, we used it on the Japanese, not the Germans, on Asians, not Europeans—they ignore the fact that it was available too late for use in Europe. When President Truman in December 1950 spoke in terms taken to imply that we might use it in Korea or China, there was an outburst in all Asia, which was particularly violent in India and Pakistan. Other hints since then that the bomb might be used against the Chinese have produced similar reactions.

Thirdly, as Asians, Indians and Pakistanis have subjected the American profession of democracy to criticism in the light of situations in Asia. Respecting China, America is censured as opposing that nation's unification. India and Pakistan officially regard the People's Government as the regime which the Chinese want. The United States, too, should recognize it, they maintain, or at least admit it to membership in the United Nations, whether liking it or not. The press in each country and the public interested in international affairs generally express the same sentiment. The United States in supporting Chiang and enabling him to hold Formosa, has been, in Indian and Pakistani eyes, supporting a wrong, because a repudiated, government.

In respect to Korea, the press and public of these two nations again question the American position, which they see as blocking Korean freedom. They refer back to the end of the Russo-Japanese war when the United States and Britain approved the Treaty of Portsmouth (1905) and the delivery of Korea to the Japanese and comment that American interest in checking communism there now is not based on a concern for the Korean people but a desire to promote power politics. The United States has been supporting a leader, Syngman Rhee, they say, whose own South Korean people had shown their lack of confidence in him in elections four weeks before the Korean crisis was precipitated, when his party had had a setback that cost it control of the legislature, and he and that legislature have been in conflict since.

With regard to Japan, Pakistan approved the American position, but India sees the United States as imposing a treaty which, though affirming sovereignty for Japan, denies it the freedom to make its own defense arrangements and deprives it of territories.

The United States is not considered by Indians and Pakistanis to have a clear record on the issue of colonialism. Though our actions respecting the Philippines are commended, we appeared to them for a long time to be of two minds about Indonesia. They see us as aiding the French to retain Indo-China and supporting a political head Bao Dai in whom the people have no confidence, and in helping France to hold Tunisia. They maintain that our policy has been determined only by a desire to retain the aid of France against the U.S.S.R. in Asia and Europe, and not by any wish to meet the aspirations of the people in Indo-China and Tunisia. The United States is also charged with helping the British maintain their unpopular position in Malaya, where with large resources in men and arms they have still not been able to crush the opposition, which is small in numbers but strong through the moral support of the anti-imperialist population. Here too the American motive is considered to be maintenance of an Anglo-American alliance against communism at the expense of Malay nationalist goals. When the United States votes in the United Nations with the colonial powers against the

Asian-Arab and Latin-American countries (and the Soviet bloc), as it did in November 1952 in the Trusteeship Committee on the issue of continuing the special committee to report on economic, social, and educational conditions in underdeveloped lands, it loses again in Indian and Pakistani estimation.

Muslims in Pakistan frequently claim that the United States opposes the unity and economic development of Islamic nations in the Near East, being concerned, they say, to procure oil, support the British, and check Russian influence and communist progress. They interpret American support of Israel in the same way.

The United States is often charged by India and Pakistan with being indifferent to their real economic and social welfare and moved to give such help as it does only to "use" them for anti-Russian purposes. They complain that America asks their support and affirms that it will be to their advantage to side with America, but allots them only a fraction of the economic aid it bestows upon Europe, although their necessity is greater. America is charged, along with Britain, with doing nothing to remove racial discrimination throughout the world. It influences the Security Council, people in India and Pakistan say, to act promptly where its own interests are affected, as in the case of Korea in June 1950, but lets their affairs drag along interminably, as in the quarrel over Kashmir, which has been pending since the end of 1947. Each nation, of course, contends that a just solution of this would be in its favor!

The opinion of many Indians and Pakistanis in large terms is that the United States has only one motive in all its international relations, and that is to check the U.S.S.R. Their comment is that this aim is not primary in their eyes, that having been drawers of water and hewers of wood for the West in the nineteenth century they do not propose to become cannon-fodder for it now in the twentieth. The United States is suspected of playing its own game, and any other nation making an alliance with it, they often say, should walk carefully, keep its eyes open, and look out for sudden unilateral action that could be embarrassing to an unprepared companion.

Conversely, the British, who were viewed in India as ogres before the war, are now admired for political liberalism and realistic conduct in the face of adversity and crisis. Britain is no longer considered potentially harmful to India and Pakistan, since it has declined in power. It is being remembered less and less for disrupting India's internal economy, obstructing her industrial advance, imposing political domination, and practicing race discrimination, and more and more for having introduced modernism into the subcontinent and for having furnished examples under the Labour Government in attacking economic and social situations which India and Pakistan might profitably imitate.

In India and Pakistan the opinion seems, in 1952, to be growing that the U.S.S.R. is expansionist and has designs on them. Toward the end of 1951 some Indians were saying that abstention from the cold war was unwise, among them being Dr. B. R. Ambedkar, leader of the Scheduled Castes Federation. He contested the 1951–1952 elections with direct Western alliance as a platform plank, but lost. Nevertheless other Indians, including Nehru as quoted above in this and the preceding chapter, seem also to be moving toward this view. The United States has received much Indian and Pakistani and general Asian-Arab support in the United Nations. In due time this attitude may lead to a positive approach in Indian and Pakistani relations with the United States, one of giving as well as receiving.

At the same time the United States also needs to promote a positive approach in its relations with these two nations. How can we convince them that we have genuine friendship for them, that human goodwill is an element in our foreign policy, that we are possessed of sagacity in international affairs, that we are reliable as allies? Radio and moving-picture propaganda will not do the job. This is frequently blatant and inept, often not understood, generally discounted. To most people in India and Pakistan it seems to be only words, when concrete help is what they ask for.

To gain the confidence and coöperation of India and Pakistan we do not need to retreat from our major international aims. We can continue to oppose U.S.S.R. expansion; we can restrain Japan; we can promote our interests in the Near East; we can maintain the United Nations position in Korea. Doubtless government leaders in India and Pakistan do not feel that it would be in the best interests of their own countries if the United States should do exactly what their press and public have often demanded in respect to China and Korea. Nehru seems to acknowledge that the United States cannot recognize China while Chinese soldiers are killing ours. The United States, in accepting, even with amendments, India's proposal for resolving the Korean armistice deadlock, seems likely to win not only India but also Pakistan and other Asian nations to closer coöperation in world affairs.

By allying itself with the movement for progress now strong in Southern and Southeastern Asia, the United States would win prestige there. Colonialism is on the way out; but, whenever we appear to be on its side, we strengthen communism by throwing it and nationalism into alliance. The reverse is, as Nehru has often remarked, that the achievement of nationality in Asia operates to weaken communism.

The most important item in a positive American approach to India and Pakistan is to give them help in solving their problems of population and production. That is to cut out the ground from under communism's feet. It is a mistake to ask only: Are you for America or Russia? Are you for democracy or totalitarianism? There are other questions which the two nations consider more basic. It is as though one were to demand of a starving man, "Are you a Republican or a Democrat?" and he were to answer, "I am hungry."

The basic questions of the two countries are: How do we eat? Do we run ourselves? Are we as good as other people? How can we become strong? Who will help us? If the United States can convince them that it itself is the answer to the last question and then help them in finding answers to the others, they may give us the answers we want to our own questions.

We happily made a start by signing an agreement with India on January 5, 1952, by which each side contributed $54 million to a pool called the India-American Technical Coöperation Fund. This was to be used chiefly for increasing food production and rural community development. Our part of the sum came from the fund set up under the Mutual Security Act of 1951. An additional sum of $45.4 million was made available later. This is only a small portion of that needed, and Ambassador Bowles was reported as having proposed to the Senate Foreign Relations Committee, on January 16, 1952, that we put in a billion dollars to be made available during a four-year period on the basis of half-loan, half-gift. This proposal is being taken seriously in India, which hopes that our Congress will implement it. Pakistan accepted $10 million early in 1952 under the Point Four program, and in September 1952 effected a $15 million loan through the Export-Import Bank. That is only a fraction of what it could use. Assistance, when not accompanied by military, political, or economic demand, does not arouse Asian suspicions of our motives, and Nehru was reported on February 28 to have found "not the slightest objection" in the terms of the $54 million gift in January. The Department of State seems willing for such gifts or loans to be made without strings attached; debates in Congress indicate a less clear-cut view there.

By such assistance we help Indians answer the first, most immediate, and most critical of their questions, that which concerns eating. Private philanthropic agencies, too, notably the Ford Foundation, are helping find the answer to that question. India and Pakistan also wish help in building up industry which the United States can supply, and technical advice on social service problems.

Economic and technical assistance, however, is not all that those countries want. They want certain psychological assurances as well. One of these is that Americans look upon them and other Asians as equals. Indians and Pakistanis often complain of an arrogance of wealth and a self-righteousness in the attitude of our representatives at the United Nations. These include uncivil remarks made on the floor to representatives of India and Pakistan and reported in the press. More serious is their feeling that the smaller or less powerful nations are slighted. President Prasad, speaking at the opening of the new Indian Parliament on May 16, 1952, complained of this situation and added, "Gradually the noble aims of the founders of the United Nations and the Charter they framed appear to be getting blurred."

It is doubtful, of course, that our country will ever succeed in winning the confidence of India and Pakistan, and of other Asian nations, as long as it practices color discrimination. Though this last question seems to many Americans to be purely domestic and is so argued by southern congressmen, it has serious international connotations. It is one on which Russia is always represented in Asia as having a clear advantage over America.

The point in American national behavior which Indians and Pakistanis most often mention as indicating limited international sagacity is the current preoccupation with communism and the adoption of "containment" of Russia as the dominant if not sole motive of foreign policy. This seems to them a negative and inadequate view of world affairs. The McCarran Act, the attention which Senator McCarthy has secured, the various loyalty oaths demanded by State governments or educational or other private institutions, the attacks upon officers in the State Department and private citizens who write as scholars about foreign peoples and not in terms of denunciation, the witch-hunting fomented in government departments, the attack upon American personnel employed in the United Nations—all these are inter-preted in the newspapers of those nations as showing that the United States is in the grip of an irrational phobia. They speak of Britain as calmer and wiser in these matters.

India and Pakistan, as also other Asian countries, want American relations with them to rest upon mutual knowledge and respect. When we carry our economic, social, political ideas and techniques to Asia, Asians are sensitive to any expressions of paternalism or condescension or patronage or any tinge of contempt for them. They do not want an echo in secular fields today of Bishop Heber's religious characterization of them in the nineteenth century as "men benighted" while he and his associates' souls were "lighted with wis-dom from on high."

As Asian countries learn from and about America, they feel that there are things which it is worth while for Americans to learn from and about them. The process, they think, should be two-way. They have a point. The less than one hundred persons in the United States competent in some aspect or another of the national life of India and Pakistan are not sufficient to supply the country with the information it should have. It will acquire the respect for India and Pakistan which those countries deserve only when it has trained very many times that number and has established a continuing process of training others.

If we do not so inform ourselves about India and Pakistan and other parts of the world, we risk the alternative of losing our pres-ent position of world leadership. As Governor Dewey has said (May 19, 1952), "We need every friend we can get . . . whether their skins are black, brown, yellow, or white." Europe and Asia alike want to know that we have a genuine interest in them for their in-trinsic worth. This is especially true of Asians, who feel at a greater disadvantage with Americans than do Europeans. We might be instructed by what has happened to Great Britain, in its time of world-leadership as full of self-complacency as ever has been known. During the Kipling era, at the end of the nineteenth century, one of her great men, Lord Curzon (George Nathaniel Curzon), quite unself-consciously put the spirit of empire into the dedication of a book, *Problems of the Far East: Japan-Korea-China* (first edition 1894, second edition 1896). This reads: "To those who believe that the British Empire is, under Providence, the greatest instrument for good that the world has seen and who hold, with the writer, that its work in the Far East is not yet accomplished this book is inscribed."

As Governor General of India (1899–1905) in the days of paternalistic administration, Lord Curzon was one of the country's greatest rulers, doing much of large and enduring value for it. But he had one grievous lack. He was not aware that Indians, as well as British, had capacity for ruling and thinking. Nor did the country which he represented. Barely more than a half century after the second edition of his book was published, the Empire had to give up India, the brightest jewel in the British Crown and the Empire's most valuable possession. It had to give up others of its Asian holdings as well. What it now retains in Asia is only a fraction of what it had in 1900. The British Empire's work is almost finished in the Far East and South Asia. The very term "Empire" has gone out of fashion with the imperial idea itself, to be replaced by the term and conception "Commonwealth." Unawareness was the first element of decay at the Empire's root, unawareness of the importance of Asians, of Asians' opinions, and of Asian abilities.

Asians are willing to be our partners in world affairs, but they want us to recognize that they have a claim as valid as our own to a position of dignity among the peoples of the world. Their self-respect demands that we have respect for them as they do for us. Then they will take common action with us to advance their interests as well as ours.

Appendix I. Political Divisions and Population of India and Pakistan

I. *India.* The following figures are taken from the summary announcement of the Census of India 1951.

	Land Area in Square Miles	Population 1951
Part A States		
1. Assam *	54,084	9,129,442
2. Bihar	70,368	40,218,916
3. Bombay	115,570	35,943,559
4. Madhya Pradesh	130,323	21,327,898
5. Madras	127,768	56,952,332
6. Orissa	59,869	14,644,293
7. Punjab	37,428	12,638,611
8. Uttar Pradesh	112,523	63,254,118
9. West Bengal	29,476	24,786,683
Total Part A States *	737,409	278,895,852
Part B States		
1. Hyderabad	82,313	18,652,964
2. Jammu and Kashmir *		
3. Madhya Bharat	46,710	7,941,642
4. Mysore	29,458	9,071,678
5. Pepsu	10,099	3,468,631
6. Rajasthan	128,424	15,297,979
7. Saurashtra	21,062	4,136,005
8. Travancore-Cochin	9,155	9,265,157
Total Part B States *	327,221	67,834,056

* Area and population figures for the State of Jammu and Kashmir, and population figures for Tribal Areas of Assam not included.

Jammu and Kashmir. The area of the State is 82,258 square miles. 1941 Census population was 4.02 millions. The population strength was determined under the Constitution (Determination of Population) Order, 1950, as 4.37 millions as on 1–3–1950.

Part B Tribal Areas of Assam. Census Operations have not been carried out there. A local estimate (unverified) indicates a population strength of 560,631 persons.

I. *India* (Continued)

	Land Area in Square Miles	Population 1951
Part C States		
1. Ajmer	2,425	692,506
2. Bhopal	6,921	838,107
3. Bilaspur	453	127,566
4. Coorg	1,593	229,255
5. Delhi	574	1,743,992
6. Himachal Pradesh	10,600	989,437
7. Kutch	8,461	567,825
8. Manipur	8,620	579,058
9. Tripura	4,049	649,930
10. Vindhya Pradesh	24,600	3,577,431
Total Part C States	68,296	9,995,107
Part D Territories and Other Areas		
1. Andaman and Nicobar Islands	3,143	30,963
2. Sikkim	2,745	135,646
Total Part D Territories, etc.	5,888	166,609
Grand Total	1,138,814	356,891,624

II. *Pakistan.* The following figures are taken from the Pakistan Government's Census estimates for 1951.

	Land Area in Square Miles	Population 1951
Western Pakistan *		
Punjab Province	62,000	18,814,000
Sind Province	48,140	4,619,000
North-West Frontier Province	14,260	3,239,000
North-West Frontier Tribal Areas	25,000	2,460,000
Baluchistan (Commissioner's Province)	54,460	622,000
Baluchistan States	79,500	556,000
Bahawalpur State	17,500	1,820,000
Khairpur State	6,000	320,000
Karachi (Federal capital area) †		1,118,000
Total Western Pakistan	306,860	33,568,000
Eastern Pakistan		
East Bengal	53,920	42,119,000
Grand Total	360,780	75,687,000

* Figures for Junagadh (area 3,438 square miles) not included—see Chapter 9.
† Area included in Sind.

Appendix II.   Election Results in India, 1951–1952

The following tables are printed by permission of the *Far Eastern Survey* from an article by Richard L. Park, "Indian Election Results," published in its issue of May 7, 1952. They are not official.

There are no figures from the Jammu and Kashmir State, because elections were not held there. In Table IV, to reconcile the figures of "Total," it is necessary to note that no elections were held for three constituencies in Assam and one in Uttar Pradesh (see footnotes).

TABLE I. VOTES WON BY PARTIES, HOUSE OF THE PEOPLE *

Party	No. of Seats Contested	No. of Seats Won	No. of Votes (Unofficial)	Percentage of Total Votes	Percentage of Total Seats
Congress Party	480	362	47,588,000	44.9	74.03
Socialist Party	255	12	11,129,000	10.5	2.45
KMP Party	137	9	6,147,000	5.8	1.84
Bharatiya Jan Sangh	94	3	3,180,000	3.0	0.62
CPI and Allies	70	27	5,723,000	5.4	5.52
Ram Rajya Parishad	57	3	2,014,000	1.9	0.62
AISCF	32	2	2,438,000	2.3	0.41
Hindu Mahasabha	30	4	954,000	0.9	0.82
Other Parties	194	30	11,023,000	10.4	6.13
Independents	453	37	15,792,000	14.9	7.56

For explanation of abbreviations, see Table V.

* HOUSE OF THE PEOPLE:

Number of eligible voters	176,000,000
Number of votes invalidated (appr.)	1,635,000
Number of valid votes polled	105,987,318
Percentage of total eligible voters	60.2

TABLE II. VOTES WON BY PARTIES, LEGISLATIVE ASSEMBLIES *

Party	No. of Seats Contested	No. of Seats Won	No. of Votes (Unofficial)	Percentage of Total Votes	Percentage of Total Seats
Congress Party	3,278	2,248	43,548,000	42.5	68.58
Socialist Party	1,793	126	9,939,000	9.7	3.84
KMP Party	945	77	5,072,000	4.9	2.35
Bharatiya Jan Sangh	732	32	2,869,000	2.8	0.98
CPI and Allies	587	180	6,148,000	6.0	5.49
Ram Rajya Parishad	304	32	1,230,000	1.2	0.98
AISCF	213	12	1,742,000	1.7	0.36
Hindu Mahasabha	206	20	871,000	0.8	0.61
Other Parties	1,376	261	10,144,000	9.9	7.93
Independents (5,681 candidates)	2,596	291	20,903,000	20.4	8.88

For explanation of abbreviations, see Table V.

* STATE LEGISLATIVE ASSEMBLIES:

Number of eligible voters	176,000,000
Number of votes invalidated (appr.)	1,126,000
Number of valid votes polled	102,465,619
Percentage of total eligible voters	58.2

TABLE III. ALLOCATION OF SEATS IN THE HOUSE OF THE PEOPLE
(Total number of members 499*)

States	Total No. of Seats	Congress Party	Socialist Party	KMP Party	AISCF	Bharatiya Jan Sangh	Hindu Mahasabha	Ram Rajya Parishad	CPI & Allies	Independents	Other Parties
Part A States											
Assam	12	11	1	—	—	—	—	—	—	—	—
Bihar	55	45	3	—	—	—	—	—	—	1	6[a]
Bombay	45	40	—	—	1	—	—	—	—	3	1[b]
Madhya Pradesh	29	27	—	—	—	—	—	—	—	2	—
Madras	75	35	2	6	—	—	—	—	8	15	9[c]
Orissa	20	11	1	—	—	—	—	—	1	2	5[d]
Punjab	18	16	—	—	—	—	—	—	—	—	2[e]
Uttar Pradesh	86	81	2	—	—	—	1	—	—	2	—
West Bengal	34	24	—	—	—	2	1	—	5	—	2[f]
Part B States											
Hyderabad	25	14	1	—	1	—	—	—	7[g]	1	1[h]
Madhya Bharat	11	9	—	—	—	—	2	—	—	—	—
Mysore	11	10	—	1	—	—	—	—	—	—	—
Patiala & East Punjab States Union	5	2	—	—	—	—	—	—	—	1	2[i]
Rajasthan	20	9	—	—	—	1	—	3	—	6[j]	1[k]
Saurashtra	6	6	—	—	—	—	—	—	—	—	—
Travancore-Cochin	12	5	—	—	—	—	—	—	4[l]	2[m]	1[n]

TABLE III. (*Continued*)

States	Total No. of Seats	Congress Party	Socialist Party	KMP Party	AISCF	Bharatiya Jan Sangh	Hindu Mahasabha	Ram Rajya Parishad	CPI & Allies	Independents	Other Parties
Part C States											
Ajmer	2	2	—	—	—	—	—	—	—	—	—
Bhopal	2	2	—	—	—	—	—	—	—	—	—
Bilaspur	1	—	—	—	—	—	—	—	—	1º	—
Coorg	1	1	—	—	—	—	—	—	—	—	—
Delhi	4	3	—	1	—	—	—	—	—	—	—
Himachal Pradesh	3	2	—	—	—	—	—	—	—	1	—
Vindhya Pradesh	6	4	1	1	—	—	—	—	—	—	—
Kutch	2	2	—	—	—	—	—	—	—	—	—
Manipur	2	1	1	—	—	—	—	—	—	—	—
Tripura	2	—	—	—	—	—	—	—	2	—	—
Total	489	362	12	9	2	3	4	3	27	37	30

For explanation of abbreviations, see Table V.

* Elected		489
Nominated by the President to represent		
Jammu and Kashmir State	6	
Anglo-Indian community	2	
Part B Tribal Area of Assam	1	
Andaman and Nicobar Islands	1	10
Total		499

a Jharkhand Party—3; Lok Sewak Sangh—2; Janata Party—1.
b Peasants and Workers Party—1.
c Commonweal Party—3; Tamil Nad Toilers Party—4; Muslim League—1; Forward Bloc (Marxist)—1.
d Ganatantra Parishad—5.
e Shiromani Akali Dal—2.
f RSPI—1; USO—1.
g People's Democratic Front—7.
h Peasants and Workers Party—1.
i Shiromani Akali Dal—2.
j Most of the six Independents are ex-rulers of Princely States of Rajasthan.
k Krishikar Lok Party—1.
l United Front of Leftists: CPI, RSPI, and the KSP—4.
m One of the two Independents was supported by the United Front of Leftists.
n Travancore Tamil Nad Congress—1.
o Raja of Bilaspur (Ex-ruler of Bilaspur State).

Appendix II

TABLE IV. ALLOCATION OF SEATS IN LEGISLATIVE ASSEMBLIES

States	Total No. of Seats	Congress Party	Socialist Party	KMP Party	AISCF	Bharatiya Jan Sangh	Hindu Mahasabha	Ram Rajya Parishad	CPI & Allies	Independents	Other Parties
Part A States											
Assam	108	76	4	1	—	—	—	—	1	14	9[a]
Bihar	330	240	23	1	—	—	—	1	—	13	52[b]
Bombay	315	269	9	—	1	—	—	—	1	17	18[c]
Madhya Pradesh	232	194	2	8	—	—	—	3	—	23	2[d]
Madras	375	152	13	35	2	—	—	—	62	62	49[e]
Orissa	140	67	10	—	—	—	—	—	7	21	35[f]
Punjab	126	97	1	—	—	—	—	—	4	4	20[g]
Uttar Pradesh	430	390	18	1	—	2	1	—	—	14	3[h]
West Bengal	238	151	—	15	—	9	4	—	28	10	21[i]
Part B States											
Hyderabad	175	93	11	—	5	—	—	—	42[j]	14	10[k]
Madhya Bharat	99	75	4	—	—	4	11	2	—	3	—
Mysore	99	74	3	8	2	—	—	—	1	11	—
Patiala and East Punjab States Union	60	26	—	1	1	2	—	—	2	8	20[l]
Rajasthan	160	82	1	1	—	8	2	24	—	35	7[m]
Saurashtra	60	55	2	—	—	—	—	—	—	—	3[n]
Travancore-Cochin	108	44	12	—	—	—	—	—	32[o]	11[p]	9[q]
Part C States											
Ajmer	30	20	—	—	—	3	—	—	—	4	3[r]
Bhopal	30	25	—	—	—	—	1	—	—	4	—
Coorg	24	15	—	—	—	—	—	—	—	9	—
Delhi	48	39	2	—	—	2	1	—	—	4	—
Himachal Pradesh	36	24	—	3	1	—	—	—	—	8	—
Vindhya Pradesh	60	40	11	3	—	2	—	2	—	2	—
Total	3283	2248	126	77	12	32	20	32	180	291	261
Electoral Colleges											
Kutch	30	28	—	—	—	—	—	—	—	2	—
Manipur	30	10	1	—	—	—	—	—	2	1	16[s]
Tripura	30	9	—	—	—	—	—	—	12	6	3[t]
Total	90	47	1	—	—	—	—	—	14	9	19

For explanation of abbreviations, see Table V.

[a] Garo National Council—3; Mizo Union—3; Khasi and Jaintia National Federated States Conference—1; Khasi and Jaintia Durbar—1; All People's Party—1. Three seats allotted to Naga Hills have not been filled as no candidate from Naga Hills constituencies submitted nomination papers.
[b] Jharkhand Party—32; Janata Party—11; Lok Sewak Sangh—7; Forward Bloc (Marxist)—1; Ganatantra Parishad—1.

TABLE IV. Footnote references (*Continued*)

° Peasants and Workers Party—14; Kisan Kamgar Paksh—3; Khedut Sangh—1.

ᵈ Peasants and Workers Party—2.

ᵉ Tamil Nad Toilers Party—19; Krishikar Lok Party—15; Commonweal Party—6; Muslim League —5; Forward Bloc (Marxist)—3; Justice Party—1.

ᶠ Ganatantra Parishad—31; Independent People's Party—3; Forward Bloc (Marxist)—1.

ᵍ Shiromani Akali Dal—14; Forward Bloc (Marxist)—2; Zamindar League—2; Lal Communist Party—2.

ʰ Praja Party (Uttar Pradesh)—2; RSPI (Uttar Pradesh)—1. Polling in one constituency of Uttar Pradesh State Legislative Assembly was postponed because of the death of a candidate.

ⁱ Forward Bloc (Marxist)—11; Forward Bloc (Subhasist)—2; Gurkha League—3; USO—4; United Progressive Bloc—1.

ʲ Peoples Democratic Front—42.

ᵏ Peasants and Workers Party—10.

ˡ Shiromani Akali Dal—19; Lal Communist Party—1.

ᵐ Krishikar Lok Party—7.

ⁿ Girasdars—2; Khedut Sangh—1.

° United Front of Leftists—consisted of CPI, RSPI, and the KSP—32.

ᵖ Five of the 11 Independents were supported by the United Front of Leftists.

ᵠ Travancore Tamil Nad Congress—8; Cochin Party—1.

ʳ Purusharthi Panchayat—3.

ˢ Manipur National Union—3; Achumba Pamba Congress—2; Praja Santhi Party—3; Gandhi Sebok Sabha—1; Kuki National Association—3; Manipur Zelengrong Union—1; Mao Mariam Union—2; Mizo Union—1.

ᵗ Ganatantra Sangh—3.

TABLE V. INDIAN POLITICAL PARTIES

ACHUMBA PAMBA CONGRESS: "Genuine Congress Party"—*Moderate.* Party of Congress dissidents. Confined to Manipur State.

ALL INDIA SCHEDULED CASTES FEDERATION (AISCF): *Liberal.* Party leader: Dr. B. R. Ambedkaar.

ALL PEOPLE'S PARTY: *Moderate.* Confined to Assam.

BHARATIYA JAN SANGH: "Indian People's Party"—*Hindu Conservative.* Party leader: Dr. S. P. Mookerjee.

COCHIN PARTY: *Liberal.* Anti Travancore-Cochin Union. Separate Cochin State is the main demand. Confined to Cochin State of Travancore-Cochin Union.

COMMONWEAL PARTY: *Conservative.* Non-Brahmin caste Party. Confined to a few districts of Madras State.

COMMUNIST PARTY OF INDIA (CPI). Leaders: S. A. Dange, A. K. Ghosh.

CONGRESS PARTY: *Liberal-Moderate Socialist.* Leader: Sri Jawaharlal Nehru.

FORWARD BLOC (Marxist): *Neo-Communist.* Leader: Pandit Shilbhadra Yaji.

FORWARD BLOC (Subhasist): *Radical Socialist.* Leader: Sri R. S. Ruikar.

GANATANTRA PARISHAD: "Republican Party"—*Conservative.* Confined to Bihar and Orissa States.

GANATANTRA SANGH: "Republican League" —*Conservative.* Confined to Tripura.

GANDHI SEBOK SABHA: "Gandhi Service League"—*Moderate.* Confined to Manipur.

GARO NATIONAL COUNCIL: *Moderate-Liberal.* Confined to Garo Tribe in Assam.

GIRASDARS: "Landlords' Party—*Conservative.* Confined to Saurashtra.

GURKHA LEAGUE: *Conservative.* Confined to Darjeeling district of West Bengal.

HINDU MAHASABHA: "Hindu League"— *Hindu Conservative.* Leader: Dr. N. B. Khare.

INDEPENDENT PEOPLE'S PARTY: *Moderate.* Confined to Orissa State.

JANATA PARTY: "People's Party"—*Conservative.* Confined to a few districts of Bihar State.

JHARKHAND PARTY: *Moderate.* Scheduled Tribes State Party. Confined to a few districts of Bihar. Leader: Jaipal Singh.

JUSTICE PARTY: *Moderate Conservative.* Confined to Madras State.

TABLE V. (*Continued*)

KERALA SOCIALIST PARTY (KSP): *Radical Socialist*. Confined to Travancore-Cochin Union.

KHASI AND JAINTIA DURBAR: *Conservative*. Party of Khasi and Jaintia Tribal chiefs. Confined to Khasi and Jaintia Tribes in Assam.

KHASI AND JAINTIA NATIONAL FEDERATED STATES CONFERENCE: *Liberal*. Confined to Khasi and Jaintia Tribes of Assam.

KHEDUT SANGH: "Peasants League"—*Liberal*. Confined to Gujarat part of Bombay State and Saurashtra.

KISAN KAMGAR PAKSH: "Peasants and Workers Party"—*Neo-Communist*. Confined to Maharashtra part of Bombay State.

KISAN MAZDOOR PRAJA PARTY (KMP Party): "Peasants, Workers and People's Party"—*Liberal*. Party leader: Acharya J. B. Kiripalani.

KRISHIKAR LOK PARTY: "Peasants Party"—*Liberal*. Confined to Andhra part of Madras State, and Rajasthan. Party leader: Prof. N. G. Ranga.

KUKI NATIONAL ASSOCIATION: *Moderate Conservative*. Confined to Kuki Tribe in Manipur State.

LAL COMMUNIST PARTY: "Red Communist Party"—*Neo-Communist*. Confined to Punjab and Patiala and East Punjab States Union.

LOK SEWAK SANGH: "People's Service League"—*Liberal*. Confined to a few districts of Bihar State.

MANIPUR NATIONAL UNION: *Sectarian, Moderate Conservative*. Against Manipur's merger in Assam. Confined to Manipur State.

MANIPUR ZELENGRONG UNION: *Moderate Conservative*. Confined to Zelengrong sub-tribe of Naga Tribes of Manipur State.

MAO MARIAM UNION: *Sectarian, Moderate Conservative*. Confined to Mao and Mariam sub-tribes of Naga Tribes of Manipur State.

MIZO UNION: *Sectarian, Conservative*. Confined to Mizo Tribe of Assam and Manipur States.

MUSLIM LEAGUE: *Muslim Conservative*.

PEASANTS AND WORKERS PARTY (Shetkari Kamkari Paksh): *Neo-Communist*. Confined to Marathi speaking districts of Bombay, Hyderabad, and Madhya Pradesh States. Party leader: S. S. More.

PEOPLE'S DEMOCRATIC FRONT: *Neo-Communist*. Confined to Hyderabad State.

PRAJA PARTY (Uttar Pradesh): "People's Party"—*Conservative*. Party of Uttar Pradesh landlords. Confined to the State of Uttar Pradesh.

PRAJA SANTHI PARTY: "People's Peace Party"—*Conservative*. Organized by the ex-ruler of Manipur State. Confined to Manipur State.

PURUSHARTHI PANCHAYAT: "Refugee Association"—*Moderate*. Confined to Ajmer State.

RAM RAJYA PARISHAD: "God Rule Party"—*Hindu Conservative*. Party leader: Swami Karapatri.

REVOLUTIONARY SOCIALIST PARTY OF INDIA (RSPI): *Radical Socialist*. Confined to West Bengal, Uttar Pradesh, and Travancore-Cochin States. Party leader: Jogesh Chatterjee.

SHIROMANI AKALI DAL (Sikh Party): *Sectarian Conservative*. Confined to Punjab and Patiala and East Punjab States Union. Party leader: Master Tara Singh.

SOCIALIST PARTY: Party leader, Jayaprakash Narayan.

TAMIL NAD TOILERS PARTY: *Sectarian Conservative*. Confined to a few districts of Madras State.

TRAVANCORE TAMIL NAD CONGRESS: *Liberal*. Confined to Tamil speaking districts of Travancore-Cochin State. Merger of these districts with the Tamil Nad part of Madras State is the main demand.

UNITED FRONT OF LEFTISTS: *Neo-Communist*. Confined to Travancore-Cochin State. Constituted by CPI, RSPI, and the KSP.

UNITED PROGRESSIVE BLOC: *Neo-Communist*. Confined to West Bengal.

UNITED SOCIALIST ORGANIZATION (USO): *Radical Socialist*. Confined to West Bengal.

ZAMINDAR LEAGUE: "Landlords' League"—*Conservative*. Rural Rights Party. Confined to Punjab.

Appendix III.   Suggested Reading

Of the voluminous literature on India and Pakistan I have selected for mention works in English which, as far as I know, are either in print or are available in good libraries. Within those categories, however, I have omitted many good books since the total number is large. Many of the books listed here contain bibliographies to guide further reading.

Of general works a brief highly compressed 200-page survey of the area is *India, Pakistan, Ceylon* (Ithaca: Cornell University Press, 1951), edited by W. Norman Brown. This consists of articles written by a number of authors for the *Encyclopedia Americana*, treating geography; economic development; anthropology and sociology; languages; literature; dancing, music, and drama; architecture; sculpture and painting; religion and philosophy; law; archaeology; two thousand years of history down to 1707 A.D.; the British conquest and empire 1707–1947; India and Pakistan 1947–1950. The chapters all have brief bibliographies. Other general treatments have less scope but more depth. The most authoritative work is the *Cambridge History of India* (1922–1937), planned in six volumes, but the second was never published. This is available in the United States through the Macmillan Company in New York. There are several good one-volume histories, of which probably the most widely used is Vincent A. Smith, *The Oxford History of India*, 2nd edition revised by S. M. Edwards (New York: Oxford University Press, 1923; there have been more recent impressions). Another is *The Cambridge Shorter History of India* (New York: The Macmillan Company, 1934), edited by H. H. Dodwell. In some ways a more thought-provoking book than either of these is that by W. H. Moreland and A. C. Chatterjee, *A Short History of India*, 2nd ed. (New York: Longmans, Green and Company, 1945). Another valuable work is R. C. Majumdar, N. C. Raychaudhuri, and Kalikinkar Datta, *An Advanced History of India* (London: Macmillan, 1946).

The geography of the subcontinent is well and interestingly covered in George B. Cressey, *Asia's Lands and Peoples*, 2nd ed. (New York: Mc-Graw-Hill, 1950). This book relates India and Pakistan geographically to the rest of Asia, and in addition takes a wide view of geography as a subject. Older standard works are L. Dudley Stamp, *Asia,* 8th ed. (New York: Dutton, 1950), and Cameron Morrison, *A New Geography of the Indian Empire and Ceylon* (London: Nelson, 1926).

Because the subcontinent has had such an important development of human culture it would be easy to fill many pages with references to worthwhile works dealing with that as a whole or in part. For prehistoric cultures there is a well-written inexpensive scholarly book in the Pelican Series by Stuart Piggott entitled *Prehistoric India to 1000 B.C.* (1950). In its bibliography are cited many other works. It could be supplemented by E. J. H. Mackay's *Early Indus Civilizations* (London: Luzac and Company, 1948), which describes the important Harappa culture in brief but satisfactory form, and by *The Vedic Age* (London: Allen and Unwin, 1951), which is a work edited by R. C. Majumdar and A. D. Pusalker, and written by a number of Indian scholars, giving an Indian approach to the beginnings of civilization in their country. A lively and scholarly book in spite of its strange title is R. E. Mortimer Wheeler's *Five Thousand Years of Pakistan* (London: Royal India and Pakistan Society, 1950). This describes the Indus Valley cultures admirably. The late Professor A. A. Macdonell's short volume, *India's Past* (New York: Oxford, 1927), is still an excellent summary of the development of native Indian civilizations, and the few revisions it needs can be made without great difficulty. Another valuable work is *The Legacy of India* (New York: Oxford, 1937), edited by G. T. Garratt, a collection of essays by various scholars on different aspects of India's civilization, such as religion, science, art, and other. It includes a chapter on Muslim culture in India. Another good book is that by Paul Masson-Oursel, Helena Willman-Grabowska, and Philippe Stern called *Ancient India and Indian Civilization* (one of the History of Civilization Series), which was translated from the French by M. R. Dobie (New York: Knopf, 1934). Still another is H. G. Rawlinson, *India: A Short Cultural History* (New York: Appleton-Century, 1938), which gives more prominence to Muslim elements in Indian civilization than do the works mentioned above.

For architecture, sculpture, painting, there are two good inclusive works: Ananda K. Coomaraswamy, *History of Indian and Indonesian Art* (New York: Weyhe, 1927), and V. A. Smith, *A History of Fine Art in India and Ceylon,* 2nd ed. revised by K. deB. Codrington (New York: Oxford, 1930), of which the former is perhaps the more satisfactory to use. On architecture specifically there is an excellent two-volume work by Percy Brown entitled *Indian Architecture* (Bombay: Taraporevala, 1942), of which the first deals with Hindu and Buddhist architecture and the second with that of the Muslims. A quite different type of work, which analyzes the intellectual content equally with, if not more than, the structural, stylistic, and iconographic features is Stella Kramrisch's two-volume *The Hindu Temple* (Calcutta: University of Calcutta, 1946). For sculpture, bronzes, textiles, and painting there is a recent work *The Art of India and Pakistan,* by K. deB Codrington, John Irwin, and Basil Gray, edited by Sir Leigh Ashton (New York: Coward-McCann, 1950), which is a survey based upon the exhibition of art from India and Pakistan held at Burlington House, London, 1947–1948. The traditional Hindu, Buddhist, and Jain literature may be studied in Moriz Winternitz's large three-volume German work, of which the first two volumes have been translated into English by S. Ketkar and published as *A History of Indian Literature* (Calcutta: University of Calcultta, 1927, 1928). A. Berriedale Keith's *History of Sanskrit Literature* (New York: Oxford, 1928) is standard for the period after the Veda. A short but now largely outdated work is A. A. Macdonell, *A History of Sanskrit Literature* (New York: Appleton, 1914). It does not seem within the scope of this Appendix to list works on the vernacular literatures, which for the most part are not well reported.

Of the legion of books on Indian religions, the briefest of over-all works that has scholarly merit is J. N. Farquhar, *A Primer of Hinduism* (New York: Oxford, 1912), frequently reprinted in both England and India. For specific periods the following books may be recommended. The *Religion of the Veda* by Maurice Bloomfield (New York: Putnam's, 1908), a short work that is at once scientific, vivid, and readable. Much longer is the standard two-volume work of A. Berriedale Keith, *The Religion and Philosophy of the Veda and Upanishads* (Harvard University Press, 1925). *The Thirteen Principal Upanishads* translated by R. E. Hume, 2nd ed. revised (New York: Oxford, 1931), is by far the most reliable rendition of those works into English, though sometimes hard reading. The many smooth renderings of those texts, whether singly or in collections, are all too often sectarian or misleading or meaningless. By far the best interpretation and translation of the frequently translated Bhagavad Gita is Franklin Edgerton, *The Bhagavad Gita,* 2 vols. (Harvard University Press, 1944). On Buddhism in India a good work is the short treatment by T. W. Rhys Davids, *Buddhism, its History and Literature,* 3rd ed. (New York: Putnam's, 1918). A long and valuable general treatment of Hinduism and Buddhism is Sir Charles N. E. Eliot, *Hinduism and Buddhism,* 3 vols. (London: E. Arnold and Co., 1921). For Jainism see Margaret Sinclair Stevenson, *The Heart of Jainism* (London: Milford, 1915), or the article by H. Jacobi in the *Encyclopedia of Religion and Ethics.* On the lower religion very good books are Bishop Henry Whitehead's *The Village Gods of South India,* 2nd ed. (New York: Oxford, 1921), and L. S. S. O'Malley's *Popular Hinduism* (New York: Macmillan, 1935). Reform movements in modern Hinduism are best treated in J. N. Farquhar, *Modern Religious Movements in India,* 2nd ed. (New York: Macmillan, 1931). Another work of less scholarship but more enthusiasm is Romain Rolland's *Prophets of the New India,* translated from the French by E. F. Malcolm Smith (New York: Boni, 1930). A recent easily read book on the Sikhs is that by J. C. Archer, *The Sikhs* (Princeton: Princeton University Press, 1946). There is no small inclusive work on Indian philosophy but there exists a two-volume work by Sir Sarvepalli Radhakrishnan, *Indian Philosophy* (New York: Macmillan, 1923, 1927), and a work already in four volumes with more to come by S. N. Dasgupta, *A History of Indian Philosophy* (New York: Macmillan, 1922–1949). Possibly the average general reader would be satisfied initially with the descriptions of the various systems given in the general works on Indian civilization mentioned above. A very suggestive work is Sir Sarvepalli Radhakrishnan's small book, *The Hindu View of Life* (New York: Macmillan, 1927). A recently published and very readable book on aspects of Indian thought is Heinrich Zimmer, *Philosophies of India,* edited by Joseph Campbell (New York: Pantheon Books, 1951). Another book by this same gifted writer is *Myths and Symbols in Indian Art and Civilization* (New York: Pantheon Books, 1946). For the thought of Islam in India see Muhammad Iqbal, *The Reconstruction of Religious Thought in Islam* (Lahore: Civil and Military Gazette, Ltd., 1944).

Anthropological works of high value are J. H. Hutton, *Caste in India* (New York: Macmillan, 1946), and G. S. Ghurye, *Caste and Race in India* (New York: Knopf, 1932), both of which are at once anthropological and sociological in approach. A recent and excellent demographic work, which also treats social structure and change, is Kingsley Davis, *The Population of India and Pakistan* (Princeton: Princeton University Press, 1951). On village life an account at once reliable and interesting is Gertrude Emerson, *Voiceless India,* 2nd ed. (New York: John Day, 1944). Other sociological works are Margaret Read, *The Indian Peasant Uprooted* (New York: Longmans, Green, 1931), a study of the factory population of India, and Mohinder Singh, *The Depressed Classes* (Bombay: Hind Kitabs, 1947). The most recent study of the Muslims is Wilfred C. Smith's *Modern Islam in India,* 2nd ed. (London: Gollancz, 1946). On language a small easily procurable and authoritative pamphlet is that by S. K. Chatterji, *Languages and the Linguistic Problem,* Oxford Pamphlets on Indian Affairs, No. 11, 3rd ed. (New York: Oxford, 1945).

For the economic structure and development of India, standard works are Vera Anstey, *Economic Development of India,* 4th ed. (New York: Longmans, Green, 1942); P. A. Wadia and K. T. Merchant, *Our Economic Problem* (Bombay: New Book Co., 1945); G. V. Jathar and S. G. Beri, *Indian Economics,* 2 vols., 8th ed. (London: Oxford, 1947–1949). A well-known and still valuable book is Daniel H. Buchanan, *Development of Capitalist Enterprise in India* (New York: Macmillan, 1934), and another is D. R. Gadgil, *Industrial Evolution of India,* 4th ed. (London: Oxford, 1944). An instructive work, now a classic, is M. L. Darling, *The Punjab Peasant in Prosperity and Debt,* 4th ed. (London: Oxford, 1947).

Surveys and appraisals of India under Britain have been many but most are either ardently pro- or ardently anti-British. A carefully worked out description in just over a hundred pages is that by Daniel and Alice Thorner in the chapter "India and Pakistan" in *Most of the World*, a large work on the peoples of Africa, Latin America, and the East today, edited by Ralph Linton (New York: Columbia University Press, 1949). A much longer treatment is that by Sir Reginald Coupland, published in England in three volumes and republished in the United States in a single volume as *The Indian Problem* (New York: Oxford, 1944), a reasoned defense of the British position. A briefer study by the same author is *India: A Restatement* (New York: Oxford, 1945). A Marxist interpretation is found in R. Palme Dutt's *India Today* issued in short form (London: Gollancz, 1940) and reissued later in enlarged editions (Bombay: People's Publishing House, 1947, 1949; London: Collet, 1950), interesting in the light of the many communist victories in the 1951–1952 elections. There is a briefer form of this work entitled *The Problem of India* (New York: International Publishers, 1943). Much affected by it is Kate Mitchell's *India Without Fable* (New York: Knopf, 1942). Edward Thompson and G. T. Garratt wrote a work, *The Rise and Fulfilment of British Rule in India* (New York: Macmillan, 1934), which defends and at the same time criticizes the British regime. An objective study of the East India Company's operations is found in Holden Furber, *John Company at Work* (Harvard University Press, 1948). An account of the terms on which British capital was attracted to invest in the Indian railways appears in Daniel Thorner, *Investment in Empire* (Philadelphia: University of Pennsylvania Press, 1950).

The rise and development of nationalism is carefully and fully outlined up to the last part of the interwar period in William Roy Smith, *Nationalism and Reform in India* (New Haven: Yale University Press, 1938). An exceedingly informative study of social elements in the nationalist movement is A. R. Desai, *Social Background of Indian Nationalism* (Oxford, 1948). The development of India's governmental institutions is found in A. B. Keith's *Constitutional History of India* (London: Methuen and Co., 1936). An analysis of India's new constitution, very short, is found in Sir Ivor Jennings, *The Commonwealth in Asia* (New York: Oxford, 1951). The official *History of the Indian National Congress* is a two-volume work by B. Pattabhi Sitaramayya (Madras: Law Printing House, 1935, 1947).

Books against and for partition of India are Rajendra Prasad, President of the Republic of India, *India Divided*, 3rd ed. (Bombay: Hind Kitabs, 1947), and B. R. Ambedkar, leader of the Scheduled Castes Federation, *Pakistan, or the Partition of India*, 3rd ed. (Bombay: Thacker, 1946). An interesting book which has had the blessing of the Pakistan government is Richard Symonds, *The Making of Pakistan* (London: Faber and Faber, 1950). It deals with cultural as well as political matters. A valuable work is that by C. N. Vakil and associates, *The Economic Consequences of Divided India* (Bombay: Vora, 1950).

Studies of the two countries since independence and partition are, first, T. Walker Wallbank, *India in the New Era* (Chicago: Scott, Foresman, 1951), a thoughtful work. Margaret Bourke-White in *Halfway to Freedom* (New York: Simon and Schuster, 1949) describes vividly and trustworthily what she saw in 1947–1948, when the nations were coming into existence. Andrew Mellor in *India Since Partition* (New York: Frederick A. Praeger, 1951) ably carries the story forward in 150 pages. Clare and Harris Wofford, Jr., in *India Afire* (New York: John Day, 1951), record their impressions of a hasty visit in 1949; its most valuable parts are accounts of leaders in the Socialist Party. A rather quick journalistic survey is found in H. B. Pithawalla, *Introduction to Pakistan* (London: Probsthain, 1948). A book surveying India's relations with other Asian countries and treating especially India's attitude toward communism is Werner Levi, *Free India in Asia* (Minneapolis: University of Minnesota Press, 1952).

Relations between India and (or) Pakistan and the West are discussed in a symposium edited by L. S. S. O'Malley, *Modern India and the West* (London: Oxford, 1941). Of special interest to Americans is Lawrence K. Rosinger, *India and the United States* (New York: Macmillan, 1950). The same author edited *The State of Asia* (New York: Knopf, 1951), in which he wrote the chapter on India and Holden Furber that on Pakistan. A small and compact work is Percival Spear, *India, Pakistan, and the West* (New York: Oxford, 1949). The most recent work is Maurice Zinkin's *Asia and the West* (New York: Institute of Pacific Relations, 1951), which treats the major aspects of the socio-economic organization of Asia, the condition of the several nations there, the needs to be met for giving them adequate development, the state of their trade, and their requirements of dollars. The various sections on India and Pakistan and the accompanying tables are very enlightening.

Personalities have played a large part in the development of modern India and Pakistan. Gandhi has been the one most frequently written about. A few books on him are as follows. First, his two-volume autobiography published in 1927–1929 in India, entitled *The Story of My Experiments with Truth*, republished in Washington with the title *Gandhi's Autobiography* (Public Affairs Press, 1948). Of the studies of him the trilogy by C. F. Andrews, his close associate, published by Macmillan is the most satisfactory: *Mahatma Gandhi's Ideas* (1930), *Mahatma Gandhi: His Own Story* (1930); *Mahatma Gandhi at Work: His Own Story Continued* (1931). Of the many biographies of him one was recently published in the United States by Louis Fischer, *The Life of Mahatma Gandhi* (New York: Harper, 1950).

Jawaharlal Nehru, one of the most articulate living writers of English has published a number of books. One of these is his autobiography published in the United States as *Toward Freedom* (New York: John Day, 1941). Another is *The Discovery of India* (John Day, 1946), which gives his view of the various phases of historic Indian civilization. A very recent small work is *Talks with Nehru,* a discussion between him and Norman Cousins (John Day, 1951), in which Nehru gives his views on certain international problems, especially that of communism versus democracy.

Of Jinnah there is a biography by M. H. Saiyid, *Mohammad Ali Jinnah: A Political Study* (Lahore: Ashraf Press, 1945). Rabindranath Tagore published his *Reminiscences* (latest edition, London: Macmillan, 1946), and J. Edward Thompson published a literary biography of him, *Rabindranath Tagore: Poet and Dramatist* (New York: Oxford, 1926). Marjorie Sykes is author of a biography of him, *Rabindranath Tagore* (New York: Longmans, Green, 1945). There is a three-volume biography by L. J. L. D. (Earl of) Ronaldshay, *The Life of Lord Curzon* (New York: Boni, 1928). Selected speeches by important figures are Lord Mountbatten, *Time Only to Look Forward* (London: N. Kaye, 1949); Vallabhbhai Patel, *On Indian Problems* (New Delhi: Publications Division, Ministry of Information and Broadcasting, Government of India, 1949); Jawaharlal Nehru, *Independence and After* (New York: John Day, 1950); Liaquat Ali Khan, *Pakistan: Heart of Asia* (Harvard University Press, 1951). The autobiography of a highly sensitive Indian, recently published, is Nirad C. Chaudhuri, *An Unknown Indian* (New York: Macmillan, 1951).

Novels by Indians writing in English include, as examples, Mulk Raj Anand's *Coolie* (London: Hutchinson, 1947) and *The Village* (London: Jonathan Cape, 1939), and Dhan Gopal Mukherji, *My Brother's Face* (New York: Dutton, 1925).

An Englishman's memoirs recently published is General Sir Francis Tuker's *While Memory Serves* (London: Cassell, 1950). An earlier work of an English civil servant is Walter R. Lawrence, *The India We Served* (Boston and New York: Houghton Mifflin, 1929).

A study entitled *Indian General Elections, 1951–52,* has been prepared by the Indian Political Science Association under the editorship of S. V. Kogekar and Richard L. Park and is to be published by Vora and Company, Ltd., Bombay, 1953.

For current news the best service is furnished by the *New York Times,* which has for a number of years kept excellent correspondents in New Delhi. The present incumbent is Robert Trumbull. In 1952 it stationed Michael James in Karachi.

Note on Pronunciation of Words Transliterated from Sanskrit and Other Oriental Languages Cited in This Index

Speakers of English should stress the next to the last syllable when it is long, otherwise the first long syllable before it. A long syllable is one containing a long vowel (*ā, ī, ū*) or a diphthong (*e, o, ai, au*) or a vowel followed by more than one consonant (but note that usually *h* following a consonant indicates aspiration of the consonant and does give length to the syllable).

The sounds of the vowels are roughly as follows:

a like *u* in English up	*ū* like *oo* in English soon
ā like *a* in English bar	*e* like *a* in English take
i like *i* in English sin	*ai* like *ai* in English aisle
ī like *ee* in English sheen	*o* like *o* in English so
u like *u* in English pull	*au* like *ow* in English how

In the case of consonants pronounce as follows:

c like *ch* in English chin	*ś* and *ṣ* like *sh* in English hush
g like *g* in English gun	*ṅ* like *n* in French sens

The sounds represented by *t, d,* and *n* are made with the tongue against the back of the teeth; the sounds represented by *ṭ, ḍ,* and *ṇ* are made with the tongue turned farther back than in the case of the English sounds. The aspirate sounds *th, kh, ph* are much like the sounds of *t, k,* and *p* in English tin, kin, pin (as distinguished from the sounds in English stun, skin, spin). The aspirates *dh, gh, bh* are like the combinations in English roundhouse, doghouse, clubhouse. In Arabic words the sound ' is the glottal stop; the sound ' is a deep laryngeal, which is not pronounced in India but lengthens the adjacent vowel.

The following abbreviations are used: Skt. for Sanskrit, Ar. for Arabic, Pers. for Persian.

INDEX

2

Date Due